Donne's Idea of a Woman

Donne's Idea of a Woman

Structure and Meaning in *The Anniversaries*

Edward W. Tayler

Columbia University Press
New York

Columbia University Press
New York   Oxford

Library of Congress Cataloging-in-Publication Data

Tayler, Edward W.
  Donne's Idea of a woman : structure and meaning in
The Anniversaries / Edward W. Tayler.
      p.   cm.
  Includes bibliographical references and index.
  ISBN 0-231-07594-4
    1. Donne, John, 1572–1631. Anatomy of the world.
2. Donne, John, 1572–1631. Of the progres of the
soule.   3. Elegiac poetry, English—History and criti-
cism.   4. Woman (Philosophy) in literature.   I. Title.
PR2248.T3   1991
821'.3—dc20   91-11902
  ⊗   CIP

Casebound editions of Columbia University Press
books are Smyth-sewn and printed on permanent and
durable acid-free paper

Printed in the United States of America

c   10   9   8   7   6   5   4   3   2   1

Frontispiece Art: The marble monument in St. Paul's is
modeled on a life-size painting for which Donne himself, dressed in his death-size winding sheet, provided
the model (Photo Richard Wollman)

Permission to reprint Wallace Stevens's "Anecdote of
the Jar" is acknowledged to Faber & Faber Ltd. and to
Alfred A. Knopf, Inc. (from *The Collected Poems of
Wallace Stevens* by Wallace Stevens; copyright 1923 and
renewed 1951 by Wallace Stevens; reprinted by permission of Alfred A. Knopf, Inc.).

To My Students

Contents

Preface

In this book I aim to set the record straight: about what John Donne meant when he said that "he described the Idea of a Woman and not as she was," and about the structure, and therefore the meaning, of The Anniversaries. Nothing in the various "new historicisms" can help us define "Idea," and nothing in structuralism or poststructuralism can help us understand the "mimetic" and "ecstatic" structure of The Anniversaries. Disappointing but true, and not only for these poems. Although I am concerned primarily with the two greatest poems written between *The Faerie Queene* and *Paradise Lost,* I have the usual hopes that my mild-mannered polemic may have some effect on the way we read Donne's other poems and other works of the period.

The object of inquiry consists of five poems, three by Donne himself and two commendatory poems that on internal evidence—corroborated by Ben Jonson's comments—may be attributed with absolute certainty to Joseph Hall. *The First Anniversarie,* originally entitled *An Anatomy of the World,* first appeared in octavo in 1611, preceded by Hall's "To the Praise of the Dead, and the Anatomy" and followed by Donne's "A Funerall Elegie." *The Second Anniversarie,* subtitled *Of the Progres of the Soule,* appeared in octavo in 1612, preceded not only by Hall's "The Harbinger to the Progres" but also by a reprint of the edition of 1611, provided with a new title-page headed *The First Anniversarie,* which demoted the original title to subtitle. The five poems had become a book, and The Anniversaries had become in the technical, generic sense "companion poems," radically altering the purpose and meaning of the first edition of 1611.

These companion poems crown, and exhaust, the multifarious traditions that went into their making. The elegies written by various hands after Donne's death refer mainly to The Anniversaries and confess, with notable unanimity, that The Monarch of Wit has exhausted the elegiac vocabulary that might be used to lament his passing, that his royal appropriation of the language and conventions of the elegiac mode have made it impossible for any verses but his own to serve as his elegy. Donne had indeed created a language of mourning and consolation that, like the language of *Paradise Lost,* might be travestied but not imitated. Joseph Hall and Thomas Carew understood what Donne was about; Jasper Mayne understood the "Anniverse" well enough to know "That wee are thought wits, when 'tis understood"; and Dryden, confessing that he had "not succeeded to the same Genius," understood enough to realize that in *Eleonora* he could hope to emulate only a part of Donne's grand design. In more recent times, however, The Anniveraries have been widely—almost, one could say, systematically—misunderstood.

As teachers we ought not, I think, to encourage our students to impose their own habits of reading, acquired through cultural indoctrination, upon the older poets; and we owe it to ourselves, as well as to our ancestors, to try to get it right, which in the last analysis means to get it different from ourselves. The same caveats apply to "theory" (now more or less synonymous with "ideology"), for theory by its very nature actually authorizes the "translation" of other people's words into alien terms, and in any case theory in its application, so far as I can tell from reading a huge amount of it, invariably eventuates in an habitual response. To the dead as to the living (Milton reminds us that "books are not absolutely dead things") we have our obligations, moral and psychological; and the first of these, if we aspire to surcease of solipsism, must be to try to understand others—and that is why we retain the idiom for it—in their own terms. Exegesis before eisegesis.

In writing this book I am conscious of owing a great deal

to the living as well as the dead, not only to many a good book but also to many a good teacher at Amherst and Stanford; I think particularly though certainly not exclusively of Theodore Baird, of C. L. Barber, of Reuben Brower, of G. Armour Craig, of Benjamin DeMott, and of Walker Gibson; of L. V. Ryan, of George Sensabaugh, of V. K. Whitaker, and of Yvor Winters. (It will harm no one if I like to think of those teachers who are now gone as possessing a "life beyond life" in their students.) As for more immediate obligations, I have benefited from the advice and encouragement of James Biester, Kathy Eden, Eve Keller, Chris Moustakis, Anne Lake Prescott, Peter Rudnytsky, James Shapiro, June Siegel, and Richard Wollman. Stanley Fish and David Kastan commented incisively on what became chapters 4 and 5; Louis Martz on part of what is now the Introduction; Paul O. Kristeller, James Mirollo (to whom I am indebted for innumerable other courtesies), and Stanley Stewart on the entire manuscript. Frank Kermode, W. W. Kerrigan, and Joseph A. Mazzeo have tended to my education over a period of many years. Even such an impressive sum of scholarly insurance (as Douglas Bush used to say) cannot possibly insure the bearer against error, but it does allow me to express my deep gratitude to what I persist in thinking of as a community of scholars. I am also very grateful for the humane, concerned efficiency of Jennifer Crewe and William F. Bernhardt of Columbia University Press, and as always I owe a great debt of gratitude to the officers and staff of The Huntington Library. Sherri Geller and Lee Morrissey provided invaluable research assistance.

At the end of this Preface a word of disclaimer and then a word of impersonal thanks. The disclaimer: In the following chapters I use a lot of lump-together words like "Aristotelean," "Platonist," "Thomist," "perspectivist," and the like; and I want to say at the outset that I don't mean too much by these words because Renaissance thinkers did not "read" their "auctores" as we do. (If on occasion it seems that I have not paid proper heed to the "neoplatonisms" it may be because the historians of philosophy and of pictorial art have left many literary scholars with the erroneous impression that the language of fine art is to be identified with the language of Neoplatonism.) Renaissance thinkers, unlike

Thomas Stanley in the later seventeenth century, were not much interested in what we would now think of as The History Of Philosophy; many of these writers, though by no means all of them, wanted to lump it together rather than split it apart. They found the true and the useful and the beautiful wherever they could look for it, in a plethora of assimilable incompatibilities from Jerusalem, Baghdad, Athens, and Rome; they read Plato through Cicero and Augustine, Aristotle through the Arabic commentators and Augustine, Augustine through Aquinas, and so on. There were aristoteleanisms and platonisms and alhazenisms and a variety of old-time medleys: St. Paul and the man whom Erasmus called St. Socrates, as well as the stoicisms, atomisms, and hermeticisms of the time were assimilated, often without much in the way of critical detachment, by ravenous Renaissance readers in search of beauty and truth, perhaps in something like the way that omnivorous college students devour L. Ron Hubbard's *Dianetics,* Kant's *Critique of Pure Reason,* and Derrida's "On a Footnote in *Being and Time*" at a sitting—and then go on to relate Martin Buber's I-Thou relationship to the deplorable "Eurocentrism" of their instructors.

In the notes I cite, by way of impersonal acknowledgment, many of the older scholars, such as D. C. Allen, Charles M. Coffin, Rosalie Colie, Edmund Gosse, H. J. C. Grierson, Victor Harris, Frank Manley, Louis Martz, Wesley Milgate, Marjorie Hope Nicolson, George Potter, and Evelyn Simpson. If I were not working more or less exclusively with The Anniversaries, I would have to invoke more often names such as Meyer Abrams, Erich Auerbach, Ernst Robert Curtius, Ernst Kantorowicz, Frank Kermode, Paul O. Kristeller, A. O. Lovejoy, Joseph A. Mazzeo, Georges Poulet, and Leo Spitzer. Scholars such as these have given us our texts, our notes, our commentaries, our bibliographies, and our background information, which is to say that they have given us the history of our ideas and ourselves. Without them we could not possibly begin to know enough, much less could we be secure enough, to dismiss their labors as the mistaken legacy of late nineteenth-century positivism. I honor, as best I can, their memory, since I cannot aspire, with my learning, to stand in their company.

This book is dedicated to my students—for they both read, and understand. They have taught me much, about The Anniversaries in particular and about Renaissance literature in general. Many of them now teach and write better than their teacher, which is as it should be.

 Donne's Idea of a Woman

Introduction

Doubtless Aristotle should not have assumed that nature remains always and everywhere the same, just as fire burns both here and in Persia. Human Nature no longer exists for us except as a debilitating fiction on which our innocent ancestors relied, an ort or remnant left over from the complex of ideas that R. G. Collingwood calls "substantialistic metaphysics" and Jacques Derrida "logocentrism." Yet even if whatever it is that the abstraction "human nature" may be presumed to denote turns out to be as transitory as a literary theory, we need not invoke this or any other transcendental concept to hear ancestral voices, nor do we need to have, concealed about our persons, a transhistorical core of being in order to trace the record of bygone words. We need some learning and a willingness, sometimes as if to a foreign language, to listen. (Even if we suffer, as we tend to do these days, from severe kleidophobia, we need to take note of our symptoms —not take refuge in them.)[1] In the case under consideration, we need to know something about the "Idea" that informs The Anniversaries, and we need to be able to listen to the way the structure of the poems "speaks" to us of what used to be called, with greater exactitude than we now think necessary, essence and ecstasy.[2]

Literary critics, taking their own "linguistic turn" after the apotheosis of Ferdinand de Saussure, regularly make obeisance to the ways in which language shapes thought and channels feeling, but the widespread—systemic, epistemic—misunderstanding of

Donne's Anniversaries (*An Anatomy of the World, Of the Progres of the Soule*) shows how easily amnesia may set in when we come to the actual experience of reading and interpreting. Like *Lycidas* and *Hamlet*, The Anniversaries have come to function as hermeneutical barometers in the sense that the commentary on them seems to betray rather more about the critics and their cultural climate than about the poems themselves. With respect to The Anniversaries the weather outlook is not good. Part of the trouble lies in our tendency to talk about "discourse" and "language" instead of about what words once meant, now mean, or may well mean. Since our words, to a greater or lesser degree, manage to do more or less of our thinking for us (otherwise we just couldn't get along), the case against yet another new "discourse" is not that it is "merely fashionable" but rather that its novelty may beguile us into thinking that we have found some new truth about ourselves and our world.

This new and different description of the nature of things may prove to be a semantic engine of Copernican, Newtonian, Darwinian, or Freudian efficacy. More likely, not. And when the semantic machine—manufactured at home or imported from France— keeps turning out the same product regardless of what has been fed into the mechanism, it does not mean that we have penetrated the veil that has hitherto shrouded reality.[3] It means that we have a semantic engine of such efficiency that it can be operated even by persons who cannot follow the urbanely fallacious argument of Donne's "Nocturnall," who cannot hear the grace notes of Campian's "When thou must home to shades of vnder ground," and who cannot appreciate the twist-of-feeling in Montaigne's "Upon some Verses of Vergil."

We harbor different emotions about ourselves and our world if we have grown accustomed to think in terms of *nature* and *art* rather than *heredity* and *environment, generation* and *corruption* rather than *momentum* and *inertia, res et verba* rather than *signifiant* and *signifié,* or *substance* and *accident* rather than *matter* and *energy.* Such pairings carry with them, for a given culture at a given time, the lure of ultimate amplitude; glamorous polarities like these function as determinative locutions, circumscribing what need and need not be said about some thing at some time. If we have secured the object of inquiry in *space* and in *time,* we do not customarily begin to worry its whereabouts in the fifth dimension. It is as if, in assigning the proper valences to each term of the pair, the subject, whatever it may be, has been exhausted with respect to its significance, so that its worrisome enigmas appear to have been explained and its troublesome questions answered. Such words, provided that they still possess the glamor of completeness for a given time and place, have for their users the weight and heft of emotional inevitability. Such words cradle our minds, affording us the illusion of wholeness and appearing to insulate us from intellectual contingency.

They function also to focus our disagreements, serving to delineate areas of cultural struggle in which we are made to experience what Wallace Stevens calls the "clashed edges of two words that kill." Yet even in their most chaotic moments of semantic bloodletting these grand pairs demarcate the lines of argument and dictate, if not (always) the outcome of conflict, then at the very least the terms in which the outcome must be understood and implemented. Pairs like these function as conceptual archetypes, bearing the burden of culture and attracting into their orbits (I am thinking now of Donne in particular) subordinate distinctions— attribute, property, essence, shadow, entelechy, resultant, and the like. The subsidiary terms *mean* in relation to each other even as they interact with the determinative terms. When we find ourselves, for example, in proximity to *essence* and *accident*, "time" will be that in which it takes things to-come-to-be, "motion" will be viewed as *generation* or *corruption,* and "change" will be thought of as a transition from *potency* to *actuality.* The result, a complex of thought and feeling: the determinative or controlling terms, together with their subordinate clusters, help us package the past, deal with the present, and configure the future—everywhere providing the words that define the certain or at least delimit the probable and possible. We not only think *about* such words, we think more or less adequately *with* them.

Most of us today, I am guessing, live in a world of matter and energy, signifiers and signifieds. Some still seek the causes of effects by trying hard to maintain what some still call "objectivity" in a blizzard of indeterminacies, and one of our more venerable indeterminacies, if we are literary critics, is The Symbolist Symbol that, in the case of John Donne, Elizabeth Drury has become. It seems also that many of us think of our eyes as lenses, in action how like a video camera; that our minds are passionate computers, shuttling binary digits with sufficient rapidity and enough feeling to get along in the world, all the while adjusting and readjusting the hereditary cranial mechanism by means of cybernetic feedback from the environment. Although the lens, like the mirror-eye that Aristotle and Donne relied upon, may be thought to perceive objects, neither the lens nor the eye perceives itself, which prompts modern popularizers to wonder whether there may be someone (a trendy homunculus) living inside the computer and peering out through the video camera. We see the face across the table, seek in its special contours some special knowledge; and even when the face comes late to breakfast, we may summon it to mind in re-membrance—and then become aware of the difference. Now whether this sense of difference, awareness of the here as against the then, constitutes self-consciousness, or whether consciousness of self derives from the interaction of one half of the brain with its sibling, or whether the ghost in the slab of flesh owes its existence to cybernetic programming, or whether the self is merely, in Morse Peckham's phrase, the precipitate of culture—such questions, for us, remain to be resolved.

Donne also lived in an uncertain world, in personal ways more dangerous than our own, and there may somewhere be a weak analogy for us in his notorious declaration—wit for him, often *angst* for his modern critics—that "new Philosophy cals all in doubt." But of course for Donne many of our questions simply did not exist, or had answers within another framework of think-ing about thinking. Living as he did in a world not of matter and energy but of being and essence, his understanding of causes was Platonic, Aristotelean, Augustinian, Thomist; and he knew he could not know a cause, or indeed anything else, by "maintaining objectivity"—but only by conforming his mind to the object, only by achieving union or "same as" with the object.

Donne's eyes, like the eyes of Aristotle and Aquinas, more nearly resemble a mirror than a lens. Man is made in the image of God, and as Aquinas explains, in what became the standard gloss on 2 Cor. 3.18, St. Paul's glass or mirror re-presents the "human mind," which "reflects the likeness of God in a higher way than creatures of lower degree."[4] In this mental glass or mirror we may expect to find reflected the image of Mistress Elizabeth Drury, "not as she was" but as *species intelligibilis expressa*. The poets of the Renaissance, like all poets inveterate namers, had before them the example of the first poet Adam, whose "intuitive" or nondiscursive comprehension of the animals on parade allowed him to affix to each the one right word that signified its "essence." For the Renaissance poet who aspired to an approximation of prelapsarian vision, the function of what Sir Philip Sidney calls "our erected wit" is to overcome our "infected will" and to reveal essence. This Donne accomplished in The Anniversaries. When the poet fails in the task, he writes bad metaphysical verse, he "clevelandizes"; when he succeeds, he achieves the kind of verbal swank—T. S. Eliot's "alliance of levity and seriousness"—that we associate with the finer specimens of "metaphysical wit."

Although the majority of modern scholars seem to concur with those seventeenth-century readers who thought The Second Anniversary a matchless example of metaphysical wit, The First Anniversary has always posed special problems that I feel I must confront as directly as possible. Since all literary criticism necessarily presupposes a story—usually untold, often unknown to the critic—of the origins of the work of art, it may help in this instance simply to suppose the worst in the way of cynical etiologies, in which case the odious tale might go something like this. Although Donne had never set eyes on Mistress Elizabeth Drury, he had enough acquaintance with the inner workings of the Drury household from conversations with his sister Anne to persuade himself that he might be able to turn the death of the young girl to his personal advantage.[5] Actuated by motives utterly venal, he contrived to exploit the grief, perhaps the guilty grief, of Sir Robert Drury in order to secure his patronage. Not wanting to spill too much ink without the certain prospect of financial gain, Donne began by sending up "A Funerall Elegie" as a trial *epitaphium recens,* hoping that it might arrive in time for the early funeral; if not, perhaps in time to be attached to the hearse over the grave at the later burial (17 December 1610); or at least in time to be read by someone in the Drury household who possessed sufficient literary discrimination to appreciate witty hyperbole in the elegiac mode, and who might then recommend the poet for one or more of the customary funereal and post-funereal rituals.

The "Elegie" is a modest masterpiece, incorporating themes and images—the book, the balsamum, the clock, and so on—that might bear repetition or even elaboration in a more ambitious elegy. Elizabeth Drury, "cloath'd in her Virgin white integrity" (75), had "yeelded to too long an Extasie" (82); "her death wounded" the world (21), for she, "being spent, the world must needes decrepit bee" (30); all "Nature . . . cannot such another show" (34–35). The poet even produced for the occasion those extraordinary lines that were to become, in their later variations in The Anniversaries, the "conceit" that best communicates the "patterne" of Mistress Elizabeth:

> One, whose cleare body was so pure, and thin,
> Because it neede disguise no thought within.
> 'Twas but a through-light scarfe, her minde t'enroule,
> Or exhalation breath'd out from her soule.   (59–62)

Such praises might well insinuate the poet into the good graces of those who mourned, and he did indeed receive the commission to write a Latin inscription for the monument at Hawstead, which in turn must have provided him with the opportunity to exert in person the force of his considerable charm. Sir Robert and Lady Drury, enchanted by Donne himself and properly impressed by his secretarial skills, offered him patronage in return for services he was to render during an extended tour of the Continent.

Although the license to travel with a rather grand retinue was granted in early July of 1611, Sir Robert's "businesses" kept him in England until early November. In the interim Donne, looking for ways to consolidate his lucrative position with his brand-new patron, rummaged through the drawers in his cabinet and came up with some verses he had of late composed on the fashionable topic of the decay of the world.[6] These verses, redolent though they were with recondite learning and unsuitable though they were to this particular occasion, he scissored into their component parts; and then, thinking of his wife and his children and himself, he stitched the sections together again with transitions made up of praise and lament for Mistress Elizabeth—and presented the grieving parents with a fair, and apparently seamless, copy. When the Drurys, consoled (we may assume) and pleased (we may infer), urged publication, Donne felt he had no choice but to comply. In November of 1611 he saw *An Anatomy of the World / Wherein, by Occasion of the Untimely Death of / Mistris Elizabeth Drury the Frailty and / the Decay of this whole World is / Represented* through the press, though his experience with the patronage system had taught him that hyperbolic praise is best reserved for those to whom it is addressed . . . While in France with the Drurys Donne fulfilled the next clause in his unwritten contract by composing in December of 1611, on the anniversary of Elizabeth's death, the "Progres of the Soule." This too was published, along with a reprint of the first edition, sometime before April of 1612— and Donne continued his lucrative association with Sir Robert.

I tell the story this way not because I accept its venal implications.[7] To reduce human motives to their basest dimensions generally misses the point. Not only is it ungenerous to a great poet, one who in The First Anniversary made note of the moral fact that "wicked is not much worse than indiscreet," but also it exhibits total insensitivity to the ways in which human motivations may find legitimate if often ambivalent expression within a social, political system dominated by patronage—a system that, I have to add, is not all that alien to our own. I offer the cynical account merely to make explicit what critics often assume, and to point to the obvious conclusion—that we cannot dismiss *An Anatomy* (or salvage it) by impugning (or justifying) Donne's "sincerity." Whatever his motives, and even if the poet did indeed cobble The First Anniversary together from segments of another poem provisionally entitled the "Decay of this whole World," he would still need some principle, some poetic rationale, to establish a connection between these apparently unrelated materials and the demise of a fourteen-year-old whom the poet had never met. If he had done his hypocritical worst, he would have to do that much the better to make the recalcitrant materials cohere.

The Anniversaries, though much-admired and much-pilfered in the seventeenth century, proved controversial from the moment of publication. They are undeniably major works, the most sustained efforts of Donne's quirky career, and they are the works through which Donne was best known by the wider public during his lifetime (the other poems, circulating in manuscript, reached only a limited audience).[8] Apart from a couple of commendatory verses, The Anniversaries were the only poems that Donne permitted himself to publish, and he immediately came to regret the decision. The poems explain how we know, how we love, how we mourn, and how we achieve union, but they do so, as Joseph Hall points out in "The Harbinger to the Progres" (24–25), in ways perceptible only to those who possess "better eyes." The wit of The Anniversaries remains inaccessible to the wider public or those of "vulgar sight."

Not that the poems strike one as atypical. They are merely much longer and, sometimes, more intensely realized versions of the learning and ingenuity that appear elsewhere in Donne, but publication of this kind of esoteric verse opened the poet to adverse criticism not only from those who might feel slighted but also from those who would have concurred with the sentiments of William Drummond's letter to the King's physician Arthur Johnston. Drummond, referring to what we now call "metaphysical verse," complains that "some Men of late (Transformers of every Thing)" have "endeavoured to abstract" poetry to "*Metaphysical* Idea's, and *Scholastical* Quiddities," with the consequence that Homer, Vergil, Petrarch, Bartas, and other poets of the tradition, even "if they were alive, and had that Language," would be unable to "understand, and reach the Sense of the Writer."[9] What goes for the older poets goes for us: we cannot, lacking acquaintance with Donne's "*Metaphysical* Idea's, and *Scholastical* Quiddities," hope to "reach the Sense of the Writer."[10]

Ignorance of the poet's vocabulary (his conceptual archetypes and "*Metaphysical* Idea's") has led, over the centuries, to increased misunderstanding. No longer do we hold to the correspondence theory of truth, to the identity of knower and known in knowing, to the union of form and matter in substance, to definition according to essence, to the ocular model of mind, or to the doctrine of intentional species. No longer do we believe that it takes virtue to see straight. Yet it is out of this matrix of theories and convictions that Donne wrote The Anniversaries, and it is to this complex of thoughts and feelings that we must look if we are to understand the language of the poems and the epistemological conceit on which they are based.

According to Drummond, Ben Jonson, whose considerable learning did not in this case include the pertinent "*Metaphysical Idea's,*" managed to provoke Donne into one of his rare explanations. Jonson, so it seems, had twitted Donne by complaining that the "Anniversarie was profane and full of Blasphemies"; and Jonson then seems to have added sarcasm to injury by claiming that "he told Mr Donne, if it had been written of the Virgin Marie it had been something." Donne, goes the account, "answered that he described the Idea of a Woman and not as she was."[11] Since Drummond's "Conversations" records no reply, we find ourselves in the presence of a unique anecdote—one in which Jonson did not get the last word. The anecdote has had quite the opposite effect on the modern critics. Having recourse only to the *Oxford English Dictionary,* the modern critics can have no idea what Donne could have meant by *idea;* having no idea of the meaning of *idea,* they can form no idea of the epistemological conceit on which the poems are based. In consequence, they feel compelled to turn Mistress Elizabeth Drury into A Symbol.

Although we no longer hear much anymore about man as the symbol-making animal, no one doubts that the "symbolist movement" was far more than a literary fad summed up by Arthur Symons in 1899; habits of mind that might be called "symbolic" form the basis for ways of talking that now cluster around terms like "representation" and "ideology." With respect to The Anniversaries, William Empson appears to have inaugurated the anachronistic enterprise in 1935 by roundly declaring that "the only way to make the poem sensible is to accept Elizabeth as the Logos."[12] Although Charles M. Coffin conceded in 1938 that "Christ is not named in either of the Anniversaries," Coffin remained convinced that "He is definitely figured forth as Elizabeth Drury."[13] In 1947 Louis L. Martz, in the single most important essay on the poems, proposed in the course of an argument mainly concerned with structure that Donne had "transmuted" Elizabeth Drury into the "symbol of a virtuous soul."[14] It was an answer too modest in its dimensions and too close to the truth to satisfy the likes of Empson (or later scholars), and since Martz had allowed the word "symbol" to creep into his formulation, it was easy for others, ignoring whatever might be meant by "virtuous soul," to go right on with the business of substituting one symbol for another.

By 1950 Marjorie Hope Nicolson had persuaded herself that the "she" of the poems signified Elizabeth Drury but that the "shee" (the so-called double-shee, two "e's" rather than one) symbolized the Virgin Mary, Astraea, and Queen Elizabeth; then disarmingly admitted in a footnote that "there is at least one other 'She' and 'Shee' I cannot yet identify." [15] In 1951 D. W. Harding detected in Mistress Drury a symbol of lost motherhood, and in 1952 Marius Bewley discovered that the poems are *"private* jokes" celebrating surreptitiously Donne's apostasy in the person of the dead teenager who "symbolizes the Catholic Church." [16] Not many years later, Frank Manley, in the Commentary as well as the Introduction to his definitive edition of The Anniversaries, ranged learnedly from Jung's *anima* through the Shekinah of the Christian Kabbalists to come up with *sapientia creata* as the most appropriate label for whatever it is that Mistress Drury symbolizes. [17] Not to be outdone, Richard E. Hughes in 1967 proceeded from St. Lucy (and "all lovely women") to the "Shekinah, the neo-Platonic Paradisal Woman, the eternal consort of God in Proverbs, Dante's Beatrice, [and] the Augustinian *Sapientia,*" concluding that the teenager symbolizes "absolute beauty, absolute peace, absolute fulfillment" and that in consequence she is "truly archetypal." [18] Although this kind of list, beginning with Empson and reaching one of its climaxes here, may impress even the most solemn among us as hilarious, it is nevertheless sobering to reflect that the situation may be taken as a microcosm of the profession of literary studies.

Other candidates—Patrick Mahony's "almighty World Soul," P. G. Stanwood's "saintly embodiment of God's free gift of sanctifying grace," and Barbara K. Lewalski's "poetic symbol" of the Protestant regenerate soul—all seem a trifle pallid in contrast to the bolder colors painted by Manley and Hughes, though Lewalski's thesis in particular has impressed a wide range of reviewers. [19] Given the current lacunae in lexicographical knowledge, still other candidates will be herded forward according to the fashion of the moment, as for example the fashionable notion, now almost out of fashion, that all poems are really about poets and poetry. Ruth A. Fox proposed in 1971 (the time was ripe) that we read "to forget Elizabeth Drury in order to remember Donne," that in consequence the poems "express" the "evolution of *shee* into the soul of Donne" the poet; and in 1975, the time still being ripe, Anthony F. Bellette declared Elizabeth Drury to be an "invented and manipulated figure" symbolizing the "poetic act that embodies her."[20] Some mothers and fathers may surmise that Sir Robert would be displeased (he was an exceeding choleric man) to find out that his daughter had been invented and manipulated, but in fact he would not have understood the meaning of either word.

More recently, Thomas Docherty, "drawing extensively on post-structuralist theory," proposes a "more theoretical and critical reading," which "repudiates entirely the modernist construction of Donne as a poet of ethical, cultural and political Individualism." In his final consideration of the exchange between Jonson and Donne about "Idea," Docherty concludes that "Donne's remark here indicates the admission of guilt: the poem pretends to be about Elizabeth Drury, a commemoration of that person; but in fact it is about an idealized notion of woman and has worked to commemorate the name of Donne rather than that of Drury." The self-styled "postmodernist," after having sketched earlier on in the book a preliminary though promising definition of *idea* according to the "Thomist manner of thought," finally ends up with a Neoplatonic "idealization" and a "modernist" new label for Drury (another version of the "Donne" proposed by Fox and Bellette): "the poet is none other than Elizabeth Drury."[21]

Earl Miner sums up the perennial problem as well as anyone, and the language he employs betrays the fundamental assumptions behind all these well-intentioned efforts to use Donne's riposte about "idea" to provide a "symbolic" solution. "The problem for most readers," observes Miner, "is that the death of a fourteen-year-old girl does not seem to rank as a cause with the fall of man or new assumptions about the nature of the world. But having chosen to raise these matters," Miner continues, "Donne really had no choice other than the one he took: to make her an *idea* or *symbol* [my emphases], a grand exemplum of causes operating in the world." Two points seem crucial here. Miner, in common with other modern scholars, tends to think straightforwardly in terms of causes and effects, even though Miner himself would agree, I think, that Donne's understanding of causation and temporal process differs from our own; and Miner, in common with other modern scholars, construes Donne's "ideas" in terms of "symbols," as though the words were interchangeable ("idea or symbol," he writes). As Miner puts it elsewhere, the "formal subject [Mistress Elizabeth Drury] is transformed into a kind of counterpart image for the self, a symbol, or as Donne [himself] said, an idea of a woman." [22]

It is precisely this kind of thinking that eviscerates the argument of Barbara Kiefer Lewalski's *Donne's "Anniversaries" and the Poetry of Praise,* tellingly subtitled "The Creation of a Symbolic Mode." Because this learned book is the only full-length treatment of the subject and because it has been received with approbation in most quarters, I must make particular the grounds of my disagreement. Since Lewalski began by assuming that Elizabeth Drury must be a symbol of something, her primary task then became to determine the "theoretical and theological bases for Donne's characteristic transformations of particular individuals into all-encompassing symbols" (107). This task, in turn, requires the use of anachronistic procedures that Lewalski elsewhere, and rightly, deplores. Correctly noting the "absence of contemporary discussions of symbolism in the theoretical treatises of the period," Lewalski proposes nonetheless "that Elizabeth Drury functions in these poems as a poetic symbol, somewhat as modern critics understand that term—that is, as 'an object which refers to another object but which demands attention also in its own right, as a presentation' " (142–43, here quoting Wellek and Warren but later adverting even to Coleridge on the "translucence . . . of the Universal in the General," and so on).

It is not surprising, then, to find that Lewalski agrees almost entirely with Martz's claim that Donne "consistently attempts to transmute the girl into a *symbol* [my emphasis] of virtue that may fitly represent the Image and Likeness of God in man." [23] Having acceded to the notion that Elizabeth is a "symbol" of the

"Image and Likeness of God in man," Lewalski must then go on to claim, in deference to her polemical thesis, that Martz's "conception of the restored image and likeness of God in man as being grounded in human virtue is a *Catholic* [my emphasis] idea, whose substantive meaning is at a very far remove, I shall argue here, from Donne's understanding of these terms" (114). I am assuming that "whose" refers to "Catholic idea" and "terms" to "image and likeness," but in any case the drift seems clear enough: Lewalski believes that Mistress Drury "functions as a poetic symbol" of the "Image and Likeness of God in man" but stands prepared to argue that what is symbolized is the Protestant rather than the Catholic image of God in man.[24] Commitment to anachronism on a large scale (the meaning Lewalski attributes to "Idea" informs the argument of the whole book), along with the over-simple dichotomy between Catholic and Protestant, can hardly fail to introduce a degree of incoherence into the practice of historical interpretation.

In Chapter IV, "The Ordering Symbol: The Restored Image of God in Man," Lewalski begins by attempting to distinguish four main theories about what Elizabeth Drury "symbolizes," allowing in only one instance (Frank Manley's introduction to his pioneering edition) that the argument starts off with what may be considered a "genuine symbol"; but for Lewalski even Manley's "discussion finally becomes both nebulous and arbitrary." Lewalski therefore seeks to define a "symbolic dimension which is neither nebulous nor arbitrary, and which can relate Elizabeth Drury to all that is discussed in both poems." Accordingly, Lewalski takes as her point of departure—as she says, "everyone does"—Donne's statement about the "Idea of a Woman," and points out that hitherto it has been interpreted, wrongly, in "generalized Neoplatonic terms." Instead of appealing to the Neoplatonists, then, Lewalski proceeds to quote (112–13) from Donne's sermons in an attempt to extract a "precise, consistent, and clearly relevant gloss upon the term 'Idea.' "

The first passages quoted are standard examples of Augustinian exemplarism—nothing distinctively Protestant here—and refer explicitly to the ideas or patterns laid up in the mind of God, the "models" that He employed in creating the world and the creatures in it. The next passage quoted constitutes a variation on the first line of argument, this time to support the contention that *idea* not only means "image of God" in general but also signifies in particular the Calvinist "restoration of the image of God in man through grace."

If we provide a little more context for what Lewalski quotes, it appears that Donne starts from the usual exemplarist position (fundamentally Neoplatonic and Augustinian, though often Donne claims Bernard as his immediate source), that "God had from all Eternity an internal pattern, an *Idaea,* a pre-conception, a form in himself, according to which he produc'd every Creature" (*Sermons,* IV, 98). The preacher then explains that we too must conduct ourselves according to "Rule and Precept," though we human beings also need "Example." For one who desires to be a "new Creature," it is Christ Who is "thy *Idaea,* thy Pattern, thine Original," and all of us should therefore adopt a "Calling in this world, and . . . propose to our selves the Example of some good, and godly man in that Calling, whose steps we will walk in" (IV, 99). Lewalski does not quote the last sentence, perhaps because it plainly indicates reliance on the exercise of "human virtue" un-aided by extraordinary grace (Donne assumes the action of pre-venient grace, as did Milton, who also rejected Calvin on predestin-ation and free will). Standard homiletic procedure, though not "Protestant" in the sense that Lewalski uses the word in this con-text.

What Lewalski tries to make of those passages she does quote raises further dubieties. Lewalski infers from the first quoted passages (ideas in the mind of God) that Donne is "identifying the Idea of mankind as the image of God," though the passages them-selves make absolutely no mention of the "Idea of mankind." From the next passage (Christ as exemplar) Lewalski infers that "idea" means the "restoration of the image . . . through grace," though the preacher himself fails to mention that all-important word "grace" and in this instance seems to lay a good deal of emphasis, if I may offer a little more context, on human virtue (closer to Martz's position, which has to be oversimplified before Lewalski can undermine it): "But that thou mayst put thy self into the way to this [putting on the new man, Christ Jesus], it is usefully said, *Enim vero, certum vitae genus sibi constituere,*" and therefore you ought to imitate "some good, and godly man . . . whom we will make our precedent." Lewalski's tendentious inferences—to say nothing of the suppression of context—lead to some very large conclusions indeed: "It is evident then that for Donne the Idea of a man, or of a woman, is—quite precisely—the image of God, since that is the pattern by which God created mankind, and Christ the true Image of God is the pattern by which he restores mankind" (113). These propositions may seem logical but they are not in their ramifications theological; a severe theologian such as St. Thomas or Dean Donne would not find Lewalski's arguments unexceptionable.

Since the "idea" is the pattern, the "pre-conception" *by* which God creates, the "idea" *is* ("quite precisely") the image of God in man. In other words, and to adopt the analogy most often used in the Schools and the Renaissance, the "idea" or model according to which the architect builds the house *is* the house! Further difficulties lurk obscurely in Lewalski's formulations, for they might be said to entail the implication that Donne, in order to write the poem, had access to the "ideas" in the mind of God, an implication calculated to make even Malebranche hesitate. The proposed sense of the word "idea" can be the principle by which God wrote the poem of the world; because it is divine, it cannot be the principle by which Donne wrote The Anniversaries. The explanation actually explains nothing—but implicitly refers the mystery of artistic creation to the mind of deity.

Having equated the exemplar with the exemplum, the blueprint with the house, Lewalski can proceed to the linking supposition: "we may suppose that [Donne] undertook to praise the image of God created and restored in" Elizabeth Drury. To show that Donne must have had in mind the Protestant rather than the Catholic "image of God," Lewalski quotes from Augustine, Bernard, Aquinas, Luther, and Calvin; and Chapter IV, "The Ordering Symbol," reaches its foregone conclusion: "Donne's ordering symbol . . . has its basis . . . in his definition of the Archetype or Idaea of the human person in terms of the image of God he or she bears, and specifically in the multiple perspectives which Donne's Protestant theology permitted him to employ in analyzing a regenerate Christian as the restored image of God" (140).

If we were to take Lewalski's conclusion and translate it back into Donne's reply to Jonson, we would get something like the following: I described the Calvinist regenerate image of God in a woman and not as she was. Then what was she? and how can this theological generality be made to relate to the imagery and structure of the poem? Makes no usable, precise (theological or artistic) sense, though perhaps it does help to explain why Lewalski disclaims any intention of providing detailed, critical analyses of the poems themselves.[25] This kind of reasoning cannot explain how Donne managed to convince himself that he could see an "Idea," nor can it elucidate the cognitive processes by which he accomplished the task in the poems. And it cannot suggest how we in reading the poems are to arrive at our own vision of it.

The real problem with this kind of argument lies not with the reductive conclusion (Donne's supposedly advancing a particular kind of Protestantism), nor even with the questionable logic of the argument itself, but rather with the way the thesis reverses the poet's own procedures in the poems. It gets it all backwards with respect to these poems to begin with God rather than man, to begin with the sermons about the deity rather than the poems about Drury. We need to know first of all about ideas in the poet, in the poems, and in us—not about God's Ideas, though Donne in the poems does hint at the nature of the divine ideas. It is certainly not part of my purpose to question the relevance of the sermons to Donne's thought in 1610–12, only their applicability in this particular instance. Lewalski's procedure obliges us to try to understand the poems by first using the sermons to scrutinize the Divine Ideas; and then, instead of moving directly to The Anniversaries, we are obliged to construct A Symbol.

Donne begins, on the other hand, where his Thomistic epistemology obliges him to begin—not with the Divine Ideas but with "Sense, and Fantasy" (The Second Anniversary, 292); and then the poet shows in the poems how the human mind, which must always get its start from "Sense, and Fantasy," reaches its intelligible ideas and finally moves toward union with the mind of God. To start from the other direction not only reverses the poet's own procedures but also deflects attention from what an "idea" might be *in* the human mind and from what "image of God" might refer to *in* The Anniversaries.

Since Lewalski began by assuming that Elizabeth Drury must symbolize something, the symbolic something, in accord with the Protestant thesis, must be the restored image of the regenerate Protestant soul. Now it is of course quite true as an item of orthodox belief that Elizabeth Drury was created in the image of God, and it is likewise true that the poet in The Second Anniversary tells us that she "kept" the image "in such reparation" (455–56) that she seems to have escaped some of the consequences of the Fall; but absolutely nothing in the poems indicates that the image had been "restored" to its pristine condition through an access of extraordinary Protestant grace, nor is there anything to suggest that the poet wants us to regard her as a member of Calvin's "elect" who are predestinate to salvation through no effort of their own. It is also quite true that in his sermons Donne has recourse to Augustinian exemplarism, to the doctrine that God creates according to His "ideas" or "patterns" and that He pronounces the creature good insofar as it answers His "idea." And it is likewise true that Donne in his sermons meditates on God's having created the souls of human beings according to the appropriate "idea" laid up in the divine mind from all eternity. This "idea" is not, however, of Calvinist extraction. The "idea" according to which God creates human beings is an "idea" of Himself in the specific sense that He is The Trinity. Human beings are created as "images" of the Trinity. Indeed, Lewalski herself quotes Donne's asseveration "that there was a concurrance of the whole Trinity, to make me in *Adam,* according to that Image which they [the Persons of the Trinity] were, and according to that Idea, which they had pre-determined," though she does not draw the necessary inferences from this passage—or from the others like it.

In the sermons the word "Idea" is *not* exclusively or necessarily a synonym for "Image of God" in man but is the principle of artistic production *by* which God creates *whatever* it is that He creates. Donne's point is *not* that "Idea" *is* the "Image of God" (Protestant or Catholic); that is Lewalski's misconstrual of this and other passages in the sermons, which makes it theologically impossible for God to determine how well the image, to bring Milton to bear on the commonplace, "answers His great idea." The point is rather that God in general creates whatever He creates according to the pertinent models or "Ideas" laid up in the divine mind, and that in the particular case of human beings He creates souls according to the "Idea" of the Trinity. This is to say, and this is the theological and poetic point, that the human soul may be considered the "Image of God" because it is so created as to constitute in itself a "trinity" of memory, understanding, and will (and all those other trinities elaborately enumerated by Augustine in *De Trinitate*), which does not mean, however, that the image of God in man *is* the Father, the Son, and the Holy Ghost—not to mention a renovated Protestant. There is nothing peculiarly Calvinist or Protestant about a belief that is central to the theology of Augustine and Aquinas.

It follows from these tedious but necessary theological distinctions that Donne could not possibly have been telling Jonson that he had not been writing a poem about the death of Sir Robert's daughter but had been describing one of God's divine Ideas; and it becomes further evident, with this conclusion in mind, that Lewalski makes not one but two crucial errors: the first about the meaning of "idea" in the sermons, the second that this (misconstrued) meaning explains Donne's use of the word "idea" in the retort to Jonson. In the exchange with Jonson the word signifies neither "Image of God" in the sense proposed by Lewalski, nor the divine principle of artistic creation (as expressed in Donne's sermons), but rather the end-product of a specifically human process of intellectual abstraction (to be elucidated in chapters 1–3).

Insofar as we too assume that Donne's use of the word *idea* may be taken as somehow vaguely synonymous with *symbol,* precisely to that extent shall we feel compelled to ask, Symbol of what? and then to provide answers ranging from the Shekinah of the Kabbalah through Augustine's *sapientia* to Jung's *anima* or the "poetic act." Or Image Of God In A Renovated Calvinist. Surely it must be evident that we do not need any more names for Elizabeth Drury, any more new labels for what she supposedly symbolizes. (Literary critics invent new and newer names for old and older works of art, making them symbolical, allegorical, representational, ideological.) Instead of confusing the symbol with the thing symbolized, we need to confront the fact that the "she" of The Anniversaries is Elizabeth Drury. Instead of asking what she symbolizes, we need to know what Donne, in an age before Descartes and Locke and Coleridge, could have meant by the word *idea*. Although Donne uses the word in a number of the major and minor significations noted in the first and second editions of the *OED* (particularly those associated with Augustinian exemplarism), the dictionary entries do not adequately explain Donne's rather more colloquial retort to Jonson. For the proper explanation we must turn to the history of words, and then to the meaning and structure—in this case structure is meaning—of The Anniversaries themselves.

The Idea of a Woman

Although Jonson acknowledged that he "esteemeth John Done the first poet in the World in some things," Jonson's education, excellent though it was in some other things, did not equip him with the specialized information needed to understand the *"Scholastical"* conceit on which "Dones Anniversarie" turns, with the consequence that he found blasphemy rather than epistemological wit:

> That Dones Anniversarie was profane and full of Blasphemies: that he told Mr Donne, if it had been written of the Virgin Marie it had been something to which he answered that he described the Idea of a Woman and not as she was.[1]

If Jonson actually said this, or something very much like it, his comments and his use of the singular "Anniversarie" might seem to imply that he had just The First Anniversary (1611) in mind, though *An Anatomy* received the head-title *The First Anniversarie* only in 1612 when the two poems were published together and became, in the technical sense, "companion" poems.[2] Jonson, hard-drinking master of what Puttenham calls "Ironia, or the Drie Mock," may simply have made up the anecdote in an effort to shock the complacent laird of Hawthornden into literary sensibility. (The next observations read: "That Done for not keeping of accent deserved hanging," and "That Shaksperr wanted Arte.") Or the anecdote may have insinuated itself into Drummond's mind in this particular form simply because it was part of a venerable tradition of metaphysical put-downs. In antiquity they used to circulate the old wheeze about Antisthenes (sometimes Diogenes the Cynic) and Plato, in which Antisthenes is made to say that he can see a horse but not the Idea of horse, and Plato replies: That is because, my dear Antisthenes, you have eyes but no mind.[3] Or Drummond may have been misled by Jonson's sack-slurred speech, writing "Anniversarie" for "Anniversaries" and "the Idea of a Woman" for "his Ideal of a Woman." Or just about anything else . . . that might be imagined to emanate from that "rockie face" bent forward over the "mountaine belly" during a long evening of meat, drink, and verse.

I bring up these doubtings not because I believe the anecdote inauthentic (after all, it *sounds* like Jonson, and like Donne) but because we cannot dismiss (or salvage) the poems on the basis of Jonson's *obiter dicta*. We can, it is true, assume that "Idea" means "symbol," in which case we may do just about anything we please with the anecdote, and therefore with the poems; but as I have indicated in the Introduction this procedure simply encourages us to substitute in unending series one or another name, according as they become fashionable in literary criticism, for that of Elizabeth Drury. The problems remain. And in any case, an analysis of what Donne implies *in* The Anniversaries about how human beings get an "idea" ought to accompany any attempt to impose *on* the poems a meaning derived solely from an independent interpretation of the anecdote in the "conversations."

Under five main rubrics the editors of the *Oxford English Dictionary* seek to distinguish the major senses of *idea,* along with numerous specimens of lesser lexical fry. Although the editors note that the word is analogous in sense and derivation to the Latin *species* and are aware that other senses of "idea" become current during the latter part of the sixteenth century, they emphasize, as do the critics of The Anniversaries, the "developed Platonic sense." (The editors of the second edition of the *OED* have not substantively improved on their predecessors in this respect.) Yet it is, precisely, the historical interaction of *species* with *idea* that produces, during the latter part of the sixteenth century, the non-Platonic meaning of *idea* that pertains to Jonson's anecdote.

Some time after I had objected to the "platonizing" tendencies of Donne's critics and traced the meaning of Donne's use of "idea" (in a paper delivered at an MLA session directed by W. W. Kerrigan in 1983), Emily and Fred S. Michael published their own objections and pointed to still another "ordinary-language" meaning of "idea" in the late Renaissance (then, as now, there were *many* such meanings); namely, that of "corporeal ideas in seventeenth-century psychology."[4] In order to illustrate the prevailing but inaccurate view of the history of the word "idea," which happens to be, and not coincidentally, the history of the word as (mis)understood by those writing on The Anniversaries, the Michaels quote Anthony Kenny's "standard" account:

> The word 'idea' is now at home in ordinary language; but it is a word like 'quality' and 'intention,' which was once primarily a philosophical technicality. Its modern use derives, through Locke, from Descartes, and Descartes was consciously giving it a new sense. Before him philosophers used it to refer to archetypes in the divine intellect; it was a new departure to use it systematically for the contents of a human mind.[5]

The Michaels seek to correct this historically inaccurate account by documenting a "pre-Cartesian non-Platonic use of 'idea,'" namely, "ideas as corporeal images," and they make their case amply and well, though in the process they come close to ignoring the senses of "idea" most relevant to Donne's The Anniversaries and to the anecdote related by Drummond.

In their account of what was going on in "ordinary language," the Michaels show themselves mainly concerned with writers like Descartes and Gassendi who, whatever their differences, tend to draw fairly sharp distinctions between "corporeal ideas" and "general notions"; to phrase it prejudicially, the Michaels point to a real-enough dualistic tradition that would be associated in Donne's mind with the "new philosophy," a tradition that he knew, and could use, as he knew and could use the technicalities of alchemy or Paracelsian medicine, but which he did not happen to use in writing The Anniversaries.

Their emphasis on "corporeal ideas" leads the Michaels to note but not to explore in detail the "ordinary-language sense" of "idea" under their second rubric, namely, "images, plans, or gen-

eral notions in a human mind"; and it leads them, under the third
rubric, to separate this "ordinary-language sense" from " 'image,'
'phantasm,' 'species,' 'sensibilia,' 'simulacra,' " and the like. The
result: unnecessary and unhistorical compartmentalization with respect to Donne. In the Aristotelean-Thomist tradition, familiar to
Donne from his Oxford training (in that "Catholic" Hart Hall)
and his later reading, the "ideas" under the third rubric (images,
phantasms, species) do not belong in a separate category, for they
are in fact used—indeed, it was believed that they *must* be used—
in the process of cognition to gain access to "ideas" in the "ordinary-language sense" of "general notions." These are the "ideas"
that allow us to ascend into what Donne, near the end of a long
tradition, calls the "watch-towre"—from which coign of vantage
we may "see all things," including Mistress Drury, for what they
truly are.

In order to elucidate this use of "idea" and its connection
not only to Drummond's anecdote but also to the "watch-towre"
of Donne's The Anniversaries, I need to embark on a philological
excursus that may seem trivial to some but that means a good deal
to those who want their own terms to be understood, insofar as
possible, on their own terms.

Plato employs *idea* and its neutral equivalent *eidos* almost
interchangeably in his earlier work, whereas Aristotle, probably as
part of his effort to dissociate himself from the Theory of Ideas,
tends to use *eidos* or "form" fairly consistently. The Romans hesi-
tated over both words, then propagated their linguistic vacillations
through the medieval period and into the Renaissance. On most
occasions the Roman writers translated, rather than transliterated,
both *idea* and *eidos,* and in a variety of ways: as *imago,* as *figura,* as
exemplar, as *forma,* as *species.* On occasion, however, the Romans
simply transliterated the Greek *idea,* adopting this seminal word
into the Latin language and in this way effecting momentous changes
in the history of thought. The transliterated *idea* underwent its
own vitally ambiguous developments in relation to the various
words used to translate *eidos* and eventually emerged in the vernaculars bearing its own (considerable) weight of meanings.

Some sense of the complexity of the situation may be
gathered from the writings of Cicero, which already betray the

tendency to allow the Platonic *idea* to descend precipitously from its transcendental realm and to serve far less exalted purposes.[6] Cicero, the primary purveyor of Greek culture to Latin Christendom, expresses reservations in *Topica* 7.30 about the usual translation of the Greek *eidos*. The "Latin authors," he explains, use *species,* "not a bad translation, to be sure, but inconvenient if we wish to use different cases" (the dative and genitive plurals were not current until later).[7] In consequence, Cicero says that he himself "should prefer *formis* and *formarum,*" though elsewhere he bends to customary usage or, as in *The Orator* 29.101, *formam et speciem* appear in tandem as synonyms. In 1 *Academica* 9.33 Cicero notes that "Aristotle was the first to undermine [Plato's] Forms," but the word that H. Rackham translates for the Loeb edition as "Forms" is in fact *species;* and in 8.30–31 Cicero notes that the Greek *idea* may properly be called *species* (nos recte speciem possumus dicere), though here again Rackham gives "form" for *speciem.* For the sake of consistency within the Platonic tradition, modern translators tend to use "form" (or "idea"), but the unintended effect has been to obscure the linguistic evolution of *species* that helps make sense of Donne's reply to Jonson.[8] It remains a fact that commentators from Moerbeke to Zabarella, and poets from Dante to Donne, draw on a word-cluster that centers in *species* as well as *forma* and *idea;* and of these the history of the word *species* is not only the least well known but also the most important.

In the *Tusculan Disputations* (1.24.57–58) and in the opening pages of *The Orator* Cicero performs one of those extraordinary feats of linguistic prestidigitation that by intensifying ambiguity leads to revolutions in thought. In the *Disputations* Cicero, working his way toward his own encomium of memory, considers en route Plato's doctrine of *anamnesis*. After summarizing the way that Socrates in the *Meno* elicits the geometrical proof from the "totally ignorant" boy, Cicero draws what he evidently believes is a "Platonic" inference: "in no other way was it possible for us to possess from childhood such a number of important ideas [notiones], innate and as it were impressed on our souls [quasi consignatas, Zeno's and Aristotle's image of the seal in wax] and called *ennoiai,* unless the soul, before it had entered the body, had been active in acquiring knowledge." Then, in the very next sentence,

Cicero gives the word *idea* in Greek, calls attention to the fact that he means to use it in Plato's sense ("only that exists which is always constant to its nature" or immutable), and observes that it is what "we Latins" call "species" (nos speciem).

The conflation, or confusion, of terms is (astoundingly) noteworthy. For Plato an "idea" in the technical sense of The Theory of Ideas or Forms is not a thought nor is it derived from the senses. It is an object of thought, and the senses represent an impediment to its realization in thought. Yet Cicero nevertheless seems quite prepared to make deliberate use of the Stoic word *ennoiai*, which refers to notions in the mind that have been acquired through experience by way of the senses, in the same context as Plato's *ideas*, which refer rather to immutable notions that subsist in a transcendental realm and are, precisely, *not* acquired through the senses. Cicero, in other words, seems to want to be able to talk about "ideas" as *objects* of thought (found through "recollection" of the Platonic realm in which they subsist) *and* about "ideas" as thoughts in themselves, rattling around in the minds of human beings.[9]

The same tendency, to conflate or even to confuse, appears perhaps even more clearly in *The Orator* 2.7–3.10.[10] Cicero begins his inquiry by appealing to a modest variety of Platonism in which the perfect orator cannot be a "copy," for the original invariably excels the copy, as does the face the mask. The ideal cannot "be perceived by the eye or ear, nor by any of the senses," though we may grasp it through the exercise of mind. Since we may, even in contemplating the works of the greatest artists, imagine a more beautiful work, we must assume that Phidias, for instance, did not use a person as a model but rather "in his own mind there dwelt a surpassing vision of beauty" (species pulchritudinis). It is just such an "intellectual ideal" (cogitatam speciem) that we must use in imagining in "our minds" the "ideal of perfect eloquence" (perfectae eloquentiae speciem animo); "with our ears we catch only the copy." These "patterns of things" (has rerum formas explains *ideas*, given in Greek by Cicero and translated "patterns" by H. M. Hubbell for the Loeb edition), Cicero continues, are called "ideas" by Plato (appellat *ideas*).

Here again Cicero associates the Latin *species* with the

Greek *idea,* and here again he clearly wants to be able to regard the "ideas" as having the dignity and perfection of Platonic exemplars, functioning not only as objects of thought (cogitatam speciem) to which the artist looks in creating but also as thoughts themselves within the mind, such as the "idea" of perfect eloquence (speciem animo).[11] As early as Cicero, then, Plato's transcendental Ideas could be identified with innate *species,* exemplary still but now locatable within the human mind; and Ideas might also function as perfect notions within the mind that serve to guide the artist in making the art object: thoughts themselves as well as objects of thought.

To repeat the important—and perhaps startling—fact: since at least the time of Cicero, "ideas" may be found in the human mind as well as in a transcendent realm at the upper end of Plato's Divided Line.[12] The history of the "Platonic" usage has been written many times and may be briefly sketched. In Philo, Seneca, and elsewhere the "ideas" are made to appear in the divine as well as the human mind. In Plotinus the "ideas" become aspects of *nous* and appear, though undifferentiated, in the higher principle of the One and the Good; ideas in the soul of the world and in all other souls then become copies at some remove from *nous,* itself inferior to the One or the Good. Doubtless Plotinus thought he was providing an explanation of Plato's hierarchy of values and of the way the world proceeded by "emanation"; in any case, Plotinus' version of Plato made a perfect kind of sense to Augustine. Augustine, bedeviled by the dualisms of Manicheanism, records in *The Confessions* his intellectual agony and then, at long last, his intellectual conversion to the position of the Neoplatonists. Probably while reading Plotinus in the translation of Marius Victorinus, Augustine came to assume that when Plotinus spoke of the One and the Good he must have been reaching toward the concept of the Christian deity.

Thereafter, the "ideas" become, for Latin Christendom, "ideas" in the mind of God (as well as in the mind of man), the "exemplars" used by the deity as a blueprint in creating the world and all things in it on the analogy of the artist who uses the "idea" to make the work of art. Ficino accepts the "interpretation" of Augustine, and most later thinkers up until the time of Descartes supposed that this must have been one of the things that Plato had meant all along when he spoke of Ideas as the original archetypes for the things of this world.[13] The "ideas" exist in the mind of the Christian God as the *archai* or principles that He had, so to speak, in mind when He went about the business of The Six Days.[14] This kind of Augustinian exemplarism appealed to Donne, and it appears again and again in his sermons as a way of explaining how God created the world and the creatures in it. It is not, however, in itself a way of accounting for Donne's answer to Jonson, which depends on the meanings acquired by *idea* in its relation to *species* during the second half of the sixteenth century.

Like *forma* and *idea, species* is an all-purpose word, bearing technical meanings in areas as seemingly diverse as optics and theology; and, like *forma* and *idea,* it is radically ambiguous, referring both to appearance or outer form and to essence or inner form.

The medieval writers all show themselves well aware of the multiple acceptations of *species,* and they all begin, as was the custom, with etymological ancestry. John of Salisbury is typical, but clearer than most:

> The word 'species' likewise has several senses. Originally it meant 'form,' which consists in the general lineaments of constituent parts. Hence *speciosus* [beautiful appearance] and *formosus* [beautiful shape] mean the same. Later [the word] 'species' came to be employed to signify what is predicated in answer to the question 'What is it?' concerning things that are numerically distinct [in this way shifting the sense from outward appearance to inner form, the essence or quidditas]. . . . Boethius ascribes a third meaning to species, when he says that the substantial form of a species is referred to as a species, as when humanity is called the species of man.[15]

And so on, as the meanings continued to multiply. During the twelfth century the Schoolmen working on the older Greek texts generally translated *eidos* as *forma,* whereas those working on the Arabic texts usually gave *species,* with the consequence that the two words became more or less interchangeable by the end of the thirteenth century, taking on additional meanings from each other and from the diverse traditions with which they were associated;

rubbing a seminal word against another seminal word creates intellectual ferment, which often produces new and different configurations of thought.[16] Pierre Michaud-Quantin distinguishes dozens of senses of *species,* ranging from *species aeviterna* (Platonic Idea in Bernardus Silvestris) through the plural *species* denoting the sensible aspects of the bread and wine in the Eucharist to the *species radiosa* of Roger Bacon, which make the world go round and round.[17]

By the thirteenth century the meaning of species-as-resemblance became loosely organized into an epistemological "system" that will almost certainly be labeled, after the coinage of David Lindberg, "perspectivist" and that survives well into the seventeenth century.[18] This unsystematic system included theories of light, divinity, vision, optics, physics, and cognition; it reached its most ambitious heights of speculation in Roger Bacon, its widest dissemination in the writings of John Pecham and Witelo, and its most sophisticated codification in the doctrine of "intentional species." This doctrine (as is usual in this matrix of assumptions) mediates a tandem of dualisms, that between the external object and the organ of sense, and that between the senses and the intellect. In the sense most relevant to The Anniversaries, *species* could refer to the intelligible form of an object, that which can only be "seen," to adopt the old metaphor, by the "eye of the mind."

Out of the nomen-clutter there emerged, around the middle of the sixteenth century, a linguistic tendency to read Plato and Augustine back into Aristotle and St. Thomas.[19] Pomponazzi, for example, seems to move easily from ideas in the mind of deity to *idea quae est in mente nostra, quae est species,*[20] and C. C. J Webb, following Sir William Hamilton's "Supplementary Dissertations on Thomas Reid," has drawn attention to one of the more revealing moments in the history of this particular linguistic evolution, which may be thought to culminate in Descartes.[21] Melanchthon, whose Aristoteleanism is in the service of Lutheran Protestantism, on occasion resembles Cicero in failing to differentiate sharply between the Peripatetics and the Academics; indeed, as part of the effort, not confined to Melanchthon, to reconcile Aristotle and Plato, Melanchthon argues that "ideas" are *imagines in mente.*[22] In his *De Anima* (Lyons, 1555) he takes the next (cognitive) step and uses *idea* for *actus intelligendi* and in his commentaries for *universalia*.[23] J. C. Scaliger in *De Subtilitate* denounces such usages as neoteric, abusive;[24] and Reid notes, rightly, that "*Melanch.*" is in the margin. Seldom is it possible to demarcate a stage in linguistic evolution with greater exactitude: the word *idea* has become synonymous with what was known in the perspectivist tradition as the *species intelligibilis*.

Scaliger had about as much influence on linguistic drift as most conservatives. Goclenius in his *Lexicon* seems to accept the meaning favored by Melanchthon, Fracastorius uses *ideae* as synonymous with *universalia (species intelligibiles)*,[25] and popularizers like Blundeville simply assert that when Plato said *idea* he had *species* in mind all along.

Blundeville inquires, rhetorically, what "species [be] called of the Greeks?" and answers: "It is called *Idea*," and then without hesitation he proceeds to an Aristotelean definition; "which is as much to say, as a common shape conceiued in the mind, through some knowledge had before of one or two *Individuums* hauing that shape." Blundeville then explains that "such shapes or *Ideae* are said also to be perpetuall,"

> Because they continue in the mind, though the things themselues cease to haue any being: as the shape of a Rose continueth in our minds in the cold heart of Winter, when there is no Rose indeed. And this is the true meaning of *Plato* touching *Idea,* that is, to be perpetuall in the mind, not separate from mans intelligence, as some men faine.

Blundeville assumes that he knows what Plato meant because he knows from Aristotle and the Schoolmen that "vniuersalities are always to bee comprehended in mans mind, but not *Individua:* which, because they are infinite, there can be had of them no certayne science or knowledge."[26] Blundeville, in effect, records the triumph of Melanchthon over Scaliger, and his exposition of the "true meaning" elucidates Donne's justification of himself to Jonson—not an Augustinian exemplar, not even a Platonic-Augustinian "ideal," but rather an Aristotelean-Thomist "idea."

For Blundeville *species* is a "vniuersall word" signifying what Plato really meant by *idea,* and this philosophical interpretation coincides well enough with what had happened in linguistic practice during the course of the second half of the sixteenth century. The transliterated Greek word *idea* and the preferred Latin translation *species* had undergone separate but parallel evolutions through the Middle Ages and into the Renaissance—but then, and rather suddenly, they reverse their lexical functions. *Species,* that is, starts out the relevant part of its linguistic life as a translation of *idea.* During the latter part of the sixteenth century, however, the transliterated loan-word *idea,* now comfortably at home in the English language, becomes a synonym, even a substitute, for *species,* particularly for what in the lexicon of the Schools and the "perspectivists" was called *species intelligibilis:* the intelligible species, the intelligible idea. *Idea* is a "vniuersall word" synonymous with *species.* In short, Donne told Jonson that "he described" the intelligible species of a woman "and not as she was."

There may be some tendency on the part of modern readers to try to imagine the intelligible species or "vniuersall word" as some kind of common denominator. This is not what Aristotle or Aquinas meant, and this is not what Donne has in mind in The Anniversaries. The "idea" defines that which makes the thing what it really is. What finally counts for Donne is the ability, as he says in The Second Anniversary, to get "up unto the watch-towre," and to get up there one has to be, primarily though not exclusively, an Aristotelean, or at least an "aristotelean-platonist" in Blundeville's sense. If Donne indeed told Jonson that "he described the Idea of a Woman and not as she was," the word "idea" can only refer, in this context, to the "vniuersall word" or intelligible species. To "see" the "Idea" of Elizabeth Drury we must use the eye of the mind, not Plato's eye of the mind (unless it is Blundeville's Plato) but Cicero's eye of the mind.

The qualification "and not as she was" indicates that Donne had in mind the basic distinction between essence and accidents. When in the context of this distinction we "see" the Idea we do not see A Symbol, nor ought we to think in terms of causes and effects. Rather, we come to know Elizabeth for what makes her what she is, no longer occluded from our view by the individuating properties of matter, which are unintelligible.[27] This last point, one of the possible consequences of hylomorphic theories of "sub-

stance," has absolute importance for The Anniversaries, for we
tend to think that particulars are easier to understand than universals, whereas for Donne the "idea," in Blundeville's words, may
"bee comprehended in mans mind, but not *Individua*." Donne
alludes to this epistemological fact when, toward the close of The
First Anniversary, he boasts of his "great Office" as the poet of
memory and adds, "Nor could incomprehensiblenesse deterre /
Me" (469–70). It is not merely a compliment to Mistress Drury,
the *topos* of inexpressibility that assures Sir Robert that the illimitable memory of his daughter, which seems to be "matter fit for
[saintly] Chronicle, not verse," cannot be reduced to ordinary
versifying. It is also an allusion to the epistemological obstacle, the
material accidents of Elizabeth Drury that may not "bee comprehended in mans mind."

We are now in position to scrutinize Elizabeth Drury a
little more closely, first as she was and then as she is, and always
will be, in idea. She seems to have been quite slim, and, even for
those days, rather short, so let us say that she is almost four-foot-
two and with eyes of blue—and with any number of other accidental properties you may care to grant her. By all means make
her visible to what the poet, in The Second Anniversary, calls
"sense, and Fantasy"; but since she remains obscured by the individuating conditions of matter, she is still, to speak strictly, unintelligible; she "deterre[s]" us through her "incomprehensiblenesse."
Although we are told in The First Anniversary that "all Impressions came" from her, she remains, "by Receivers impotencies"
(415–16), unknowable to those "who lodge an In-mate soule" (6).

In this life the proper reception of these "Impressions"
(the word is technical, exact, "perspectivist") is the closest approximation we have to angelic "intuition" (the word is technical,
exact, "perspectivist"). Sir Thomas Browne proclaims that "no
man truely knows another," for God "onely beholds me, and all
the world, who lookes not on us through a derived ray, or a
trajection of a sensible species, but beholds the substance without
the helpe of accidents, and the formes of things, as wee their
operations." Browne knows that "according to *Aristotles* Philosophy" there must be a "body or Medium to hand and transport the
visible rayes of the object unto the sense," but he has faith that "if

in our glorified eyes, the faculty of sight & reception of objects I could thinke the visible species there to be as unlimitable a way as now the intellectuall."[28] It is by the "unlimitable" species, the "intellectuall" species, that we must see Elizabeth Drury, and Milton in the person of his sociable archangel (5.486–90) offers the radical assurance—Donne would not have permitted himself to go quite so far—that our comprehension of her in this manner is not entirely different from the angels' "intuitive" (*intueor*, immediate enlightenment) knowledge of essences:

> Fancy and understanding, whence the Soul
> Reason receives, and reason is her being,
> Discursive, or Intuitive; discourse
> Is oftest yours, the latter most is ours,
> Differing but in degree, of kind the same.

Our minds, shaped by the principles laid down in Aristotle's *De Anima*, must move discursively, but our apprehension of the "intellectuall" species is in its own way "illimitable" in dealing with the "incomprehensiblenesse" of Elizabeth Drury; these cognitive processes, at least for those committed more to Browne's "comparative way" of the rationalists than to the "negative way" of the mystics, differ according to Milton "but in degree, of kind the same."

In Donne's entirely traditional formulation in The First Anniversary, the process begins when "to our eyes, the formes from objects flow" (316), which is to say that the *species sensibilis,* the sensible species, flow from the girl to our eyes where they are impressed on the organs of sense, then channeled within through the agency of the bodily "spirits" to become expressed species or sensuous representations. Yet she remains unintelligible, incomprehensible. Passing through the *sensus communis,* the expressed species of the girl is once again impressed, on this occasion in the glass or mirror of the imagination where for the first time "she" becomes available to the intellect. The understanding functions under two aspects, the passive and mirrorlike *intellectus possibilis,* and the active, lamplike *intellectus agens.* The active intellect illuminates (Plato's trope used, desperately, by Aristotle) the sensuous image of the girl, making it possible for the first time to comprehend the object in and through the image of the object discerned in the fantasy (or the memory). In other words, the active intellect expresses the intelligible species from the image of Elizabeth Drury "as she was" and impresses it upon the passive or potential intellect, where it is actualized as an expressed intelligible species. The object known and the knower are now identical: "it is both the object and the wit." The knower now possesses, in what Aristotle calls The Place of Forms, "the Idea of a Woman and not as she was."

If Drummond's anecdote is true, and truly reported, Donne's diction and phrasing coincide with the philological evidence: Donne told Jonson that he described the intelligible species of a virtuous young woman. Speaking of her "as she was," the poet laments her in elegiac hyperbole. Speaking of the "Idea of a Woman," the poet's "hyperbolic" statements simply convey what is true about the young woman, about us, and about the fallen world in which we live.[29] If we are good, and of good understanding, we too may find that we are, to use the phrasing of The Second Anniversary, "growne all Ey" so that we too may "see all things despoyld of fallacies," reflected in the *claritas* of that which makes them what they are. Then we shall know Elizabeth Drury as now the poet knows her and offers to "name" her, and we shall understand the epistemological conceit on which The Anniversaries turn, the "hinge" (to use Jonson's word) on which they pivot. The anecdote does not, however, constitute sufficient evidence in itself either to support these generalizations or to lend them the necessary specificity. The Anniversaries must supply the corroborating evidence; the poems themselves must authenticate and give meaning to Donne's reply to Jonson. In Donne's universe of discourse, we must "up unto the watch-towre get" to see the "Idea of a Woman."

The Watch-Towre (1)

Donne may well have tried to explain his witty hyperboles to Jonson. Donne certainly sought to justify
himself to his friends in April of 1612. Writing from Paris Donne
acknowledges that he has heard "from *England* many censures of
my book, of M^{ris.} *Drury*" but strongly protests that his fault lies
only in allowing the poems to be printed: "against my conscience,
that is, against my own opinion, that I should not have done so."[1]
What has not been noticed—and yet is crucial to an understanding
of the poems—is that Donne sought to justify his procedures
before as well as after the fact.

The opening lines of The First Anniversary constitute in
effect an act of literary criticism by posing an invidious contrast
between two kinds of readers: those who are able to "see" (the
verb is crucial) Elizabeth Drury, themselves, and the poem, and
those without the wit to "see, and Judge" either Elizabeth Drury,
themselves, or the poem. These last, as the poet later suggests in
The Second Anniversary, ought to be reckoned amongst those
who have failed to ascend to The Watch-Towre:

> When wilt thou shake off this Pedantery,
> Of being taught by sense, and Fantasy?
> Thou look'st through spectacles; small things seeme great
> Below; But up unto the watch-towre get,
> And see all things despoyld of fallacies. . . .   (291–95)

Restricted to "sense, and Fantasy," these unknowing ones cannot, to formulate it in terms of the ternate series that Donne prescribes in The First Anniversary, "see, and Judge, and follow worthinesse" by remembering the "rich soule" of Elizabeth Drury. The poet contrasts those (readers) "who know" with those (readers) who merely "lodge an In-mate soule":

> When that rich soule which to her Heaven is gone,
> Whom all they celebrate, who know they'have one,
> (For who is sure he hath a soule, unlesse
> It see, and Judge, and follow worthinesse,
> And by Deedes praise it? He who doth not this,
> May lodge an In-mate soule, but 'tis not his.)[2]

The obligation laid upon the reader—as a requirement for reading the poem!—is nothing less than *nosce teipsum,* to know thyself: not of course in the sense recommended by Freud, nor yet in the sense advocated by Socrates, but rather in the specific sense intended by Donne and those Renaissance Christians of his persuasion.

When Donne posits his two kinds of readers in the opening lines of The First Anniversary and recurs to the distinction in The Second Anniversary, he is practicing his usual exclusionary tactics, marking himself off less or more successfully from those who merely "lodge an In-mate soule," just as in, say, "A Valediction" he differences himself from those whose "soule is sense" and who in consequence can only participate in "dull sublunary lovers love."[3] These tactics leave the critics in an extremely vulnerable position.

All literary criticism necessarily involves some kind of selection and translation: selection of certain elements of a work to the exclusion of others, translation of these elements into the vocabulary of psychoanalysis, of cultural materialism, of deconstruction, of Coleridgean symbolism, or whatever kind of discourse proves congenial to the critic and meaningful to her audience. In the case of The Anniversaries, however, the poet consciously and aggressively intervenes not only in the process of selection (by defining the proper activities of the proper reader, by disqualifying all others) but also in the process of translation (by drawing attention to his own technical vocabulary, by disqualifying other nomenclatures). In The First Anniversary he anticipates the adverse criticism he in fact received, and he attempts to render it invalid in advance, defining those who do not know themselves as those who cannot hope to "see, and Judge" the worth of Elizabeth Drury or the poem.

The poet demands that his intentions be acknowledged for what they are, which by tendentious implication means that the reader, in order to be numbered among those who are in the know, must "select" those features of the work ("see, and Judge, and follow") made salient by the poet, and by the same token must "translate" as little as possible simply in order to be considered for the honorific category of those "who know." By implication the modern reader must seek to reanimate the dead idiom of "see, and Judge, and follow" or consign himself to the unenviable classification of those who "lodge" a transient "soule." The older meanings of "see, and Judge, and follow" before their demise, as well as their connections to the "rich soule" of Elizabeth Drury and to the souls of those "who know they'have one," formed part of Donne's purposes as he wrote, which is to say that the poet committed the intentional fallacy before I could implicate myself in the endeavor. Neither party to the exchange can avoid the fallacy. Nor should we try to avoid it: the intent to divine the intent of the other initiates the process of interpretation, and it is, after all, the least that we owe each other. The epistemological conceit governing The Anniversaries lends itself well to this wished-for correspondence of intents, for Donne explicitly intends intention, and his community of those "who know," intending the intention he intends, act to preserve—against the forgetfulness of those who do not know themselves—the intentional meaning of intentional meaning.

Donne's intention must of course receive its formulation in the available language, in the terms associated with the conceptual archetypes that the inhabitants of his particular time and place employed in making their psychological predicaments intelligible to themselves and to each other. With respect to the opening lines of The First Anniversary, the triadic formula of "see, and Judge, and follow" cannot be, to take the obvious contrasting example, the Freudian triad of superego, ego, and id but must be what

Donne, following Bernard who follows Augustine, calls "a trinity from the Trinity."[4] In *Paradiso* XXIV Dante the Pilgrim, catechized by St. Peter, shows that he knows himself by confessing his belief in the Trinity, three Persons in one essence. This credo, sealed upon his mind *(mente mi sigilla),* becomes a "spark" that "dilates into living flame" and "scintillates" within his mind like a star in heaven; and in Canto XXXIII—sight, except for St. Bernard's Prayer, solely takes the place of sound in this Canto—Dante receives the final vision of the *Commedia,* the three circles of three colors that remain inaccessible even to this poet's *alta fantasia,* and yet within this ineffable vision of the Trinity, Dante, his mind again illuminated by a "flash" *(da un fulgore),* seems to see the Image of Man "painted with our own likeness" *(pinta della nostra effige).* Here Dante ends the *Commedia,* with the *lume reflesso* of the Trinity that reveals his image and *l'amor che move il sole e l'altre stelle;* and here Donne begins the meditations of The Anniversaries.[5]

In Shakespeare's *Measure for Measure* Isabella provides the most economical and eloquent formulation of the conceptual archetype that lies behind Donne's "trinity from the Trinity":

> But man, proud man,
> Drest in a little briefe authoritie,
> Most ignorant of what he's most assur'd,
> (His glassie Essence) like an angry Ape
> Plaies such phantastique tricks before high heauen,
> As makes the Angels weepe: who with our spleenes,
> Would all themselues laugh mortall.[6]

In this context "glassie" signifies "mirrorlike" and alludes to the scriptural fact of man's having been created in the "image" of God. "But man," as Sir Walter Ralegh notes in his *History of the World,* "is ignorant of the essence of his own soul."[7] Man is "most ignorant" of his essential self—what it means to him to have been created in the mirror-image of his Creator—even though "he's most assur'd" of that essential self by God's own account of the matter in Genesis. Mind, according to this commanding trope, is reflecting substance, and what lies mirrored there, according to the Augustinian tradition as it finds its way into The Anniversaries, is a "trinity from the Trinity." If man is not "ignorant of the essence of his own soul," he will see reflected in the mirror of his mind the faculties of memory, understanding, and will. Then, and only then, will he be no longer "ignorant" of what he is "most assur'd" —his "glassie Essence."

As Donne puts it in *Essays in Divinity,* Pt. 2, "Certainly, every Creature shewes God, as a glass, but glimeringly and transitorily, by the frailty both of the receiver, and beholder: Our selves have his Image, as Medals, permanently, and preciously delivered." Nevertheless, in this life, by reason of the "frailty both of the receiver, and beholder," we fully "comprehend" neither "Gods Essence" nor our own. Although discursive "meditations" can take us only so far, Donne in the *Essays,* as elsewhere, nevertheless allows "reason" its own powers and takes care to specify that "we do not deny" the "sovereign power" of "common notions and generall impressions."[8] To return in this context to The Anniversaries, we may conclude that the man with the "In-mate soule" reveals the "frailty both of the receiver, and beholder" and lacks the "sovereign power" of "generall impressions"; such a man is one of those who do *not* "know they'have one," for he is "most ignorant of what he's most assur'd." Such a man (reader), according to the poet, may "lodge an In-mate soule, but 'tis not his." To put it bluntly, such a reader, because of the "frailty both of the receiver, and beholder," will fail to "see" the "glassie Essence" of Elizabeth Drury, will fail to comprehend the true connection between the death of Elizabeth Drury and the death of the world; and may even, beguiled by "sense, and Fantasy," come to imagine that the young girl is A Symbol Of Something . . .

The knowing man (reader) may be "sure" he is not "most ignorant of what he's most assur'd" if he can "see, and Judge, and follow worthinesse." These three acts—of memory, understanding, and will—form a "trinity" modeled on the Trinity. As Donne says in the sermons, "Let us therefore, with S. *Bernard,* consider *Trinitatem Creatricem,* and *Trinitatem Creatam,* A Creating, and a Created Trinity; A Trinity, which the Trinity in Heaven, Father, Son, and Holy Ghost, hath created in our soules, Reason, Memory, and Will."[9] Donne's tripartite formulation, which the poet uses in The Anniversaries as part of his intention to disqualify certain readers in advance, derives from his understanding of the human soul as a "trinity" made up of the memory (in which we "see"), the understanding (by which we "Judge"), and the will (according to the movement of which we "follow worthinesse").[10]

At least since the time of Augustine, theologians (except for some of the Reformers, notably Calvin) interpreted the scriptural fact that man is created in the "image" of God to mean that we possess within ourselves an interior "trinity"—not three Persons but three faculties in one nature. The divine analogy confers selfhood on the person; it allows Donne the terms in which to define the self or the subject—the necessary precondition of being able to read The Anniversaries. There is no way to exaggerate the significance of this analogical transfer of "natures" from God to man, either for the history of *nosce teipsum* or for the interpretation of The Anniversaries. In *De Trinitate* Augustine multiplies triads with the indefatigable ingenuity of a metaphysical poet, but his final emphasis, at least in the view of later writers, falls on remembering, knowing, and loving as the means by which we form the "inner word" and direct the soul to God; and Aquinas finds in Augustine's "trinities" a significant parallel to the "processions" of the Word and the Spirit from God.[11]

The image of the Trinity within the soul provides the foundation in human nature for participation in the eternal life of the Trinity, and not incidentally it gives Donne a way of calling attention to the nature of his "self" and its relation to other "selves" (readers), for no man is an island. As Sir Thomas Elyot puts it, "And of that same matter and substance that his soul is of, be all other souls that now are, and have been, and ever shall be, without singularity or pre-eminence of nature. In semblable estate is his body, and of no better clay (as I may frankly say) is a gentleman made than a carter, and of liberty of will as much is given of God to the poor herdsman as to the great and mighty emperor. Then in knowing the condition of his soul and body he knoweth himself, and consequently in the same thing he knoweth every other man."[12] Knowing oneself means knowing others of the "same matter and substance" as integral parts of the *corpus mysticum* of believers—or, indeed, as parts of the community of knowing readers of The Anniversaries.

In connection with the opening lines of The First Anniversary, Wesley Milgate follows Manley in citing yet another "trinitarian" passage from the sermons: "As God, one *God* created us, so wee have a soul, *one soul,* that represents, and is some image of that one God; As the three Persons of the *Trinity* created us, so we have, in our one soul, a *threefold impression* of that image, and, as Saint *Bernard* calls it, *A trinity from the Trinity* [Migne, *P.L.* clxxiv. 546–47], in those *three faculties* of the soul, the *Vnderstanding,* the *Will,* and the *Memory.*"[13] I emphasize the matter because this "trinity from the Trinity" specifies the nature of the "intended" reader of The Anniversaries and points toward the epistemological conceit on which the poems are based.

The internal trinity is not merely a theological abstraction but a psychological fact to be assumed in reading The Anniversaries and, argues Donne the preacher, during the course of daily devotions and meditations:

> And therefore be not too curious in searching reasons, and demonstrations of the Trinity, but yet accustome thy selfe to meditations upon the Trinity, in all occasions, and finde impressions of the Trinity, in the three faculties of thine owne soule, Thy Reason, thy Will, and thy Memory.   (*Sermons,* III, 154)

In *The Confessions* Augustine comes close to identifying memory with the self, and Donne follows him in this tendency in arguing that the most important of the three psychological powers or faculties is not the reason or the will but the memory. It is true that the "eye [traditionally associated with memory] is the devils doore" and that "the eare [usually associated with teaching and reason] is the Holy Ghosts first doore" (*Sermons,* VIII, 228); true that *"Knowledge* cannot save us, but we cannot be saved without Knowledge" (*Sermons,* III, 359); and true that "when we come to sin, upon reason, and upon discourse, upon Meditation, and upon plot, This is *Humanum,* to become the Man of Sin, to surrender that, which is the Form, and Essence of man, Reason, and understanding, to the service of sin" (*Sermons,* I, 225). Therefore, and even though the "Form, and Essence of man" is his "Reason, and understanding," Donne accords the faculty of memory a special role in the process of salvation (and the writing of poetry).

Noting "perversenesse in both faculties, *understanding,* and *will,*" Donne goes on to explain that "for the rectifying of the *will,* the *understanding* must be rectified; and that implies great difficulty: But the *memory* is so familiar, and so present, and so ready a faculty, as will always answer, if we will but speak to it, and aske it, *what God hath done for us, or for others.* The art of *salvation,* is but the art of *memory.*" And then Donne immediately makes this strong conclusion even more emphatic by noting its genealogy: "*Plato* plac'd *all learning* in the memory; wee may place *all Religion* in the memory too" (*Sermons,* II, 73–74). Memory has its special powers because, like the imagination, it mediates between sensation, especially the sense of sight, and the understanding. Before we may "Judge" (through wit or understanding) and "follow" (through the movement of the will), we must be able to "see" Elizabeth Drury in "memory."

It is a matter of *perspectiva,* in the Aristotelean–Thomist tradition. When "thou look'st through spectacles,

> small things seeme great
> Below; But up unto the watch-towre get,
> And see all things despoyld of fallacies. . . .
> (293–95)

Although in "Heaven" the soul "straight know'st all" (299) and has need of neither "sense" nor "Fantasy," the soul in this life, in order to see Elizabeth Drury (and become the reader of the poem), must make use of sense and fantasy (the images of the poems) to move beyond them—to ascend to the "watch-towre."

In The First Anniversary Donne—following Plato, Aristotle, Augustine, Aquinas—maintains succinctly that "sight is the noblest sense of any one" (353), a judgment explained at greater length in the sermons: "The sight is so much the Noblest of all the senses, as that it is all the senses. As the reasonable soul of man, when it enters, becomes all the soul of man, and he hath no longer a vegetative, and a sensitive soul, but all is that one reasonable soul; so, sayes S. *Augustine* (and he exemplifies it, by severall pregnant places of Scripture) *Visus per omnes sensus recurrit,* All the senses are called Seeing" (*Sermons,* VIII, 221). In The Second Anniversary the "soule" en route to the beatific vision "now is growne all Ey" (200) because sight must precede understanding:

> Onely who have enjoyd
> The sight of God, in fulnesse, can thinke it. . . .
>
> (440–41)

And so also, in degree, with more mundane kinds of vision. In the tradition in which Donne writes, sensing provides the model for thinking, and "sight is the noblest sense": an ocular model for abstractive cognition that in its later sophistications becomes an optical model for the workings of mind in general. In "The Harbinger to the Progres" Joseph Hall shows that he understood what Donne was about when the "harbinger" represents himself as "third" to the "two soules" of Elizabeth and the poet. Since "no soule" while in the body "can follow thee [Elizabeth] halfe way" or "see thy flight" that "doth our thoughts outgoe," Hall must ask "what soule besides thine owne" can "tell" and "relate" the "blessed state"? Only Donne's "Great spirit," which the "Rich soule" of Elizabeth "follow'd hast," can be equal to so great a task, and "none [other] can follow . . . so fast" or "so farre," for Donne has gone beyond "vulgar sight" and "now mak'st proud the better eyes."

The vulgar vision of some of Donne's contemporaries and of subsequent critics will not serve. To see Elizabeth Drury and to read the poems we need "better eyes," which in accord with the ancient equation between seeing and knowing implies the need for a better mind. And a better mind for Donne, though not for us, depends on virtue. Donne makes an epistemological—and misogynous—joke of the matter in "Communitie,"

> If they were good it would be seene,
> Good is as visible as greene,
>
> (Grierson, *Poems,* 32)

but Jasper Mayne is entirely serious, and his use of "good" has moral as well as esthetic force, when in his elegy on Donne he says of the "Anniverse" that it is

> Indeed so farre above its Reader, good,
> That we are thought wits, when 'tis understood.
>
> (Grierson, 382)

This system of parallels—sight, thought, virtue—corresponds to the requirements for knowing oneself and reading the poems: "see, and Judge, and follow worthinesse." The problem of "seeing" the poems corresponds to the difficulty of seeing Elizabeth Drury, "since now no other way there is," explains Donne in The First Anniversary, "But goodnes, to see her" (16–17). Just as it would be wrong to take Mayne's "good" in a purely esthetic sense, so it would be wrong to take Donne's explanation in a purely literary way, as poetic symbolism or epideictic hyperbole: Donne means that, as a matter of epistemological fact, you can't see her if you are not good, for you have "vulgar sight" and stand in need of "better eyes."

Donne notes toward the end of The First Anniversary that "incomprehensiblenesse" could not "deterre" him from writing about Elizabeth Drury (469), though he knew that publication could only expose his poems to those of "vulgar sight" who, "being dead" (63) to virtue, cannot comprehend her "rich soule." Other readers, those in the know about the epistemological conceit informing the poems, have "better eyes." They "so many weed-lesse Paradises bee" (82) and possess Edenic vision (as Glanvill notes, Adam in Eden needed no spectacles); they detect the "glimmering light" of the memory of Elizabeth, with the consequence that

> A faint weake love of vertue and of good
> Reflects from her, on them which understood. . . .
>
> (71–72)

Accordingly, Donne's conceits, his intellectual images, derive in important instances from the science of optics:

> That soules were but Resultances from her,
> And did from her into our bodies go,
> As to our eyes, the formes from objects flow.
>
> (314–16)

Those of lesser wit and purblind vision find themselves deterred by "incomprehensiblenesse" and perceive only imperfectly or not at all the subject of The Anniversaries:

> She from whose influence all Impressions came,
> But, by Receivers impotencies, lame. . . .
>
> (415–16)

It will be evident that Donne has laid down stringent requirements for a proper reading of The Anniversaries and that he has been at pains to anticipate the adverse judgments of possible detractors; if we fail to "see," it is by reason of (our) "Receivers impotencies." Since Donne's mode of defense includes such a strong component of aggressive contempt, we may sympathize with the modern critics who have apparently felt reluctant to face the fact that they come to the poems equipped with impotent receivers.

Such a critic, in need of "better eyes," remains "most ignorant of what he's most assur'd"; lodging "an In-mate soule," a "soule of sense," he does not know how his "glassie Essence" may enable him to "see, and Judge, and follow." He merely thinks he can think, whereas in actuality he lacks the wit to follow the poet whose verse, like that of Moses, "hath a middle nature" (474) between earth and heaven and is "a last and lastingst peece" (462). This kind of literary critic, his "Receiver" become "lame" by reason of its "impotencies," has been deterred by "incomprehensiblenesse," by material individuality, so that in Donne's terms he can't see the poems for what they are.

We lack the virtue to see and think aright because our minds have become preoccupied with particularity to the exclusion of the universal, the *species intelligibilis expressa*. In consequence Donne in The Second Anniversary urges us into the "watchtowre" where we may "shake off" the "spectacles" of "sense, and Fantasy" and "see all things despoyld of fallacies" (291–95): no "soule of sense" can see Elizabeth Drury except in the "incomprehensiblenesse" of her material individuality.

Although neither Plato nor Aristotle dealt with universals in the manner of the medieval theologians, the so-called realists and nominalists of the medieval period derived much of their authority from the classical philosophers. The differences between the moderate elements of both schools were perhaps not as different as many of the differences within each school, but in the interest of expository simplicity we may avoid the appeal to some third category, such as "conceptualist," and imagine that the realists consistently maintain that universals have some kind of independent existence, whereas the nominalists, though many were prepared to grant general "names" some sort of objective relation to the particulars, consistently hold that universals do not exist absolutely as things in themselves; the valiant attempts of modern Thomists like Etienne Gilson and Jacques Maritain—in spite of their gift for lucidity—to make sense of what agitated the medieval thinkers sometimes appear as ponderous, and overly qualified, as the sentence I just wrote. The metaphysical spectrum of possibilities may run from "ideas" *ante rem* (before the things of this world, in the mind of God) to "ideas" *in rem* (in the things of this world, as their forms or principles of being) to "ideas" *post rem* (in the minds of human beings); and this kind of standard formulation may do well enough, up to a point, for Donne and his view of Mistress Elizabeth Drury: her "idea" subsists *ante rebus,* in the mind of deity, it exists in her *in rebus* as form or principle of being, and it appears *post rebus* in the mind of the knowing reader. But the conventional dichotomy between "realists" and "nominalists" is so difficult to sustain in relation to particular works of the period that the terms become misleading, inaccurate, or worse.

Another way of telling the story avoids the superimposition of these categories and focuses instead on the "perspectivists," most notably Roger Bacon (ca. 1220–92), who appears to have been the leading figure in the West to model human cognition on the most advanced optical treatise available at the time—Alhazen's *De Aspectibus.*[14] Bacon's metaphysic of light, together with the "optical" or "perspectivist" treatises of Pecham and Witelo, established an "epistemology" that remained in place from the thirteenth through the sixteenth century. Although William of Ockham, among others, vigorously attacked the doctrine of *species in medio* and tried to razor such notions out of the curriculum, the syntheses of the "perspectivists" continued to guide inquiry even at Ockham's Oxford and retained their prestige as the best means of explaining cognitive processes during the time Donne attended Hart Hall.[15] These "perspectivist" tractates exfoliated into comprehensive theories about deity and the universe, about human perception and cognition. They absorbed the teachings of Augustine and the pseudo-Dionysius, of Aristotle and his Greek and Arabian commentators, of Euclid and Galen. They synthesized, however unsystematically and uncritically, the prevalent views of the world and of human cognition; their doctrines about the functioning of the senses and the mind underlie the questions that agitated the "realists" and "nominalists" and that normally receive the attentions of historians of theology and philosophy. The "perspectivists" provided answers to basic questions about perception and cognition, answers that were utilized by Donne and his contemporaries.

Such questions held special urgency for the thinkers of the medieval period because the status of ideas-as-universals appeared to involve articles of faith. Augustine had, for example, expropriated Neoplatonic theories to support Christian doctrine: instead of allowing Plato's Forms or Ideas to subsist in a transcendental realm of their own, Augustine's reading of Plotinus allowed him to transfer the Ideas to the mind of deity where as exemplars or patterns they serve the Supreme Artifex in the process of creation. As Plotinus placed the One above the Forms as well as above the Many, so Augustine allowed God precedence over the Ideas as well as over the species and particulars. It was a neat solution, one that recommended itself to Donne, though the judicious Hooker had his doubts and Puttenham, among others, utterly rejected the metaphysical sleight-of-hand.

In meditating on St. Paul and Original Sin, Augustine could avail himself of the "platonic" explanation. If men are indeed sinful before they perform any sinful act, then the "idea" Sinful Man must be conceived to be real and universal prior to and apart from its embodiment in particular fallen men. In his polemics Augustine could adopt similar positions, assuming the prior existence of the universal "idea" in order to root out heretical doctrine in particular men. Bishop Donatus of Carthage and his fellow schismatics, for example, maintained that the validity of the sacraments depended on the spiritual probity of the priests who administered the sacraments, and in combating this heresy Augustine made use of the distinction to which he recurred in *The City of God* —that the Invisible Church is real and universal apart from its particular manifestations in particular groups of men. In ways such as these, belief in universal "ideas" becomes entangled with belief itself, and then dogma may become an epistemological principle of living and dying, as when Donne in *The Devotions* movingly proclaims that "no man is an *Iland,* intire of it selfe . . . ; any mans *death* diminishes *me,* because I am involved in *Mankinde.*"[16]

Although the problem of universals seemed more pressing during the medieval period than at any other time, the problem is itself universal. We see particulars and class them under general names, regarding the particular dog or cat as individual specimens of, say, a species. Then we may come to shift our attention, as did Porphyry and Boethius, to the nature of the species themselves, inquiring whether they exist only in the mind or have some "real" existence in or even prior to the particulars. In Plato the "Ideas" or "Forms" were, at least at one stage of his thinking, regarded as more "real" than, and as ontologically prior to, the particulars of quotidian existence, whereas in Aristotle the "form" does not exist as an independent entity, transcendental or other, but is inseparable from the particular except insofar as the intellect may entertain it in the act of abstraction. For Aristotle the *psyche* is the "form" of the man; it is not an *ousia,* an independent substance, but the functioning of a particular body. It is the power or *dynamis* of living and knowing, and it has its own way of working *(energei)* and its own *telos* in the full actuality *(entelecheia)* of whatever it is. No Platonic dualism, rather a proportion: soul is to body as form is to matter.[17]

Although the operation of *nous* depends on phantasmata, its main business is to perceive the intelligible forms or universals. It is the pure capacity to know, to enter into an identity with the object, that makes all things intelligible to the thinking soul. In the less technical language of Traherne's Meditation Seventy-Three of the Fourth Century, the "Objects" outside the mind interact with the "faculties of the Soul beholding them": a "Tree apprehended is a Tree in your Mind," and a "sand in your conception conformeth your soul, and reduceth it to the Cize and Similitud of a sand," and the "Heavens magnifie your soul to the Wideness of the Heavens"; the "Spaces abov the Heavens enlarg it Wider to their own Dimensions," and "what is without Limit maketh your Conception illimited and Endless." In the succinct formulation of Meditation Seventy-Eight of the Second Century: "as Light varieth upon all objects whither it cometh, and returneth with the Form and figure of them: so is the Soul Transformed into the Being of its Object . . . , and by Understanding becometh All Things."[18] The mind, plastic to all things, becomes, in the act of knowing, one with its object. It is then, to adapt Donne's locution, a potent receiver.

In Aristotle there appears a dualism that must be overcome during the process of cognition, but it bears only a distant resemblance to the Christian dualism of body and soul or the Cartesian dualism of *res cogitans* (the thinking, feeling substance) and *res extensa* (matter extended in space). Aristotle sought primarily to deal with the dualism, apparently inherited from Plato, of "form" and the particulars of matter. Indeed, the *De Anima* may be viewed without undue distortion as Aristotle's solution to the problems raised by the absolute dichotomy between sense and intellect in Plato's Divided Line. The main problem in this context is not how the soul communicates with the body nor how mind communicates with what is not mind, but with how, in a world of sensible particulars, human beings manage the distinctively human process of abstraction, of generalization. In short, the problem is how we "up unto the watch-towre get."

Aristotle's solution in the *De Anima,* a treatise that says at least as much about sensation as it does about intellection, remains incomplete but suggestive, sufficiently suggestive to dominate thinking about thinking in the Renaissance until the time of Descartes. In the treatise Aristotle utilizes not only his basic distinction between "matter" and "form" but also the paired concepts of "potentiality" and "actuality," which he had developed to deal with the problems of "change" that had so graveled his predecessors (Donne will make witty use of the related pairing of "generation" and "corruption"). Since Aristotle assumes that successful cognition depends finally upon the reception of general ideas, he further supposes that there must exist in the human mind some power or faculty capable of receiving those ideas.[19]

The (Platonic?) dualism of sense and intellect apparently requires Aristotle to use "imagination" as an intermediate entity, a kind of halfway house for images derived from the senses. Aristotle and later thinkers seem to have had difficulty in conceiving of something being where it is not, as though the Law of the Excluded Middle were to be understood in spatial terms and then applied to the processes of thought. If the sun or the mountain cannot *be* in the mind, it was assumed that something else—a similitude, a phantasm, a "sensible species"—must be present to the mind, either in the imagination or available to the imagination from the memory, to stand vicariously for the physical object. Since thinking is "akin" to "sensing" (429a13), and since sight is sensing par excellence (428b30), "images serve as sense perceptions" for the "thinking soul" (431a8), which "thinks the forms in images" (431b2); "not the things themselves; for it is not the stone which is in the soul, but its form" (431b24).

Despite the difficulties and the ambiguities of the *De Anima,* we may be pretty sure about what Aristotle was trying to do in order to make thinking intelligible. He proceeds by way of analogy from sense perception, notably seeing, to produce a schematic account, as it were, of the soul in line with his hylomorphic conception of the "whole of nature." Nature comes in bundles of matter and form, moving from potentiality to actuality and exhibiting generation and corruption, and it is susceptible to analysis in terms of the four causes. "Since [just as] in the whole of nature there is something which is matter (and this is what is potentially all of them)" and since "there is something else which is their cause," there "must also be these differences in the soul": namely, the potential intellect, analogous to matter, "an intellect which is of this kind by becoming all things," and "another [the active intellect, analogous to form] which is so by producing all things." The second is "related" to the first "as an art to its material" and (in a Platonic metaphor) is "like light," in the "sense that light too makes colours which are potential into actual colours." The two intellects therefore stand in relation to each other as material cause to efficient cause, as "becoming all things" to "producing all things."

The intellect that resembles light is "distinct, unaffected, and unmixed, being in essence activity" (430a10), and its activity is to actualize the potentialities that allow the soul to grasp the essences of objects. In combination with the potential intellect, it makes the mind one with its object: "actual knowledge is identical with its object" (431a1). Aristotle may have felt a little uncomfortable, or at least a little undecided, about his need to posit the existence in the soul of the second intellect that resembles light, for he failed to lend it a name while nevertheless separating it from matter in ways unusual for him. His commentators, beginning with the Greeks, primarily Themistius and Alexander of Aphrodisias, did not hesitate to name this intellect *nous poietikos* (for the Latin commentators *intellectus agens*) in accord with what they assumed to be Aristotle's meaning, and in the course of explaining *De Anima* these and other commentators, primarily the Arabs, shaped Western thinking about thinking. Since Aristotle had more to say about sense than intellect in the treatise, he left precisely that much more room for the commentators; and what he did have to say allowed for a good deal of latitude in its interpretation, particularly though not exclusively in connection with that unnamed power that somehow *in actu* illuminated the power that until then remained *in potentia*.

Because one part of the thinking soul is rather casually but nonetheless explicitly denominated immortal (though Aristotle could not have been advocating the personal immortality espoused by Christian thinkers), is called separate and distinct, and is said to remain "unaffected" by the body, ideas or "thoughts" cannot *be* "images, but [nevertheless] they will not exist without images" (432a3). It is by means of the image or phantasm that the *nous* attains to its contemplation of the "forms," that the thinking part of the soul becomes "all existing things" (431b20), "identical with its object" (431a1) in the sense that it is the same as its "form" (the stone itself is not in the mind).

Because Aristotle assumes that "existing things are either objects of perception or objects of thought" (431b20), either the object of sense or the object of intellect, *we* know that he was trying to explain what is not so much a mind-body dualism, or a Christian soul-body dualism, as a sense-intellect dualism—a world divided into the particulars of sense and the generalized abstractions of the intellect. And yet there remains in this Aristotelean world enough residue of the Platonic position that the soul, or part of the soul, is somehow divorced from the procedures of sense, and is indeed in its highest part immortal, to induce Christian thinkers to persuade themselves that in *De Anima* Aristotle was describing the cognitive operations of their own minds. And, in consequence, the cognitive means by which we may ascend from "sense, and Fantasy" and "up unto the watch-towre get," where we may at last "see," and "think," the "Idea of a Woman."

The Watch-Towre (2)

The irresistible force of the *De Anima* and its multitude
of commentators began to be felt, against a background of Christian Platonism, during the twelfth century. In this
Christian-Platonic or Augustinian tradition the soul was regarded
as a spiritual "substance" possessed of *ratio superior,* devoted to
divine matters, and *ratio inferior,* concerned with the business of
this world. This soul was separate, or at least separable, from its
mortal body, and because, only because, God illuminates it, the
soul can lay claim, even after the Fall, to certain kinds of innate
knowledge and can perform relatively independent cognitive functions. This soul knew enough to deemphasize the importance of
sense perception but had no very convincing theory, as did Aristotle in *De Anima,* about how the mind managed the uniquely
human process of abstraction. The clash of this older tradition
with the "new" Aristotle eventuated as early as Bonaventure in a
synthesis that, though replete with diverse elements and irresolva-
ble contradictions, eventually became the "epistemology" of the
Renaissance.

The *De Anima,* encrusted with the Hellenistic and Arabian
commentaries that contributed to its authority, established cognitive hegemony in the School Latin, *verbum e verbo,* of the indefatigable William of Moerbeke during the second half of the thirteenth
century.[1] Aristotle seemed to be able to provide a description of
how the Christian soul could attain to the "idea" or *species intelligi-*

bilis expressa; and William of Moerbeke in turn provided most of the technical vocabulary of these mental transactions—initially to Latin Christendom but later to the vernaculars, there to be naturalized and then to be institutionalized.[2] Although the Humanists tried to offer their own, rather more Ciceronian, translations (even entitling the treatise *De Animo*), Moerbeke's version had established itself as *the* language of cognition to such a degree that the Humanists had to append Moerbekean glossaries to make their translations fully intelligible. These writers had the three-part soul of Plato's *Phaedrus;* they had, from many *loci* in Aristotle, the threefold division into vegetative soul, sensible soul, and rational soul; but it was, preeminently, in *De Anima* that these writers could find an explanation of how the rational soul actually managed to go about its business of *thinking,* an explanation of how the rational soul could begin where it had to begin, with "sense, and Fantasy," and then, triumphantly, ascend the hill of truth to see the "Idea." Poets from Dante to Donne relied upon Moerbeke, commentators from Aquinas to Zabarella (in the late sixteenth century) relied upon Moerbeke. It was this translation of the *De Anima* that established the vocabulary, the terms of discourse, that were used habitually to describe mental operations in Renaissance England: phantasia, phantasma, sensibile, sensitivum, intelligibile, intellectus patiens, intellectus agens, and the like. There is no way to exaggerate the importance of this development. From Dante to Donne, from Aquinas to Zabarella—this is the language of imagining and thinking: the vocabulary of cognition.

Thomas saw clearly that Aristotle had circumvented, in the first book of the *Physics,* where he develops the concepts of potency and act, *the* pre-Socratic problem, namely that of genesis and change as formulated in "no thing can come from nothing" and "what is does not come to be." Thomas saw clearly that the concepts of potentiality and actuality might be used, as indeed Aristotle had used them, to develop a cognitive model for the workings of the mind; and he fastened on Moerbeke's version of *De Anima* as a way of explaining how human beings managed to "see" the essence of an object. Although some ecclesiastical authorities reacted strongly against the influx of the new Aristoteleanism and on occasion branded Aquinas the main culprit, his system found its way into the schools and he himself found more favor among the Humanists than any other of the Schoolmen, almost as though they regarded him as a proto-Humanist. His formulations lent force and precision to the doctrine of intentional species as it appeared in the perspectivist tradition.

There is the world of the senses and the world of mind, mediated by imagination; there are the two intellects, mediated by images. The Christian doctrine of the immortality of the soul traditionally presupposes that the soul be separable from the body, which in turn excites the need for another mediating principle.

Western thought in general reveals the tendency to multiply intermediate entities. From the dyad comes the triad, just as the Father and the Son between Them produce the Holy Ghost. The Trinity, when sufficiently elaborated as a theological formula, may then be transferred, through the usual alchemy of metaphorical transmigration, to the souls of human beings, making of them, as in Augustine's *De Trinitate* and Donne's Anniversaries, a little trinity of memory, understanding, and will. Whether considering the mind and the body, that world and this world, the universal and the particular, the soul-as-prisoner and the body-as-prison, the philosophers and theologians seem to have assumed the necessary existence of a mediating concept or entity, the *tertium quid* that fills the need for what Plato called "participation."

Man himself is, after all, "that amphibious piece betweene a corporall and spirituall essence, that middle forme that linkes those two together, and makes good the method of God and nature, that jumps not from extreames, but unites the incompatible distances by some middle and participating natures." Man is the *vinculum* or middle link in the chain of being, and Sir Thomas Browne finds "the reall truth therein," in what he confesses might otherwise be considered "onely a pleasant trope of Rhetorick": "thus is man that great and true *Amphibium,* whose nature is disposed to live not onely like other creatures in divers elements, but in divided and distinguished worlds; for though there bee but one world to sense, there are two to reason; the one visible, the other invisible."[3] The alternative to ontological schizophrenia is the recognition of "some middle and participating natures," easy for Browne but difficult for Donne—and agonizing for Fulke

Greville, who knew what it meant to be "Created sicke, commanded to be sound."

Christianity—witness Greville's terrible dilemma and Augustine's tribulations with Manicheanism—may be thought of as
extremely in need of intermediate entities, and perhaps out of that
need extremely fertile in the dissemination of halfway points. Jesus
the Christ, theologically two natures in one person or by hyphen-
ation the God-man Who is man-God, represents only the most
spectacular instance of the need to mediate extremes and to sanc-
tion ongoing discourse, the need to preserve, and of course to
validate if possible, some sort of intercourse between the realm of
nature and the realm of deity. The doctrine of the immortality of
the soul seems to presuppose a "separable" soul, an incorruptible
soul temporarily housed in a corruptible body. But this dualistic
assumption, that the soul is not really the body and the body not
really the soul, entails a good many inconveniences for the theologian, the philosopher, and the common man or woman: the most
obvious, and easily the most discomfiting, stems from the question
of how the ghost in the machine communicates with the machine,
how the immortal and indivisible and impassible and immortal
soul of man manages to make his arms move and his mouth utter
the needed words about the immortality of the soul.

In this case the theologians and philosophers relied on the
medical profession and had recourse to the Galenic doctrine of the
spirits.[4] These convenient substances, arising as a kind of heat or
vapor from the blood, begin their physiological mediations in the
liver where they function as *natural spirits;* continuing to the heart
these comparatively gross spirits are refined, becoming the more
rarefied *vital spirits;* and then, having been communicated to the
brain, these are, by a final process of concoction and rarefaction,
transmuted into intellectual or *animal (anima,* "soul") *spirits,* most
of which then proceeded along the nerves to the organs of sense;
some remained in the ventricle of the brain to support the operations of the *sensus communis,* the imagination, the memory, and the
intellect. In *Paradise Lost* (5.483–87) the spirits, "by gradual scale
sublim'd," provide "both life and sense,"

> Fancy and understanding, whence the Soul
> Reason receives, and reason is her being;

and accordingly, Satan, "squat like a Toad, close at the ear of *Eve,*" seeks while she sleeps to control her "animal spirits that from pure blood arise" (4.805).[5] These *intellectual* or "anima" spirits were conceived to be the means by which the separable and impassible soul was enabled to communicate with the corruptible body. As Donne put it in "The Extasie" (Grierson, *Poems,* 53), "our blood labours to beget"

> Spirits, as like soules as it can,
> Because such fingers need to knit
> That subtile knot, which makes us man.

Although the spirits have now been consigned to the same discard bin as phlogiston, they did their job well enough at the time, and their particular uses included the mechanism of enamorment: the *spiritus visivus* emanates from the bright eye of the *donna,* penetrates the eye of the lover, and proceeds through the agency of the spirits to the heart where it disrupts the vital spirits, causing paleness, sleeplessness, languishing, listlessness, and other symptoms of love melancholy (the murderous glance of the basilisk operates in the same fashion). Even Descartes, who was the first important thinker of the Renaissance explicitly to reject the other main doctrine of mediation, that of the "species" or "forms," nevertheless assumed the reality of spirits in explaining the operation of his own *tertium quid,* the pineal gland. (When we speak nowadays of language as a "mode of representation" or as a "medium of communication," we exhibit the same habits of mind that created the doctrine of spirits: between mind and world, between mind and another mind, there are the intermediate entities called "words.")

Precisely analogous difficulties obtained for those Renaissance theorists who wanted to explain how immaterial mind interacts with the material world. Aristotle had taught them that objects in the external world were "impressed" on the organs of sense. In the *De Anima* and elsewhere the analogy is to a seal on wax, but he had left the exact nature of the process in doubt even in his complicated theory of how sight occurs through the "actualization" of the "diaphanous." He had here rejected the theories of extromission, that the eye emits a kind of fire that allows for sight, which inexplicably meant to many later thinkers, though not to Aristotle, that the object must therefore emit something that travels to the eye. What the something was and how it was propagated Aristotle, who could not know that he would be regarded in some quarters as the father of a theory he did not espouse, had not of course explained. The lacunae—perhaps also what was susceptible of misinterpretation or even what was simply hard to understand— allowed later practitioners of what was called the science of *perspectiva* to adapt and synthesize various aspects of the theories of vision propounded by Plato, Aristotle, Euclid, Galen, Lucretius, Al-Kindi, and, most important of all, Alhazen or Alhacen (Ibn al-Haytham).[6]

The ancients propounded theories of sight rather than light, theories of how we see rather than theories of the nature of light itself. Broadly speaking these were of three kinds: intromission (the eye somehow receives something from the object), extromission (the eye somehow goes out to get something from the object), and a combination of the two. These three suffer confused and confusing permutations as they are held by different thinkers and undergo inconsistent changes within the work of the same thinker; Aristotle, for example, can explicitly reject one theory in the *De Anima* and assume its validity in the *Meteorologica*. Since the theories also differed as the objectives of a Euclid (geometrical) differ from those of a Galen (physiological), the medieval and renaissance writers had their pick of a multitude of competing theories, and many of these writers, from Roger Bacon to Johannes Kepler, preferred to gloss over differences and inconsistencies to provide themselves with a rich, if contradictory and historically inaccurate, synthesis.

When Donne writes an "Epithalamion, or Mariage Song on the Lady Elizabeth, and Count Palatine being married on St. Valentine's Day" and praises the way the "lesser" take their "jollitie" from "thine eye" (31–32), Milgate aptly quotes Ficino (he could have used any number of platonizers) on how the "heart . . . pours . . . sparks of light through various single parts, but especially through the eyes. . . . [and] throws missiles of its own light into near-by eyes."[7] And in "The Extasie" Donne speaks from a variety of Platonisms as refined by the poets of the *dolce stil novo* and generations of Petrarchans, in which the process of enamorment is that of extromission (the *donna* and the basilisk going about their business in the same way):

> Our eye-beames twisted, and did thred
> Our eyes, upon one double string. . . .

In The Anniversaries, on the other hand, where the "formes from objects flow," Donne adopts the intromission theory that derives, in part and in some quarters, from a misunderstanding of Aristotle, that was refined by the Scholastics, that was contaminated by the atomists, and that was propagated through the optical treatises of Witelo and others. In theories of vision, as elsewhere in the Renaissance, syncretic tendencies produced a storehouse of philosophical incompatibilities and metaphysical conceits.

The medieval thinkers, in common with those in the Renaissance, had found it difficult to imagine direct communication between the soul and the external object. As with the soul and body, so with the soul and the object: it seemed necessary to posit the existence of an intermediate entity. Since the mountain is not in the mind, some cognitive surrogate must be there to take the place, as it were, of the mountain. The atomists tried to meet the problem with their intromission theories of *eidola* or *simulacra*, convoys of which peeled off the object and entered the eye. In Book IV of *De Rerum Natura*, Lucretius offers an elaborate account of vision that provides the physical or "corporeal" counterpart to the medieval doctrine of "intentional species" and emerges in the Renaissance, with a twist, as the "corporeal ideas" of Gassendi and Boyle. Lucretius explains that the objects of the external world constantly emit fine "films," and that these *rerum effigias tenuisque figuras* are propagated continuously in all directions until they strike another object, bounce off a mirror, or meet the human eye. The *membranae, exuviae, eidola, effigiae, imagines*, or *formae* later become generally known as *species visibilis*; these, when received by the sense organ, are conveyed by the spirits to the *sensus communis*, which correlates the "impressions" of the various senses and makes the "resultances" available to mind. Although this corporeal theory of intromission proved to be unsatisfactory—mainly because it was corporeal—to medieval Christians, the noncorporeal or "intentional" theories, as apprehended by thinkers less subtle than Aristotle or Aquinas, tended to become simplified in the direction of the corporeal theories.[8]

The doctrine of "intentional species," which I have mentioned before and which we now know could have been called the Doctrine Of Intentional Ideas, may be apprehended most easily in schematic form, ignoring its historical vicissitudes and the qualifications, even the rebuttals, introduced by individual Schoolmen.[9] Aristotle in *De Anima* had employed only the one word *forma* to refer to what was in the external object and to what supposedly corresponded to it in the mind. Since the medieval and renaissance thinkers had *idea* and *species* as well, they could clarify the distinction between inner and outer by using "form" for what was in the object and "idea" or (in more technical accounts of vision and cognition) "species" for what was in the mind. When in Donne, "to our eyes, the formes from objects flow," these external "realities" become (intentional) "species" within the human being.[10] Hobbes provides a schematic version of the doctrine, so accurately and concisely presented that it becomes travestied, in the first chapter of *Leviathan:*

> But the philosophy-schools, through all the universities of Christendom, grounded upon certain texts of Aristotle, teach another doctrine [than his own, of "motion"], and say, for the cause of *vision,* that the thing seen, sendeth forth on every side a *visible species,* in English, a *visible show, apparition,* or *aspect,* or *a being seen;* the receiving whereof into the eye, is *seeing.* And for the cause of *hearing,* that the thing heard, sendeth forth *an audible species.* . . . Nay, for the cause of *understanding* also, they say the thing understood, sendeth forth an *intelligible species,* that is, an *intelligible being seen;* which, coming into the understanding, makes us understand. I say not this, as disproving the use of universities; but because I am to speak hereafter of their office in a commonwealth, I must let you see . . . , which things would be amended in them; amongst which the frequency of insignificant speech is one.[11]

Then, as now, the universities institutionalize "insignificant speech," but before this "species" language of feeling and thinking lost its explanatory power, the philosophers could use it to elucidate the mechanisms of perception and cognition, John Davies could have recourse to it in understanding himself in *Nosce Teipsum,* and John Donne could use it to allow his readers to understand the "Idea of a Woman."

The doctrine of intentional species (as is usual in this matrix of assumptions) mediates a tandem of dualisms, that between the external object and the organ of sense, and that between the senses and the intellect. Accordingly, the species inside the human being were thought to be of two kinds, corresponding to the supposed division between sense and intellect: the *sensible species,* impressed on the organ of sense, and the *intelligible species,* impressed on the intellect. This division requires, of course, its own intermediate entity, in this instance the phantasy or imagination. Both sensible and intelligible species, according to function and use, must first be impressed and then expressed. The *species sensibilis impressae,* representing the likenesses of external objects, become impressed on, cause an "impression" on, the organ of sense, which then cooperates in producing the *species sensibilis expressae.* These expressed species may be "impressed" again, this time on the mirror of the phantasy, where they are once again "expressed" in order to become accessible to the intellect.

These cognitive acts provide the means by which we may get "up unto the watch-towre."

> When wilt thou shake off this Pedantery,
> Of being taught by sense, and Fantasy?
> Thou look'st through spectacles; small things seeme great,
> Below; But up unto the watch-towre get,
> And see all things despoyld of fallacies. . . .

The cognitive clarity enjoyed by those who see from the watchtower resembles heavenly vision; as Spenser notes (*The Faerie Queene,* II, ix, 47), the tower of Alma (soul) "likest is vnto that heauenly towre, / That God hath built for his owne blessed bowre." Although the closeness of the analogy varies according to the admixture of Aristotelean, Platonic, and Christian elements, the ancient *topos* of the watchtower had been commonplace for a long time before John of Salisbury got around to putting it in *The Metalogicon* (iv.17) in 1159:

In other words, reason serves as a sort of supreme senate in the soul's Capitoline Hill, where it is centrally situated [in the head] between the chambers of imagination and memory, so that from its watchtower, it may pass upon the judgments of sensation and imagination.[12]

Although John assumes, like Donne, the cognitive hierarchy that rises from "sense, and Fantasy" to the intellect, the most revealing version of the commonplace occurs in Marsilio Ficino, who resembles Donne in his concern with perspective, with the way "small things" may "seeme great" when we remain "below"; and who lends the "aristotelean" tower a Christian-Platonic emphasis congenial to Donne and quite common in the period:

> Let us climb into the high watch tower of the mind, leaving the dust of the body below; then we will gaze more closely at the divine and view the mortal from a distance. The former will seem greater than usual, and the latter smaller. So, cherishing the divine, and disregarding the mortal, we will no longer be foolish or miserable, but indeed wise and happy.[13]

Once we are "up unto the watch-towre" of the intellect, we need no longer be "deterre[d]" by the "incomprehensiblenesse" of Elizabeth Drury.

Instead of going to Aquinas, Zabarella, or Suarez to illustrate the ways in which the mind deals with the "incomprehensiblenesse" of sense perception, I will draw on a courtier's how-to-do-it-manual that matches chronologically, that shows itself aware, however uncritically, of differences between the "aristoteleanisms" and the "platonisms" of the period, and that presents the matters I have sketched in a form calculated to reach aspiring courtiers who wanted to add some shine to their polish, as well as to remind a more highly educated audience of how their cognitive processes actually worked.[14] Lodowick Bryskett, in *A Discourse of Civill Life* (London, 1606), translates, and adapts, the *Dialoghi* that Giambattista di Cristoforo Giraldi, also known as Giraldus and Cinthio, had appended to his popular *Hecatommithi*.[15] Although the translation appeared only five years before The Anniveraries, Bryskett implies that the dialogue took place in 1585, and he includes among its distinguished participants Edmund Spenser, who would have been, so runs the compliment, the likely discussion-leader had he not been occupied with his current project "in *heroical verse,* vnder the title of a *Faerie Queene*" (26–28). As a later reference to the "Angelicall Doctour" (267) suggests, and as the account itself makes clear, the Aristotle of Cinthio and Bryskett is the Aristotle of Aquinas in the translation of William of Moerbeke.

"The opinion of *Aristotle* was," according to Cinthio-Bryskett (hereafter simply "Bryskett," who might as well be the author of these commonplaces), "that our soule did not only not record any thing, but that it should be so wholy voyd of knowledge or science, as it might be resembled to a pure white paper: and therefore affirmed he, that our knowledge was altogether newly gotten; and that our soule had to that end need of sense; and that sense failing her, all science or knowledge should faile withall."[16] Bryskett explains that the "senses . . . receiue the images or formes particular of things: which being apprehended by the common sense, called *sensus communis,* bring foorth afterwards the vniuer-sals."[17] Since neither the "senses" nor the "common sense" com-prehends the "nature of things," the *sensus communis* "offereth" the "things sensible" to the "facultie *imaginatiue.*"[18]

"This done," Bryskett continues, "then the part of soule capable of reason, beginneth to vse her powers; and they are (as they affirme) two: the one *intellectus possibilis,* and the other *intellec-tus agens:* these latin words I must vse at this time, because they be easie enough to be vnderstood, and in English would seeme more harsh; whereof the first is as the matter to the second, and the second as forme to the first."[19]

> Into that possible facultie of the vnderstanding, do the kinds or *species* of things passe, which the fantasie hath apprehended, yet free of any materiall condition: and this part is to the vnderstanding, as the hand is to the bodie. For as the hand is apt to take hold of all instruments; so is this power or facultie [the possible or potential intellect] apt to apprehend the formes of all things, from whence grow the vniuersals: which though they haue their being in the materiall particulars which the Latins call *indiuidua;* yet are they not material, because they are not (according to *Aristotle*) yet in act.[20]

Although "onely things vniuersall are knowne, because they be comprehended by the vnderstanding, without matter,"

> It is neuerthelesse to be vnderstood, that the kindes of things are in this possible part thus separated from matter, but blind and obscure: euen as colours are stil in substances, though the light be taken away; which light appearing and making the ayre transparent which before was darkened, it giueth to things that illumination, by which they are comprehended and knowne to the eye, whose obiect properly colours are. [21]

The agent intellect then "worketh the same effect towards things intelligible that the Sun doth towards things visible; for it illumineth those kinds or formes which lie hidden in that part possible, dark and confused, deuoyed of place, time, and matter, because they are not particular." [22]

Bryskett then goes on to discriminate the functions of the two intellects in terms of matter and form:

> And hence it cometh that some haue said this possible vnderstanding (as we may terme it) to be such a thing, as out of it all things should be made, as if it were in stead of matter; and the other agent vnderstanding to be the worker of all things, and as it were the forme, because this part which before was but in power to things intelligible, becometh through the operation of the agent vnderstanding to be now in act.

These discriminations allow Bryskett to proceed to the crucial point, the identity of knower and known in the apprehension of truth:

> And for this cause also is it said, that the vnderstanding, and things vnderstood, become more properly and truly one selfe same thing, then of matter and forme it may be said. For it is credible, that both the formes of things and the vnderstanding being immateriall, they do the more perfectly vnite themselues, and that the vnderstanding doth so make it selfe equall with the thing vnderstood, that they both become one. To which purpose *Aristotle* said very well, that the reasonable soule, whiles it vnderstandeth things intelligible, becometh one selfe same thing with them. And this is that very act of truth, to wit, the certain science or knowledge of any thing: which knowledge or science is in effect nought else then the thing so knowne. [23]

We now have the "idea" of the thing, and not as it was. The expressed intelligible species now corresponds precisely to the form or essence of the object; the wit is the object, for "the vnderstanding doth so make it selfe equall with the thing vnderstood, that they both become one." The object, formerly obscured by reason of its accidents or the individuating properties of matter, is now comprehensible, thoroughly intelligible and illuminated in the light of that which makes it what it is. The "formes from objects" are now identical with the "species" or "ideas" in the "watch-towre" of the mind, analogous in this life to the Beatific Vision in the life hereafter: "For it is both the object and the wit."[24]

All this means that the reader of The Anniversaries has been enabled by the poet's images of "sense, and Fantasy" to ascend to the "watch-towre" and to "see, and Judge, and follow" the "Idea of a Woman": the "rich soule" of Elizabeth Drury. Her soul is rich, the gift of Christ—as the marginal gloss in the Geneva Bible on the disconcerting parable of the steward in Matthew 16 informs us: "Christ calleth the gifts which he giueth vs, riches." On the locution "rich soule" Manley first quotes I. A. Richards' two senses—"possessing much (a rich man)" and "giving much (a rich mine)"—and then offers what he terms the "best gloss," from the *Sermons* (VI, 303–4):

> Riches is the Metaphor, in which, the Holy Ghost hath delighted to expresse God and Heaven to us; *Despise not the riches of his goodnesse,* sayes the Apostle; And againe, *O the depth of the riches of his wisedome;* And so, after, *The unsearchable riches of Christ;* And for the consummation of all, *The riches of his Glory.* Gods goodnesse towards us in generall, our Religion in the way, his Grace here, his Glory hereafter, are all represented to us in Riches.

From the "watch-towre" we may see the essence or form of Elizabeth Drury, which is "rich soule" and "all" that is "represented to us in Riches."

In the "entrie into the worke" of The First Anniversary Donne makes the necessary distinction absolutely explicit and lends it meaning in terms of Christian history. This basic distinction makes clear the exact sense in which "he described the Idea of a Woman and not as she was."

First, we are told that Elizabeth Drury is dead, "Some

months she hath beene dead" (39); this is Elizabeth Drury "as she was," according to "sense, and Fantasy." Second, and in seeming contradiction, we are also told, "But long shee'ath beene away, long, long" (41); this is Elizabeth Drury considered from the "watch-towre" as "rich soule," the "Idea of a Woman and not as she was." In "Idea" she re-presents the "richness" of prelapsarian innocence and virtue. In this latter sense it is literal, or rather theological, truth that "long shee'ath beene away, long, long"—since the Fall from the Garden of Eden. Although Mistress Elizabeth has "beene dead" only a short while, her "Idea" has in theological fact "beene away, long, long"—since the Fall from the prelapsarian state of *integritas* or oneness with inner and outer nature. And in this sense the poet speaks witty truth, not hyperbole, when he claims that her loss re-presents the decay of the world; or as his subtitle for The First Anniversary claims, "Wherein, by Occasion of the Untimely Death of Mistris Elizabeth Drury the Frailty and the Decay of this whole World is Represented." Here lies the epistemological conceit on which The First Anniversary turns: high praise for the "worthinesse" of Elizabeth Drury "as she was," lament for the lost "Idea of Woman" that she "represents." Not inexcusable hyperbole but theological fact and metaphysical wit.

The watchtower stands for the height of earthly knowledge, but also it mediates, in the manner habitual with Western philosophy, heaven and earth. Much later in the dialogue (276–77) Bryskett, prompted by Cinthio and actuated by Christian commentaries on the *De Anima* and *Nicomachean Ethics,* makes even higher claims for the "watch-towre" of the mind, created in the image of his Christian Aristotle:[25]

> In consideration whereof *Aristotle* sayd, that man through contemplation became diuine; and that the true man (which both he and his diuine master agreed to be the minde) did enioy thereby (not as a mortall man liuing in the world, but as a diuine creature) that high felicitie, to which, ciuill felicitie was ordained.

There are indeed enough hints in Aristotle to make these claims seem plausible, but Bryskett knows that the grandest activity of the Aristotelean "watch-towre" enables us only to "see, and Judge" the intelligible idea, which in turn enables us, in our more contem-

plative moments, to move beyond "ciuill felicitie" to "high felicitie"; and this penultimate "high felicitie" accordingly brings Bryskett to the highest claims of Christian Platonism, to highest
"felicitie":

> And not impertinently haue the Platonikes (following their master
> in that point) sayd, that nature had giuen vs sense, not because we
> should stay thereupon, but to the end that thereby might grow in
> vs imagination, from imagination discourse, and from discourse
> intelligence, and from intelligence gladnesse vnspeakable, which
> might raise vs (as diuine, and freed from the bands of the flesh) to
> the knowledge of God, who is the beginning and end of all good-
> nesse, towards whom we ought with all endeuour to lift vp our
> minds, as to our chiefe and most perfect good: for he onely is our
> *summum bonum.*

The three stages comprising the vertical hierarchy of Aristotle's
anima culminate in "discourse" (of reason), but on this last occasion Bryskett moves up to the *ratio superior* of "intelligence," and
then from "intelligence" to what Donne in The Second Anniversary terms "essentiall joye." The "watch-towre," type of the identity of knower and known that foreshadows in this life the identity
of "the object and the wit" in the Beatific Vision, functions as the
mediating term.[26] Now we are to ascend *from* the "trinitarian"
soul, and *from* the tripartite "watch-towre" of the mind, to the
heavenly watchtower and realm of "gladnesse vnspeakable":

> For to them it seemed that the man whom contemplation had raised
> to such a degree of felicitie, became all wholly vnderstanding by
> that light [in Donne the soul is "growne all Ey"] which God impar-
> teth to the spirits that are so purged through the exercise of morall
> vertues; which vertues are termed by *Plato* the purgers of the mind:
> stirring vp therein a most ardent desire to forsake this mortall bodie,
> and to vnite it selfe with him.

In The Second Anniversary we watch the soul "forsake this mortall bodie, and . . . vnite it selfe with him": "Such doth God draw
vnto himselfe, and afterwards maketh them partakers of his ioyes
euerlasting: giuing them in the meane while a most sweet tast euen
in this life of that other life most happie."

     To ascend higher than the earthly "watch-towre," to reach

the heavenly watchtower or what Donne in The Second Anniversary calls the "first pitch" of the soul, we must turn our attention to the eloquent structure of The Anniversaries. Structure speaks, of "gladnesse vnspeakable"—when it too becomes "both the object and the wit."

F O U R

Beauties Best (1)

In The First Anniversary Donne, advertising his allegiance to the Scholastic esthetic that survived long enough for James Joyce to import its doctrines into Stephen's imaginings in *A Portrait of the Artist as a Young Man,* renders the two main principles economically: "Beauty, that's colour, and proportion" (250). And of these two, "beauties best" is "proportion" (306).[1] These commonplaces take us a long way from Hart Crane's *The Bridge,* John Berryman's *Dream Songs,* John Ashbery's *Self-Portrait in a Convex Mirror,* or T. S. Eliot's "The Love Song of J. Alfred Prufrock"—poems that exhibit what Kenneth Burke calls "qualitative progression" as distinct from "quantitative" or logical progression. In "Prufrock" the images "come and go" rather like the women talking of Michelangelo; this method of composition, which Ezra Pound imposed on Eliot's *The Waste Land* by removing a good many causal connectives, pretends to be associative rather than logical and proceeds by contiguity rather than by continuity. The poetic procedures tend to be as metonymic as that "pair of ragged claws"; and these methods may of course be compelling and moving, though in 1917 some readers, not yet habituated to this kind of poetic composition, denounced "Prufrock" for not being "poetry."

By the same token we ought not, I think, to allow habits of reading that are now second-nature to blinker our hindsight, for logical organization—"discourse" he would have called it—in

Donne's rhetorical, even "prosaic," universe of words constitutes the first "Element" of beauty in a poem. Synecdoche rather than metonymy is the master trope; syllogistic logic is the standard against which Donne's "urbanely fallacious" procedures must be appreciated—detected, measured, understood; and the "proportion" of the whole in relation to the parts is "beauties best," a mode of understanding as well as an esthetic principle. Design, symmetry, harmony, shape, pattern, structure—these make for beauty and may be *made* to express meaning (they do not signify in themselves except by convention, through their traditional associations).

It is no accident that the New Critics found themselves drawn to Donne; their particular brand of formalism represents the most appropriate response to Donne's (formalist) practice. The exception to this generalization—and the exception is of first importance—lies not in those ingenious explications of ingenious "conceits" or even of those "well wrought" structures, but in the failure of the formalists to recognize the *significances* that Donne assigns to *structure,* the ways in which the poet makes structure *mean.*

I deliberately choose "The Canonization" as a heuristic example because it used to be exemplary for the "new criticism" and was, indeed, the poem from which Cleanth Brooks—the point man for the New Critics in the United States—derived the title of his most influential work, *The Well Wrought Urn.*[2] Although the poem indisputably displays the "language of paradox" that Brooks found, disputably, to be the essence of poetry in general, I merely want to use "The Canonization" to make a preliminary point about how the structure of the work of art may become in itself a source of significance, the way in which shape may be made sufficiently eloquent to speak to us of matters unsayable or otherwise left unsaid.

> For Godsake hold your tongue, and let me love,
> Or chide my palsie, or my gout,
> My five gray haires, or ruin'd fortune flout,
> With wealth your state, your minde with Arts improve,
> Take you a course, get you a place,
> Observe his honour, or his grace,

Or the Kings reall, or his stamped face
  Contemplate, what you will, approve,
  So you will let me love.

Alas, alas, who's injur'd by my love?
  What merchants ships have my sighs drown'd?
Who saies my teares have overflow'd his ground?
  When did my colds a forward spring remove?
    When did the heats which my veines fill
    Adde one more to the plaguie Bill?
Soldiers finde warres, and Lawyers finde out still
  Litigious men, which quarrels move,
  Though she and I do love.

Call us what you will, wee are made such by love;
  Call her one, mee another flye,
We'are Tapers too, and at our owne cost die,
  And wee in us finde the'Eagle and the Dove.
    The Phoenix ridle hath more wit
    By us, we two being one, are it,
So to one neutrall thing both sexes fit,
  Wee dye and rise the same, and prove
  Mysterious by this love.

We can dye by it, if not live by love,
  And if unfit for tombes and hearse
Our legend bee, it will be fit for verse;
  And if no peece of Chronicle wee prove,
    We'll build in sonnets pretty roomes;
    As well a well wrought urne becomes
The greatest ashes, as halfe-acre tombes,
  And by these hymnes, all shall approve
  Us *Canoniz'd* for Love:

And thus invoke us; You whom reverend love
  Made one anothers hermitage;
You, to whom love was peace, that now is rage;
  Who did the whole worlds soule [ex]tract, and drove
    Into the glasses of your eyes
    (So made such mirrors, and such spies,
That they did all to you epitomize,)
  Countries, Townes, Courts: Beg from above
  A patterne of your love![3]

Structure speaks, speaks of "patterne."

The poem sings a Petrarchan commonplace, that The Lady is A Saint. The wit ranges from simple punning ("Kings reall, or his stamped face," where the meter alerts us to the double pun in the disyllabic "reall") to the quasi-blasphemous complexities of the "Phoenix ridle" and the "Mysterious" way "Wee dye and rise the same," which toy with the sexual pun on "dye" in relation to the theological "mysteries" of Incarnation and Resurrection. There is the usual play with microcosm and macrocosm, not only in larger aspects of design but also in the razzle-dazzle of local effects: the "whole worlds soule" has been alchemically "extract[ed]" from the macrocosm and been distilled into the "glasses [alchemical flasks] of your eyes," which then vertiginously become "glasses" in the sense of "mirrors," which then become "spies" in the sense of spyglasses that "epitomize" (when observed through the wrong end of the telescope) the macrocosm in the reflecting microcosm ("mirrors") of the "glasses of your eyes"! But the exercise of wit extends from these local scintillations to matters of structure.

"The Canonization" consists in five complex stanzas of nine lines apiece. The result is a linear structure that provides the poet with the opportunity for a virtuoso performance, allowing him to point an antithesis in a long line—

Wee can dye by it, if not live by love—

or use the short lines with epigrammatic brevity—

The Phoenix ridle hath more wit
By us, we two being one, are it—

but this series of fancy stanzas does not "mean" anything *as* a "structure."[4] The linear structure of the five stanzas also coincides, wittily enough, with the topical (and linear) "structure" of the ecclesiastical *processus* of canonization: (1) proof of personal sanctity urged against a Devil's Advocate, (2) practice of virtue in heroic degree, (3) examination of alleged miracles, (4) consideration of writings and remains, and (5) canonization.[5] This extrinsic structure "means" because the poet manipulates a witty parallel between the poetic stanzas and the ecclesiastical stages in the *processus,* but it means more-of-the-same rather than more-and-different.

The linear structure of five stanzas likewise coincides with the linear movement of what Burke calls "qualitative progression." The poet's theatrical utterances gradually assume the shape of a little emotional drama that moves from the defensive irritability of the first stanza, to the mixture of querulousness and truculence of the second stanza, to the flamboyant turn at the center of the poem —the third stanza. "Call us what you will." Call us the worst, for the "flye" by poetic convention if not by insectival nature embodies unclean lust and unrestrained concupiscence; and yet the poet will nevertheless, through the alchemy of wit, transform this worst of names to the best of names and "prove" us "Mysterious by this love." This turn at the center, as if on a pivot, leads into the calm assurance and reasoned distinctions of stanza four (no more shouting, no more whining); and the little drama then reaches its victorious close, at the opposite end of the emotional spectrum from the first stanza, in the triumphant certitude of the fifth stanza. It is a witty drama of conversion, a poetic "peece of Chronicle," that moves from accused sinner to adored saint.

To refer to the third stanza as the turn at the center is more than a figure of speech, for the series of repetends intrinsic to the poem invites us to see the linear structure as finally circular. Each of the five stanzas is framed by the word "love," last in the first line and last in the last line, making of each stanza a microcosmic circle that in its repetitions constitutes the greater circle of the entire poem from "love" to "love": and this is a movement that we must at last recognize as a movement from love to Love. When the lovers, having assumed their canonical office as intercessory saints, look up to find the "patterne of . . . love," they apprehend —and we know what they apprehend because structure has spoken —the perfect form, the circle of pure and endless love, that in its perfection stands for God: *Deus est sphaera infinita, cuius centrum est ubique, circumferentia nusquam.*[6] When Kenelm Digby interprets Spenser's "Frame . . . Circular," his mind moves immediately, and rightly, to the pertinent commonplace: "For, as God hath neither beginning nor ending: so, neither of these can be found in a Circle, although that being made of the successive motion of a line, it must be supposed to have beginning somewhere: God is compared to a Circle whose Center is every where, but his circum-

ference no where."[7] This "allegoricall description of *Hermes**
[**Sphaera, cujus centrum ubique, circumferentia nullibi*]," confesses Sir
Thomas Browne, "pleaseth mee beyond all the Metaphysicall def-
initions of Divines."[8] So also Donne the poet: God is an infinite
sphere whose center is everywhere and circumference nowhere,
making of deity the grandest of all metaphysical conceits—an
intellectual "image" or "idea" that cannot be visualized but must
be comprehended from the "watch-towre." And as readers we
have now been readied to complete our own poetic circle. In the
beginning we had read "For Godsake hold your tongue" as a
colloquial imprecation, as a hackneyed oath that takes the name
of God mildly in vain; but the end of the poem is our beginning,
and fold-over structure now invites us, through the circular economy of this poem, to hold our tongues for the sake of God. Conventional imprecation becomes witty truth, language reani-
mated. Structure speaks of "patterne," and encourages us to read
around.

Beauty lies not in the eye of the beholder but in the
"colour" of the object and, most of all, in the "proportion" of the
object, in the "Symmetree" of part to whole. For Donne the circle
of perfection retains, in spite of the "new philosophy," its metaphysical and esthetic prestige: the dominant trope, the circle, and
the dominant figure of speech, synecdoche.[9] When thinking ad-
vances in terms of this trope and this figure, the dominant principle
of structure will be "proportion" in the sense of the relation of
part to whole, whole to part. The dominant power of mind,
variously called, will be Aristotle's *nous,* Augustine's *ratio superior,*
the Renaissance commentator's *intellectus,* or the *wit* of a Sidney or
Donne: this power of mind, this "erected wit," could see beyond
"colour" to appreciate "proportion"; could grasp the immaterial
"forms" or "ideas" of material objects; and could reason by synecdoche from microcosm to macrocosm, moving vertically from the
realm of nature toward the realm of grace.

These habits of mind tend to ignore or at least to minimize
the significance of linear, historical relations of cause to effect,
though the alternative view appears clearly enough in the Renaissance—among other places, in Shakespeare's *2 Henry the Fourth*
(III, i):

> There is a history in all men's lives,
> Figuring the nature of the times deceased,
> The which observed, a man may prophesy,
> With a near aim, of the main chance of things
> As yet not come to life, which in their seeds
> And weak beginnings lie intreasured.
> Such things become the hatch and brood of time. . . .

Warwick assumes that knowledge is incremental, acquired along the line of time by piling up and storing a sufficient number of particulars and precedents until there appears some intimation of future dislocations or, more important to him and the King, the possibility of relying upon something irreducible, exemplifying continuity, in human development. Truth is probabilistic, "a near aim, of the main chance of things." On the other hand, if human life is not lived exclusively along the horizontal line of history, then living in this universe of discourse may be felt to be "circular" as well as "linear," which holds out the promise that any temporal moment may be measured against the divine circle of eternity and, at least in part, understood and valued insofar as it seems in proportion to revealed truth; thinking radiates toward the circumference, rather than ranging back and forth along the line of time. Instead of depending exclusively on the past, on the horizontal accumulation of wisdom over the years, the wise man may rely also on the vertical relationship of truth-to-truth, the relations of part to whole that tend to dominate thinking about thinking in the Renaissance. The tension between these two ways of interpreting human problems—the emerging "horizontal" as against the dominant "vertical"—appears everywhere in the thinkers of the period, but I believe it is fair to say that up until the great reversal in Hobbes, the emphasis most often lies on synecdoche, on the relation of part to whole: the "proportional" relations of microcosm to geocosm to macrocosm that rely less on temporal continuity than on a kind of spatial metaphysics. "Beg from above / A patterne of your love!"

Although this habit of mind inevitably encourages the use of analogy in general, the most relevant kind of analogy in the context of Donne's practice in The Anniversaries is synecdoche, for it is this figure that best represents part-whole relations, preeminently the relations between microcosm and macrocosm. In that *aubade* to metaphysical wit, "The Sunne Rising," the poet can shrink the macrocosmic sun to the confines of the lovers' room:

> Shine here to us, and thou art every where;
> This bed thy center is, these walls, thy spheare.

Or the poet will simply announce that he himself represents a "little world made cunningly." In The First Anniversary Donne first meditates on the "rich soule" of Elizabeth Drury as the "name" and "forme" of the macrocosmic "world" (31–60), and then he promptly transforms "her vertue," through his customary (and witty) reversal of ground and figure, into the "matter" of the "new world" of which the "forme" is our "practise" (61–91). Donne's wit oscillates between accident and essence, matter and form, microcosm and macrocosm—and then he reverses the terms of the "proportion." These relations inform his tropes, and in The Anniversaries he rings multiple changes on what is really a fairly limited range of "*Metaphysical* Idea's, and *Scholastical* Quiddities"—with inexhaustible wit. His thinking, unlike ours, tends to move from synecdoche to synecdoche, circling in circles within circles.

The Anniversaries have suffered mainly from imperfect appreciation of the ways in which they are constructed—the relation of the parts to the whole and the whole to the parts, which is "beauties best, proportion." Structuralists, from Jean Piaget to Claude Lévi-Strauss and beyond, have been so successful in directing attention to so-called deep structures that they have helped deflect attention from more traditional kinds of structure, those by which writers consciously order and develop their thoughts.[10] I have in mind nothing more mysterious than what we ordinarily think of as expository techniques, the expository signals that we inherit from the logic and rhetoric of the Renaissance schoolroom.

In this connection the various movements known as structuralism have combined with other powerful influences—Romanticism, Symbolism, Imagism—to reduce interest in kinds of structure consciously devised and deliberately articulated, particularly those that display logical development; these kinds of structure, for the most part displaced from poetry during the nineteenth century, have been largely relegated to prose. When the author of

"Prufrock," for example, gingerly acknowledges that the "three strophes" of Marvell's "To His Coy Mistress" bear "*something like a syllogistic relation to each other,*" his phrasing betrays the slight embarrassment he feels in the presence of a kind of poetic structure that is not just "something like" but is in fact what the logicians of the seventeenth-century could refer to as "Conditional or Hypotheticall Syllogismes."[11] Under the circumstances it is probably not surprising that the expository (prosaic) structure of The First Anniversary, elaborated with the kind of mechanical rigor that many associate with syllogistic logic, remained undiscovered for so long; or that its discoverer, uneasy in the presence of expository techniques that, since the Romantics, have seemed more appropriate to prose than to poetry, should at first have regarded his discovery as an imperfection to be used in justifying his preference for The Second Anniversary.

Since the structure, the basic organization, of The Anniversaries remained imperceptible to readers who lacked Donne's training in logic and rhetoric, the "general feeling" among the critics, as Manley notes in his fine introduction to his pioneering edition, "was that despite a number of passages as brilliant and complex as Donne ever wrote, the poems as a whole left one curiously unsatisfied and confused."[12] We may rephrase the difficulty in terms of a modest version of the hermeneutic circle: there is no way to isolate a workable hypothesis about structure without some notion of what individual "passages" mean and how they relate to each other—and no way to assess the meaning of the "passages," however "brilliant and complex," without some notion of overall structure. The rhetorical figure for this version of the hermeneutic circle is synecdoche. In short, the difficulties stem directly from the way Donne's mind habitually worked—through synecdoche or the "proportion" between part and whole, between whole and part.

In 1947 one man had an irresistible and irreversible effect on the way experienced scholars sought to assess the achievement of The Anniversaries, and his own achievement, properly assessed, should have changed the way we approach the rest of Donne's poems; and it might also have suggested alternative strategies in trying to account for the literature of the Renaissance in general.

Louis L. Martz demonstrated conclusively that The First Anniversary "as a whole" (his analysis of the second poem proved to be imperfect) exhibits a "deliberately articulated structure" supposedly derived from the procedures of Jesuit meditation.[13] It is the structure itself, not its putative source, that possesses first importance. The First Anniversary has a clearly defined Introduction (1–90), a clearly defined Conclusion (435–74), and five main sections (91–190, "how poore a trifling thing man is"; 191–246, "how lame a cripple this world is"; 247–338, "how ugly a monster this world is"; 339–76, "how wan a Ghost this our world is"; and 337–434, "how drie a Cinder this world is"). Each of these main sections is rigorously subdivided into three parts, consisting of Meditations on the decay of the world (91–170; 191–218; 247–304; 339–58; and 377–98), Eulogies of Elizabeth Drury (171–82; 219–36; 305–24; 359–68; and 399–426), and Refrain-Morals (183–90; 237–46; 325–38; 369–76; and 427–34). This elaborate structure, so carefully and so clearly articulated, provides us with a way of beginning to deal with the perennial dilemma—that we cannot adequately weigh the relative importance of the particulars without first apprehending the structure of the whole, and that we cannot adequately appreciate the significance of the structure without first comprehending the function and import of the particulars. (There is no need to invoke Schleiermacher—or to translate mighty testimonials from Gadamer and Habermas—to formulate so modest a version of the hermeneutic circle.)

I must take care to acknowledge that certain structural features of a text (poems invariably have many "structures") assume prominence only in relation to the concerns, and habits, that we bring to our reading, which explains why it will always be a nice question to distinguish persuasively between structure discovered and structure imposed. W. M. Lebans, for example, appears to have begun by assuming that Donne intended to write a classical elegy—lament, panegyric, consolation—and that in consequence The First Anniversary must consist in three, rather than (Martz's, and Donne's) five main parts.[14] Lebans, or anyone else proceeding in this way, has only to "demonstrate" that the categories associated with the classical elegy appear in The Anniversaries. This kind of demonstration depends not on the formal features of a text but on the content or topics that may be presumed to be included in the text; and at least in theory the text, brought into alignment with any number of topics or abstract categories, becomes almost infinitely malleable.[15] The persuasiveness of Martz's argument, on the other hand, derives not only from the plausibility of Donne's acquaintance with traditional conventions (classical elegy or Jesuit meditation) but also from the way that Martz can draw attention to formal elements recognizable to almost any educated reader, namely, the *repetends* (refrains, modes of address) that demarcate parts of the text at regular intervals, separating as well as connecting the various parts of the poem.

Although most scholars now accept—the evidence, especially with respect to The First Anniversary, seems overwhelming —the structural divisions proposed by Martz, some have sought to lend them meanings other than that of Jesuit meditation: for Harold Love, that of judicial oratory or, for Patrick Mahony, that of "deliberative-epideictic rhetoric."[16] Barbara K. Lewalski, the scholar who has written most extensively about the poems, also begins with Martz, but her thesis requires her to change the structure as well as its meaning, the meaning as well as the structure.

Since Lewalski apparently needs to believe—perhaps as a consequence of her Protestant or "binary" thesis, perhaps as a consequence of the "binary" principles displayed in the popular genre of the "anatomy," or perhaps as a consequence of a personal tendency toward "binary" thinking—that The First Anniversary has a "four-part argument," it must follow, for her and her thesis, that the "structure of the poem" consists of "four large sections" (binary division or two-plus-two). But "argument," considered as an abstract series of propositions or subjects, need not necessarily coincide with "sections," for the sections depend on the formal features within the work, and an abstract "argument" (about a genre of Protestant "anatomy" or whatever) may come from just about anywhere outside the work. Lewalski's procedure substitutes argumentative and topical categories for expository signposts, ignores the series of repetends *within* the poem, and arbitrarily collapses two of Donne's painstakingly distinguished sections into one—"in accordance" not with formal features observable within the poem but "with the genre of the anatomy, rather than

the five-part meditation formula which Professor Martz proposes."
This suggestion looks so much like responsible scholarship that it
has misled scholarly reviewers and, I would guess, a good many
students; the argument is, nonetheless, radically flawed in the way
it substitutes possible sources and background information for the
poet's organization of his materials.

This kind of disagreement (as between Lewalski and Martz),
when it is conducted on this level of abstraction, no longer concerns the structure of the poem itself but rather the antecedent
forms (anatomy, Jesuit meditation) that may or may not have
influenced the poet in the composition of the poem. The structure
of the apartment house, in other words, depends not on the ar-
rangement of the girders and I-beams, strategically repeated at
intervals throughout the building, but on architectural forms that
may or may not have previously occupied the site. Disagreement
of this kind stems from a confusion of the repetends intrinsic to
the work with the topical categories extrinsic to the work.

In regard to The Second Anniversary Lewalski arbitrarily
expands Donne's induction from forty-four to eighty-four lines,
which requires her to ignore such prominent formal features as the
poet's first address to his soul and in consequence causes the *entire*
"colloquy" of the first main section to disappear into the introduction; the first section, to put it another way, has been decapitated,
for it has lost the first of the three parts that are symmetrically—
"beauties best, proportion"—repeated in later sections. To destroy
artful repetition destroys meaning. Thereafter, however, Lewalski
follows Martz quite closely, except in maintaining without sup-
porting evidence from the poem itself that each of Donne's (and
Martz's) tripartite sections exhibits a "four-part argument." [17]

Even from this brief survey it will be obvious that different meanings (derived from genres such as the classical elegy, from
practices such as Jesuit meditation) may be assigned to the "same"
structures; that an antecedent structure or prior assumption—that
of the anatomy or even a thesis about Donne's Protestantism—
may be imposed on a text by the simple expedient of bypassing
some or all of its internal features, preeminently the repetends that
occur and reoccur almost verbatim at strategic points; and that
structure, when imposed from without, may obscure or even oc-

clude the methods of organization consciously introduced by the poet to lend shape to his materials. The results seem inevitable: controversy among the critics, exemplified most plainly in the inability to reach even tentative agreement about the *subject* of the poems—the identity and the significance of "she."

This situation, difficult enough with regard to The First Anniversary, becomes far more troublesome in trying to determine the more complex structure of the second of the companion poems. Martz himself came to acknowledge that in 1947 he had apprehended the structure of the second poem only imperfectly. According to his first analysis, The Second Anniversary has an Introduction (1–44), a Conclusion (511–28), and seven main sections (45–84; 85–156; 157–250; 251–320; 321–82; 383–470; and 471–510), each subdivided in ways that only at first resemble those of The First Anniversary. The first main section reveals the tripartite organization repeated throughout the whole body of The First Anniversary, being divided, according to Martz in his article of 1947 and his book of 1954, into Meditation (45–64), Eulogy (65–80), and Refrain-Moral (81–84). Martz thought that the second main section had the Meditation (85–120) and the Eulogy (121–46) but no Refrain, only a Moral (147–56). And he believed that the five remaining sections have neither Refrains nor Morals, only Meditations (157–219; 251–300; 321–55; 383–446; and 471–96) and Eulogies (220–50; 301–20; 356–82; 447–70; and 497–510).

This summary may be accepted, as I will demonstrate in detail later on, with regard to the Introduction, Conclusion, and the first section; but in the second section Martz seems to have missed the Refrain, perhaps because it varies from the first and from those in The First Anniversary; and in the third, fourth, and fifth sections he overlooked the modified Refrains and Morals (247–53; 315–20; and 379–82). He seems to have missed these variations and modifications because, I suspect, he was relieved to have left behind what he had originally felt to be the overly mechanical structure of The First Anniversary and because he was hunting for exact repetitions rather than meaningful variations or outright departures from the patterns established by the first poem; perhaps he did not see them because he was not ready to see them *as* variations. (The truism is true that we see what we want to see and fail to see what lacks meaning for us.) As for the sixth and seventh sections, I will argue that they simply do not exist in the sense proposed by Martz and that they were in fact, though I shall not argue the point, suggested to him from his study of The First Anniversary and from his discovery of what he took to be the pertinence of the Jesuit practices of seven-part meditation. Donne's final modifications (Martz's putative sixth and seventh sections) represent significant departures (not just variations) from the normative expectations created by the exact repetends of The First Anniversary.

A quarter century later, speaking on the four-hundredth anniversary of the birth of Donne, Martz again made important observations about the poems and the scholarship on them. He also proposed a new "outline [of the structure of The Second Anniversary] that represents a significant extension from [really a revision of] the outline" he had offered in his ground-breaking essay of 1947. The Introduction, Conclusion, and first two sections remain the same, but the Meditations of the other five sections are now subdivided into two parts each, and a "brief moral" (but no refrain) has now been found for each of the Eulogies of sections three, four, and five.[18] Although this later account of the structure of The Second Anniversary represents in some respects an advance on Martz's earlier analyses, it too remains incomplete and inaccurate. It looks to me like an attempt to make logical what is finally, and deliberately, not logical.

There are four main reasons that make it absolutely necessary to dwell on these different accounts of structure—apart from the hermeneutic reason that we cannot apprehend the structure of the whole without knowing the parts and that we cannot know the parts without some apprehension of the structure of the whole. Quite obviously it makes a critical difference in our appreciation of a poem if we suppose that its structure is that of the classical elegy —or that of a Jesuit meditation. Just as obviously our understanding of structure vitally affects our understanding of other aspects of the poem—imagery, tone, theme, and the like.

From these two obvious points we may adduce a third: that the *meanings* we ascribe to the poem depend upon the structure that we find in the poem or that we manage to impose on the poem. (Some critics maintain that all meanings are imposed, but if that is true—and it is not true except in some absolute sense that makes no sense—the truth of the claim invalidates the claim.) Finally, the structure or the lack of it, and whether found or imposed, may become, according to our cultural and literary presuppositions, a judgment of *value*. Martz, in what I want to regard as an atypical access of Romanticism, at first considered The Second Anniversary superior to The First because Donne had "freed [it] from [the] heavy pauses," the tighter organization, that supposedly marred the earlier effort. The poet's breaking of the "strict mold" of The First Anniversary "suggests a creative freedom that absorbs and transcends formal divisions."[19] Structure becomes value, value structure.

The influential work of O. B. Hardison, Jr., may be used to illustrate these generalizations about the critical significance of structure. Hardison apparently began by assuming that Donne, deeply influenced by epideictic theory and practice, must have written The Anniversaries in the tradition of the literature of "praise." Therefore, "it seems [to Hardison] more likely that the *Anniversaries* and [Martz's] devotional tracts resemble one another because of a common source—epideictic formulae." Hardison then observes that "it is usually assumed" (presumably by those who follow Martz) that The First Anniversary consists of an Introduction, a Conclusion, and five Meditations, but in the service of his thesis Hardison pleads that the "five meditations are [actually] subdivisions of three larger units that make up the body of the poem." Once this structure has been imposed on Donne's structure, it immediately turns out that what Martz had called a "strict mold" apparently has a "long digression imbedded in it" and that indeed a good deal of "intervening material (63–90) is digressive." (How do you recognize a digression? Simply by imposing a structure and then seeing what doesn't fit . . .) From the structure that he has imposed on the poem, Hardison then manages to draw the predictable conclusions—not only that Donne "digresses" but also that his "three major units" figure forth the "sensory, rational, and intuitive powers of the [Christian-Platonic] soul" and that the "sub-sections" contain the "rhetorical topics of funeral elegy." In short, Hardison imposes a structure on The First Anniversary to establish the thesis that began as a presupposition. As Hardison himself observes, without irony: "The difference between a three- and a five-part division . . . may seem at first trivial, but it is not."[20]

Indeed it is not. In his analysis of the structure of The Second Anniversary Hardison appears to follow Martz exactly, though without mentioning or citing him, but Hardison does change the labels affixed to sections and subsections.[21] These changes once again allow him to draw further inferences about meaning and value, for of course the rubrics themselves represent "conclusions." "If the preceding outline is acceptable," argues Hardison, "the poem cannot be read [in the way proposed by Martz? on the basis of the outline Martz seems to share with Hardison?] as the narrative of the soul's journey to heaven." How then? Since Donne must of course, in accordance with the thesis of Hardison's book, have been trying to write "praise" in the manner of "the *stilnovisti*," Hardison will want us to acknowledge, while begging the big question, that it "is one of the disappointing features of the *Progress* that Donne does not imitate the *stilnovisti* at the end of part seven." And Hardison draws the final conclusion: "Once again the best means of understanding Donne's intention is the theory of praise."[22] And once again we are back where we started, with a presiding assumption that prejudges the judgment of the work of art.

Hardison's assertions, like those of Lewalski, are advanced with the utmost seriousness. The circular nature of the reasoning stems partly from the nature of reasoning itself, partly from the influence a critic's thesis exerts over the critic, and partly, perhaps, from the unexamined assumption that structure considered as structure somehow *means* unambiguously in and of itself. In any case, Hardison's learned chapter on the structure and meaning of The Anniversaries has become part of later scholarship, not always with adequate acknowledgment. In dealing with that other, and always related, problem—the meaning of "she"—Hardison begins, accurately enough, by observing that all those troublesome allusions to Astraea or the Blessed Virgin ought to be taken, in the sense recommended by I. A. Richards, as "vehicles" or metaphors. They are "'vehicles' for a 'tenor'—the soul of Elizabeth—which is otherwise incomprehensible." But when Hardison, in accord with his epideictic thesis, immediately adds that Donne does *not* "suggest that Elizabeth is far more virtuous than anyone else," we may begin to wonder just what it is that all those spectacularly extravagant "vehicles" *do* suggest. And when Hardison, in accord with his theory of Christian epideixis, maintains that "there is nothing startling about the assertion that the virtuous Christian cultivates the image of God in his soul," we may suspect that behind this otherwise unimpeachable statement there lies some fusion or even confusion of "vehicle" with "tenor."[23] In any case it will be clear that the meaning and value of The Anniversaries (and of the "idea" of "she") involve, directly or indirectly, assumptions about structure.

Since 1947 the meaning of the structure (as distinct from the question of structure *qua* structure) of The First Anniversary has been the subject of a good deal of speculation, and this speculation inevitably includes what may be thought of as the structure of the structure—the three-part substructure that Donne methodically repeats in each of the five main sections of the body of the poem: a meditation upon some aspect of the "decay" of the world, lament-praise, and a refrain-moral. The meaning of this tripartite structure may be sought outside the poem itself—in St. Bernard, say, or in the codified procedures of Jesuit meditation as set forth by St. Ignatius and others. This "trinitarian" thinking, as I have demonstrated at some length in the previous chapter, pervades the Middle Ages and the Renaissance and may also be found in Donne the preacher, in the many passages in the sermons—most of them derived from Bernard and Augustine—on the faculties of the human soul as it is created in the image of God. "God created one *Trinity* in us; (the observation, and the enumeration is Saint *Bernards*) which are those *three faculties* of our soule, the *reason,* the *memory,* the *will.*"[24] Although this trinity of faculties of the human soul clearly has some connection with the tripartite substructure of The First Anniversary as it has been described by Martz and others, the way in which each faculty is in turn brought into play *within* the poems themselves radically changes the order and importance of these faculties as they are codified by Ignatius.

Frank Manley was, I believe, the first to perceive the

vitally important connection between the three faculties of the soul (that trinity from the Trinity) and the ternate substructures of The Anniversaries; but when he came to apply the insight to The First Anniversary, he seems to have followed the order advised by the Jesuits and assumed by Martz rather than the order devised by Donne. Manley argues that "in what Martz terms the *meditations,* Donne sends his mind back in time toward Eden [and] 'remembers' imaginatively [this would be the Jesuit use of the faculty of memory] the perfection of the first days . . . and searches out the cause for the present decay." "In the so-called *eulogies,*" Manley continues, Donne "probes the significance of a young girl's recent death and discovers in it an answer to what caused the decay. . . . And finally . . . Donne arrives at an act of will: to forget this rotten world." In other words, Manley tries to establish a correspondence between the three faculties of the soul and the three subsections of each of the five main sections of The First Anniversary in the order advocated by the Jesuits: first the memory, then the understanding, and finally the will.

It seems strange that Martz himself did not make these connections in this order, or even make these connections in any order, for it is he who has taught us so well that many poets of the Renaissance followed the Jesuit order of (1) *compositio loci* (seeing the scene in *memory*), (2) intellectual analysis of the scene (the exercise of *understanding*), and (3) the *colloquy* (with God or oneself) that ideally issues in the movement of the *will.* Perhaps Martz failed to perceive the connections because the correspondences are not nearly so exact as Manley implies, or perhaps because the exercise of the three faculties in The First Anniversary does not in fact follow the sequence prescribed by the Jesuits.

Although the third of the subsections invariably draws a moral that explicitly invites the movement of *bona voluntas* (the movement of the faculty of will in the direction of the good), the connections proposed by Manley (between the faculties of the soul and subsections of the poem) seem much less clear with respect to what Manley, following Martz, calls the "meditations" and the "eulogies." It is true, as Manley suggests, that the "meditations" usually contrast the good old days with "how poore a trifling thing" we have at present, and yet the emphasis, unfortunate if not fatal for Manley's suppositions, lies not on the "memory" of the good old days but on "understanding" why things look so bad at the moment. It is in fact, as ordinary readers recognize when they have the background information, the "anatomy" part of the anatomy of the world. The intellectual processes are not those of "remembering" (though invidious comparisons abound) but of "dissecting," of "anatomizing," of analyzing the decay evident in microcosm and macrocosm. These opening parts of the tripartite substructures, in short, depend mainly on the exercise of "reason" or "understanding" rather than on an appeal to "memory."

The second parts of the three-part substructures, on the other hand, very clearly emphasize the role of "memory." Although the praise of "she" points a sharp contrast with what the world now patently lacks, the emphasis lies not so much on judgment, on the exercise of the "understanding," as on the "memory" of the "she" who is "gone." The world "hast forgot [her] name," the poet says in the "entrie into the worke," and the second-part "eulogies," not the opening "meditations," are set in past-tense and designed to recall the one whose name has been forgotten; it is memorial exercise. In The Second Anniversary Donne makes his intentions entirely explicit when in the second-section eulogies he repeats "remember then that she" or refers directly to our "Memory" and what we "forget." Manley's observations, in short, appear to be derived from the sequence of Martz's categories rather than from The Anniversaries. Manley assumes that the enumeration of the faculties proceeds in the order recommended by the Jesuits: first the memory, then the exercise of the understanding on the imagined scene, and finally the movement of the will.

But in the passage from the sermons that I have quoted, and in the others that I cite, the "Reason" or "Understanding" comes first, and this is in fact the case with The First Anniversary as well, in which the poet begins each subsection not with a composition of place but with an "anatomy."[25] (The Second Anniversary differs yet again, for Donne begins each subsection with the "colloquy," which for the Jesuits comes third rather than first in the meditational sequence.) The First Anniversary, then, ought not to be identified exclusively with the line of Jesuit meditation studied by Martz—nor with the line of Protestant meditation advocated by Joseph Hall.[26] Although Hall's "arte of devine meditation" begins, like Donne's in The First Anniversary, with the understanding, his method, moving from "cogitations" to "affections," seems to owe a good deal to Ramism and proceeds by dichotomies rather than the "trinities" characteristic of Donne.[27]

In the first subsections of each of the five main parts of The First Anniversary Donne uses the faculty of "reason" in "anatomizing" the world; next he calls upon the "memory" in recalling the virtues of "she" who is "gone"; and finally he draws the morals that again and again encourage the "will" to reject the world. Donne would have agreed with Hall (and also with the Jesuits) that *ratio recta* or right reason ought to guide the will. Indeed, Donne the poet begins each subsection with an "anatomy," with an analysis by the "understanding," because he assumed with Donne the preacher that "for the rectifying of the *will*, the *understanding* must [first] be rectified" (*Sermons*, II, 73). And yet Donne the preacher also knew that the "understanding" is "often perplexed" and that the "will" is "untractable, and untameable." Donne in consequence puts his trust in the memory, giving to that faculty the dignity and power it had acquired in Plato and Augustine—far beyond anything attributed to it in the Jesuit "composition of place." Donne observes that "*Plato* plac'd *all learning in the memory;* wee may place *all Religion* in the memory too" (*Sermons*, II, 74). And "therefore [Donne the preacher recommends that] if thine understanding cannot reconcile . . ., if thy will cannot submit . . ., go to thine memory" (*Sermons*, II, 237).

In brief, "The art of *salvation,* is but the art of *memory*" (*Sermons*, II, 73). The "Memory," says Donne the preacher, "is often the Holy Ghosts Pulpit that he preaches in, then the understanding" (*Sermons*, VIII, 261); first the memory, second the understanding. In addition, the term "remember" possesses such a range of significations for Donne that it threatens to engulf the other faculties; the preacher takes care to note that the "word is often used in Scripture for considering and taking care," which implies that "remembering" has functions that are ordinarily reserved to "understanding" and "willing" (*Sermons*, II, 236). Remembering may even have for Donne the force of logic; the "Memory is as the conclusion of a Syllogisme, which . . . cannot be denied" (*Sermons,* VIII, 262).

Given the latitude of signification that even Donne the preacher ascribes to "remembering," we must be prepared to accept some degree of overlap in the exercise of the three faculties of reason, memory, and will in The Anniversaries, but when we consider the importance that Donne assigns to the second of these faculties, we must also expect what is in fact the case, that memory comes into play primarily in recalling the "she" who is "gone." For Donne, though not for the Jesuits, the exercise of understanding is prior in order but not in importance; memory, which is first in psychological and theological power but second in order, then leads to the movement of the will.

The understanding proceeds by anatomizing this rotten world, allowing us to "see" it for what it is and thus encouraging us to "see" the images of virtue in memory. In words that seem to describe by hindsight his practice in The First Anniversary, Donne the preacher admonishes his congregation: "Let every one of us therefore dissect and cut up himself" (it is precisely this kind of anatomy lesson that enforces the "morals" of The First Anniversary). "Whether [man] consider himself *in omnibus,* or *in singulis,*" he sees his "littleness" and notes "how poor, and small a thing Man is." Nevertheless, urges the preacher, "we may better discern our selves *in singulis,* then *in omnibus;* better by taking our selves in pieces, then altogether." The major purpose of this kind of anatomy lesson is to enable vision, to make us *see;* and we see "better by seeing [man] cut up, than by seeing him do any exercise alive; one desection, one Anatomy teaches more of that, than the marching, or drilling of a whole army of living men" (*Sermons,* I, 272–73). In Donne's judgment the end of this kind of anatomy lesson is to promote self-knowledge, to allow one to *see* oneself; in short, Donne the preacher assumes that the faculty of understanding "anatomizes" the object so that we may "see" ourselves for what we truly are. Understanding by "anatomy" precedes in order, though not in importance, the "seeing" of memory.

The First Anniversary exhibits the "method" of "anatomy" that Donne the preacher, following the *Commentarii in Eccle-*

siasten (1606) of Johannes Lorinus, supposed Solomon the preacher to have employed in composing Ecclesiastes.[28] Donne, preaching at Whitehall on the second of April in 1620, praises Solomon as both "a good Master to correct us in this world, [and] a good Master to direct us to the next"—just as The First Anniversary "correct[s] us in this world" and The Second Anniversary "direct[s] us to the next." Donne might have been describing his own aims in The First Anniversary when he explains the ultimate purpose of "Solomons Anatomy, and cutting up of the world": "Man therefore can have no deeper discouragement, from enclining to the things of this world, then to be taught that they are nothing, nor higher encouragement, to cleave to God for the next, then to know that he himself is nothing too."

It all comes down to proper vision (no impotent receiver will be equal to the task): "because there is no third object for mans love, [because] this world, and the next, are all that he can consider," Donne may make the parallel claim that "as [man] hath but two eyes, so he hath but two objects," and then the preacher may conclude that "if our love might be drawn from this world, *Solomon* thought it a direct way to convay it upon the next." This, then, is "*Solomons* method": "*Solomon* shakes the world in peeces, he dissects it, and cuts it up before thee, that so thou mayest the better see, how poor a thing, that particular is, whatsoever it be, that thou sets thy love upon in this world." And this is, indeed, Donne's own method in The First Anniversary, entitled in the first edition *An Anatomy of the World*. Man must learn to "see" the world for what it is by "anatomy," and then, because "he hath but two objects," the anatomy lesson will inevitably "convay" his gaze from "this world" to "the next" (*Sermons*, III, 47–51). This is also to "convay" our gaze from The First to The Second Anniversary where the soul is "now growne all Ey" (200).

Schematic representation of the skeletal structures of The Anniversaries will help to reveal exactly how Donne effected the transition from the first to the second poem. This kind of outline of structure will also provide graphic illustration of the organization that the poet consciously imposed on his varied materials and will show that this structure may be apprehended without recourse to theories epideictic, Jesuitical, or funereal. Most important, schematic representation will help make it clear that the organization of The Second Anniversary begins as a deliberate imitation of The First Anniversary, proceeds to a series of carefully calculated variations from the norm established by the first poem, and ends with an astonishing yet significant departure from the norm. Structure will be made to speak, to convey meanings beyond the reach of conventional discourse.

Beauties Best (2)

Although Donne, in planning or in composing The Second Anniversary, designed the poems to be "companion" poems, functioning if you will as a poetic diptych, the second does not merely reflect the first, nor is it indeed fully intelligible without its companion. The repetends of The First Anniversary (the five "anatomies," the five laments for "she," and the five refrain-morals) not only produce "beauties best" of logical progression and rhetorical symmetry but also establish for the knowing reader a *pattern of expectation*. These expectations the poet can then exploit in The Second Anniversary, first by duplicating the earlier pattern and then by diverging from it in meaningful ways. Donne uses structure to go beyond structure, making structure speak the unspeakable.

It is variation from the structural norm, not the norm itself, that bears the primary weight of meaning. The Anniversaries are, for example, written throughout in iambic pentameter couplets, two hundred thirty-seven couplets in The First Anniversary and two hundred sixty-four couplets in The Second Anniversary. That adds up to a lot of couplets, and we may find significance in their use if not in their numbers, saying for instance that in Donne the form has more flexibility than the couplets of George Gascoigne and less than the artfully enjambed verses of Ben Jonson. According to training and temperament we may find these couplets more interesting than George Chapman's fourteeners, less

interesting than Andrew Marvell's tetrameters. The point is, first
of all, that their significance depends less on what they are in
themselves than on the habitual associations that we bring to our
reading. The point is, second, that repetends like the couplets do
not mean in and of themselves because they are *invariable* in their
iteration. We may of course deem some couplets more incisive or
more slack than others, some couplets wittier or more sententious
than others; but as a structural element the couplets as couplets do
not have decisive importance, do not advertise meaning in and of
themselves. Donne's couplets constitute the norm for The Anniversaries, but without variation from the norm—a section in am-
phibrachs, a racy run of Skeltonics—there is no way to lend
internal significance to the couplets. The triadic structure of the
repetends, on the other hand, is decisive, and is meaningful, because it represents norm-with-variation and even norm-with-de-
parture.

The shift, from the norm represented by the first poem to
the norm-and-variation represented by the second, may be understood more easily if viewed as part of the larger movement that
Donne the preacher calls "*Solomons* method," which is also, at
least in part, the method by which the companion poems become
companions. It will be recalled that, according to Donne the
preacher, "if our love might be drawn from this world, *Solomon*
thought it a direct way to convay it upon the next." The First
Anniversary represents "Solomons Anatomy, and cutting up of
the world," whereas The Second Anniversary explicitly seeks "to
convay [our love] upon the next," in order "to cleave to God for
the next." Donne, that is, attempts in the two Anniversaries to
emulate Solomon, who is "a good Master to correct us in this
world, a good Master to direct us to the next."

The way the poet represents himself, his own poetic role,
within the two poems, likewise corresponds to the distinctions of
Donne the preacher in explaining "*Solomons* method." At the end
of The First Anniversary Donne aligns himself with the Song of
Moses, that "last, and lastingest peece"—"last" because it was the
last time that God spoke to Moses before he died and the Israelites
entered the Promised Land, and "lastingest" because they would
forget the "Law" but "keepe the song still in their memory" (461–

68). Not the redemptive Song at the Sea but the Song of Deuter-onomy 31.19–30,32.1–47 (Geneva) that caps the Old Law as it is embodied in the Old Testament, and is a Song of Judgment: "this song may be my witnes against the children of Israel. . . . For they are a nacion voyde of counsel, nether is there anie vnderstanding in the[m]. Oh that they were wise, then they wolde vndersta[n]d this: they wolde co[n]sider their later end." It is a Song of Wrath —these "wordes which I testifie against you this day"—to a per-verse generation who cannot see, judge, and follow the "idea" of virtue; and in consequence The First Anniversary becomes by implication the Old Testament song of darkness, diminution, and death addressed to those who are not "wise, then they wolde vndersta[n]d this: they wolde co[n]sider their later end."

In The Second Anniversary, on the other hand, Donne's poetic role becomes that of the "Trumpet, at whose voice the people came" (528)—not the voice of the Old Testament Isaiah, which "like a trumpet" could "shew the people their transgres-sions," but the voice of the New Testament preacher: "God shall send his people preachers furnished with all these abilities, to be *Tubae,* Trumpets to awaken them; and then to be *carmen musicum,* to sing Gods mercies in their ears" (see *Sermons,* II, 164 and 166).[1] The companion poems stand in relation to each other as the "trum-pet" of "transgressions" to the "trumpet" of "Gods mercies"—as type to antitype, Old Testament to New Testament, and Justice to Mercy. Donne the poet resembles Donne the preacher, who en-deavors to be like Solomon—"a good Master to correct us in this world, a good Master to direct us to the next."

"The entrie into the worke" (marginal gloss) of The First Anniversary consists of ninety lines, divided into three sections of thirty lines apiece.[2] In the first section Donne justifies his role as poet and depicts a world that, having "lost [its] sense and mem-ory," is sick unto death and ripe for anatomy; "speechlesse growne" (30), the poet must speak for it. In the second section Donne claims that the world has "forgot" its "name," which means that the poet (adopting "*Solomons* method") must begin to work on the mem-ory by using his understanding to perform an "Anatomy" (60). In the third section Donne, with urbanely fallacious logic, argues that, even though we have been "taught" by the death of "shee" that the world is "mortall in [its] purest part," nevertheless (so goes the conceit) "there's a kind of world remaining still" that may benefit from the poet's "dissectione" of the "diseases of the old" world, for men "forgoe" or "covet things" when they "their true worth know" (90).

These three introductory subsections adumbrate the tripartite organization of each of the five main sections that follow and make up the body of The First Anniversary. Each of these five main sections begins (1) with an anatomy performed by the poet on a "speechlesse" world devoid of "sense and memory," then proceeds (2) to "name" her, to awaken memory and allow us "to see her, whom all would see," and finally closes (3) with an injunction to follow "true worth." These generalizations, given the nature of the case and the clarity of Martz's argument, should need no substantiation, but my review of the criticism indicates that I must demonstrate the structure of The First Anniversary in sufficient detail to make the burden of proof fall on those who have sought to modify Martz's exposition of Donne's structure. It is easy to do, though tedious in the recounting; but it must be done, if for no other reason than that the poem cannot be understood without understanding the way it is put together. And the way The First Anniversary is put together *in relation* to the way The Second Anniversary is put together. It is the relation of the two poems that, finally, counts; that finally signifies—and, accordingly, I have had the corresponding sections of the two poems printed side-by-side on facing pages (pp. 96–97). It will be difficult, I believe, for even the most solemn theorist to evade this double-entry evidence of conscious intention, of preconceived "Idea" and architectonic "foreconceit." It is "beauties best, proportion."

Not counting "The entrie into the worke" (1–90) and the "Conclusion" (435–74), the schematic structure of The First Anniversary, based in a series of easily recognized repetends, ought to be represented in the way indicated on page 96.

Exhibited in this schematic way, the architectonic qualities of The First Anniversary will be obvious to almost anyone (who has not written on the poems). The first main section of The First Anniversary begins (1) with the assertion that "There is no health" (91) in the little world of man, demonstrates the proposition for some eighty lines, and concludes (170) that "man is a trifle, and poore thing." This section then proceeds (2) to a eulogy of "she" who was the repository of the "vertue" that man has lost (171–82). The section closes (3) with the claim that we now know "how poore a trifling thing man is" and that we must, accordingly, strive to "be more then man" (183–90). Having disposed of man the microcosm, Donne characteristically moves from one aspect of the commonplace analogy to the other; he turns our attention from the microcosm to the geocosm.

The second main section accordingly begins (1) with a logical transition that explicitly points the analogy: "Then, as man-kinde, so is the worlds whole frame / Quite out of joynt, almost created lame" (191–92). Donne demonstrates the proposition for more than twenty-five lines before concluding that "this is the worlds condition now" (219). This section then proceeds (2) to a eulogy of "she" to "whom this world" was but a "Microcosme of her" (220–36). The section closes (3) with the claim that we now know "how lame a cripple this world is" and that we must, accordingly, strive "to be none of it" (237–48). It is not merely that Donne relies upon the commonplace analogy of microcosm and geocosm; he explicitly uses it in the simile ("as mankinde, so is the worlds whole frame") that forms the transition to the second section, then ends the section with an explicit reminder ("worlds condition now"), and secures the imaginative integrity of the unit with the imagery that begins with "lame" and ends with "cripple."

And so on—throughout the rest of the three main sections of The First Anniversary. After the poet has anatomized the microcosm, the little world of man, and the geocosm, the larger world to which the microcosm corresponds, he can turn his attention, logically enough, to the two (Scholastic) elements of beauty that used to inform the microcosm, geocosm, and macrocosm—first "beauties best, proportion," and then "beauties other second Element" or "Colour"; and finally he considers the loss of correspondence between the geocosm and the macrocosm, between earth and heaven. The poet has orderly conned his commonplaces. In each instance Donne introduces his topic directly, providing transitions that remind the reader of the preceding topic and that relate

The First Anniversary

(1)   "There is no health" in man, the microcosm.

"If man were any thing, he's nothing now" (for "he lost his hart" when "shee" died).

"Shee, shee is dead; shee's dead: when thou knowest this.
Thou knowest how poore a trifling thing man is.
And learn'st thus much by our Anatomee. . . ."

(2)   "Then, as mankinde, so is the worlds whole frame. . . ."

"This is the worlds condition now, and now
She that should all parts to reunion bow. . . ."

"Shee, shee is dead; shee's dead: when thou knowest this,
Thou knowst how lame a cripple this world is.
And learnst thus much by our Anatomy. . . ."

(3)   The "worlds beauty is decayd, or gone" (this section devoted to "proportion," the next to "colour")

"Beauties best, proportion, is dead," and she, "measure of all Symmetree," is gone.

"Shee, shee is dead, shee's dead; when thou knowst this
Thou knowst how ugly'a monster this world is;
And learnst thus much by our Anatomee. . . ."

(4)   "But beauties other second Element,
Colour, and lustre now, is as neere spent."

"Perchance the world might have recovered,
If she whom we lament had not beene dead."

"Shee, shee is dead; shee's dead: when thou knowest this,
Thou knowst how wan a Ghost this our world is:
And learnst thus much by our Anatomee. . . ."

(5)   "Nor in ought more this worlds decay appeares" than in the lack of "correspondence" between "heaven and earth."

"If this commerce twixt heaven and earth" were not lost, then "Shee" and her "vertue" could still "worke . . . on us"

"Shee, shee is dead; shee's dead: when thou knowest this,
Thou knowst how drie a Cinder this world is.
And learnst thus much by our Anatomy."

The Second Anniversary

(1)   "Thirst for that time, O my insatiate soule," for the "onely
        Health" is to "Forget this rotten world."

        "Looke upward; that's toward her, whose happy state
        We now lament not, but congratulate."

        "Shee, shee is gone; shee's gone; when thou knowst this,
        What fragmentary rubbidge this world is
        Thou knowst, and that it is not worth a thought. . . ."

(2)   "Thinke then, my soule, that death is but a Groome," to light
        thy way to "Heaven."

        "Thinke these things cheerefully: and if thou bee
        Drowsie or slacke, remember then that shee. . . ."

        "Shee, shee embrac'd a sicknesse, gave it meat,
        The purest Blood, and Breath, that ere it eat.
        And hath taught us. . . ."

(3)   "Thinke further on thy selfe, my soule, and thinke
        How thou at first wast made but in a sinke. . . ."

        "To'advance these thoughts, remember then, that shee,
        Shee, whose faire body no such prison was. . . ."

        "Shee, shee, thus richly,'and largely hous'd, is gone:
        And chides us slow-pac'd snailes. . . ."

(4)   "Poore soule, in this thy flesh what do'st thou know?
        Thou knowst thy selfe so little. . . ."

        "There thou (but in no other schoole) maist bee
        Perchance, as learned . . . as she / Shee who. . . ."

        "Shee, shee, not satisfied with all this waite,
        (For so much knowledge, as would over-fraite
        Another, did but Ballast her) is gone,
        As well t'enjoy, as get perfectione.
        And cals us after her. . . ."

(5)   "Returne not, my soule, from this extasee,
        And meditation of what thou shalt bee. . . ."

        "Up, up, for in that squadron there doth live
        Shee, who. . . ."

        "Shee, shee doth leave it, and by Death, survive
        All this, in Heaven; whither who doth not strive
        The more, because shee'is there, he doth not know. . . ."

it to the current topic, and then concludes with summary lines that connect the end of the subsection to the beginning of the subsection. The poet then proceeds to a clearly defined eulogy marked by identical refrains; and then, before repeating the triple progression in the next section, closes with the appropriate homiletic injunction, different according to the topic of each section but introduced with the same words. This logical structure, each part meticulously demarcated with the same or similar rhetorical signals, seems hard to overlook and, once seen, harder still to ignore or deny—but the history of criticism suggests otherwise.

Although this skeletal structure, without which the integument of witty conceit would lack meaningful shape, does not display much in the way of Romantic spontaneity, it reveals for Donne and other University Wits "beauties best, proportion." As such it gives the impression of completeness, of being in itself a harmonious whole that exhibits *claritas, integritas,* and *proportio.* It offers the artistic illusion of being a well-wrought urn, a poetic microcosm of what the macrocosm was before the loss of proportion and correspondence. Put into relation with its companion poem it becomes far more significant.

The first 383 lines of The Second Anniversary, precisely divided into five main sections of three parts each, are consciously designed to recall the aims, methods, and pattern of the earlier poem. Schematic representation of these lines—the remaining lines of the poem fulfil another, and extraordinary, function—indicates that Donne composed The Second Anniversary with The First in mind, modeling The Second on The First in order to stimulate comparisons and contrasts between the two companion poems printed together in one volume. The two schematic representations, considered together, reveal the ways in which the poet has gone about his artistic business: first by directly imitating the earlier poem, and then by diverging from it—not all at once but through a series of calculated gradations.

The five main sections, each consisting of three subsections, that make up most but not all of the body of The Second Anniversary ought to be represented in skeletal form as I have done on page 97, facing the preceding page that outlines The First Anniversary—also in five main sections of three subsections. A glance at the facing pages, with special attention to the refrains that make up the third subsection of each of the five parts, reveals that the Second Anniversary relates to the First Anniversary as imitation to original, variation to standard, and departure to norm.

The series of repetends reveals that Donne, after "the entrance" or introduction (1–44), has constructed five main sections, each subdivided into three parts. Each of the triads begins with an analytical "colloquy" (for the Jesuits the "colloquy" comes last, not first) in which the poet directly addresses his "soul"; after the colloquy the poet in each subsection exhorts us to "remember" and "looke" toward "her" in heaven; and then in each subsection the poet repeats and varies the refrain-moral ("Shee, shee . . .") that he had established, and methodically repeated, in The First Anniversary.

The first refrain of The Second Anniversary in effect summarizes the earlier poem, which had demonstrated in *its* five main sections that, to adopt the phrasing of the second poem, this world "is not worth a thought." And yet the refrain also intimates, in its minor variations from the norm established by the repetitions of The First Anniversary, that The Second will, taking The First as its point of departure, make its "Progres" in a new direction. The First Anniversary has become by implication the model for The Second Anniversary, the standard against which the poet invites us to assess the modifications made in The Second Anniversary.

From the outline it is possible to see clearly what Donne is doing with The Second Anniversary (at least with the first 383 lines of this 528–line poem) in relation to The First Anniversary. Simply by focusing on the refrain we may observe some of the ways in which the five main sections, each divided into three parts, of the second poem have been set up to correspond to the five main sections, each divided into three parts, of the first poem. Where The First Anniversary has,

> Shee, shee is dead; shee's dead: when thou knowst this,
> Thou knowst how poore a trifling thing man is,
> And learn'st thus much by our Anatomee . . . ,

The Second Anniversary reads:

> Shee, shee is gone; shee's gone; when thou knowst this,
> What fragmentary rubbidge this world is
> Thou knowst, and that it is not worth a thought. . . .

The shift of emphasis, from "Anatomy" and *contemptus mundi* to "Progres of the Soule" and *contemplatio dei,* is entirely traditional; it fulfils expectations. What is unexpected is that this major shift in emphasis makes for such minor changes in the first refrain. Although the shift obviously requires the poet to drop the term "Anatomy" and to revise the terminal "shee is dead" (to this world) into the valedictory "shee is gone" (to the other world), in other respects the lines retain the phrasing of the earlier poem, in this way allowing the poet to make explicit the fact that the two poems ought to be read in relation to each other.

Having "corrected" us according to "*Solomons* method" in The First Anniversary and having reminded us of the "correction" in the first refrain of The Second Anniversary, the poet has readied himself to begin, and his audience to appreciate, the series of variations from the norm created by the repetitions of the earlier poem. This series forms an order in itself, a poem-within-the-poem that reveals "beauties best, proportion" and that is itself a microcosmic "progres of the soule." The very next refrain (the second in the series) accordingly repeats "Shee, shee" but drops the "knowst" that carries the associations of *contemptus mundi.* Instead, her departure "hath taught us" that "Death" must "unlocke the doore" to "Heaven." The third refrain repeats "Shee, shee . . . is gone," but now she (actively, though negatively) "chides us slow-pac'd snailes" for *not* following her to heaven. The fourth refrain again repeats "Shee, shee . . . is gone," but now she (actively, and positively) "cals us after her." The fifth refrain completes this pattern of "progres"—first by repeating "Shee, shee," then by asserting that she "by Death survives," and finally by urging that anyone who does not strive to follow her "doth *not* know" (my emphasis). The refrains therefore not only reveal, through incremental gradations, the ascending scale that moves from *contemptus mundi* toward *contemplatio dei* but also exemplify the rhetorical circle of hysteron proteron that moves from "thou knowst" (this world is worthless) to an imagined someone who "doth *not* know" (the joys of heaven). The refrains, artfully varying from the norm established in the earlier poem, constitute in themselves a little world made cunningly.

As with The First Anniversary, the tripartite structure of each of the five main sections of The Second Anniversary may seem to resemble the three-part pattern of Jesuit meditation. But here again the poet changes the order in which the three faculties of the soul are exercised, beginning each of the main sections where St. Ignatius would end, namely with the "colloquy" in which Donne speaks in direct address to his soul; and in each of these colloquies the poet emphasizes neither memory nor will but understanding. In each of the five main parts of The Second Anniversary the poet starts out not with *compositio loci* but with the hortatory, analytical admonition to his soul, proceeds then in each case to a eulogy in which the imperative is to "looke . . . towards her" and "remember then that shee," and ends in each instance with "Shee, shee is gone" (or some recognizable, and meaningful, variation) to heaven. The pattern is perfectly clear, though it is equally clear that the pattern is not that of St. Ignatius. The pattern is derivative only in the sense that it is the traditional "trinity" of human faculties derived from theological contemplation of the Trinity. Donne, in short, turns the pattern to his own uses in The Second Anniversary just as he had in The First Anniversary.

For Ignatius the colloquy comes third, after composition of place and analysis; and ideally it issues in an act of the will. For Donne the colloquy begins the process and involves not the faculty of will but the reason or the understanding. After the first main section has reminded us of the mode of The First Anniversary ("forget this rotten world"), the second section emphasizes thought: "Thinke then, my soule," says the poet, and repeats the verb throughout the section. The third main section starts with, "Thinke further on thy selfe, my soule," and the poet again repeats the verb. The fourth emphasizes what "thou knowst not," and the fifth denigrates "earthly thoughts." The second subsection of each of the five main sections stresses looking "upward" toward her and "remembering" her; each of the third subsections focuses on what we now "know" and have been "taught" about leaving this world for the next. This tripartite structure—thinking, remembering, willing—of each of the five main sections obviously reflects

the "trinitarian" conception of the human soul, but Donne's em-
ployment—and deployment—of the faculties of reason, memory,
and will remains distinctively his own.

The outline of the structure of The Second Anniversary
also indicates how carefully, and logically, the poet developed the
implications of his subtitle—"Of the Progres of the Soule." I have
in mind not only the strictly controlled modulations in the refrain,
moving for example from "Shee, shee is gone" to "Shee, shee
doth . . . survive" or from the negative "Shee, shee . . . chides us"
to the more positive "Shee, shee . . . cals us after her"; not only
the rigorously calculated gradations in the eulogies, each one moving closer to "her" as a more nearly adequate "object" in which to
contemplate deity; but also in the "progres," the movement, of
the five main sections considered as tripartite "meditations" beginning in *contemptus mundi* and ending in ecstatic *contemplatio dei*.

The first of the "meditations" sums up the theme of *contemptus mundi* that dominates The First Anniversary: "Forget this
rotten world," for "it is not worth a thought." The second meditation begins the turn from this negative view: "Thinke . . .
cheerefully" of death, for it is the only way to eternal life. The
third "advance[s] these thoughts" by meditating on "how poore a
prison" the body is; the fourth meditates on the soul itself, how it
"know'st [it] selfe so little" while in the body. The fifth meditation—

> Returne not, my soule, from this extasee,
> And meditation of what thou shalt bee—

asserts that the earlier meditations have freed the soul from the
body, not through ordinary death but through a moment of *extasis,* the "standing apart" from the body in "contemplation of
God, and heaven." As Donne the preacher says (*Sermons,* II, 210),
"I will finde out another death, *mortem raptus,* a death of rapture,
and of extasie, that death which S. *Paul* died more then once." The
poet, in other words, implies—so goes the poetic conceit—that
the earlier meditations have been successful, that they have accomplished their purpose, which is to "finde out another death . . . of
extasie." No longer need we "peepe through lattices of eies" or
"heare through Laberinths of eares" (296–97). The poet can, ac-

cordingly, exhort the soul, already "growne all Ey" (200) and now
with "new eare" (339), not merely to "looke upward" but to *be*
"Up, up" with the angels and the "blessed Mother-maid," the
patriarchs, the prophets, the apostles, the virgins: "Up, up, for in
that squadron there doth live / Shee. . . ." The "Progres of the
Soule," the result of a logical as well as an emotional progression,
is in one sense complete: the soul, out of the body, contemplates
the joys of heaven, but the poet has completed only those parts of
The Second Anniversary that at first reflect, but finally "reverse"
or "negate," the five parts of The First Anniversary.

Having reached the end of the five main sections that
correspond to, and progressively vary from, the five main sections
of The First Anniversary, Donne performs one of those incredible
feats of poetic prestidigitation for which he is justly famous and
unjustly notorious.

The fifth meditation of The Second Anniversary ends in
the usual manner, with the expected refrain, "Shee, shee doth leave
it," and the appropriate moral. Then the poet *appears* to begin a
sixth colloquy—for which there would be *no* corresponding section in The First Anniversary:

> But pause, my soule, and study ere thou fall
> On accidentall joyes, the'essentiall.
>
> (483–84)

The mode of address is plainly that of the colloquy, and the School
logic, dealing with accidents in relation to essences, is typical of
Donne in general and of these poems in particular. And yet this
colloquy is not, as in all previous instances, followed by a eulogy
of "shee" and by a refrain-moral ("Shee, shee"). Instead, our
expectations, established by the first poem and reinforced by the
second, are immediately frustrated when this colloquy is followed
by yet another colloquy, "Then, soule, to thy first pitch worke up
again" (435), and this colloquy not by the expected eulogy but by
the refrain, "Shee whom we celebrate, is gone before" (448),
which does not on this occasion, as on all previous occasions, lead
to a moral but instead to a eulogy; this refrain then followed by
yet another refrain, "shee to Heaven is gone" (467), which leads
into a peculiar transition rather than into the customary moral:

> But could this low world joyes essentiall touch,
> Heavens accidentall joyes would passe them much.
>
> (471–72)

This transition—a "colloquy" without, as it were, direct address to the soul—is then succeeded not by a eulogy and a refrain-moral but by what looks like a refrain-eulogy:

> In this fresh joy, 'tis no small part, that shee,
> Shee, in whose goodnesse. . . .   (497–98)

And this refrain-eulogy modulates from praise to praise back into what looks like an oddly attenuated version of the refrain, "Shee . . . to heaven is gone" (507–09), which is then followed by the "Conclusion" (511–28).

No wonder that commentators have been frustrated, no wonder that Martz felt the need to revise his earlier analyses! The kind of analysis to which The First Anniversary proved susceptible seems at first to work admirably with The Second Anniversary— but *only* with the first 383 lines of the 528–line poem. The Second Anniversary presents problems that do not arise with respect to The First Anniversary, and the problems seem to be exacerbated rather than ameliorated by the close resemblances of the second poem to the first. For 383 lines Donne models the 528–line Second Anniversary on the five main parts of The First Anniversary and then, instead of sequentially continuing *or* completely abandoning the repetends that signaled the three-part subsections, he commingles and confounds them: insofar as the conventions of discourse permit, the poet identifies one faculty with another, substitutes one faculty for another, and makes them, in effect, into interchangeable parts. Whatever expectations may have been aroused—and I have been implying that a good many *would* have been in the oral-rhetorical culture of Donne's time—by the five three-part meditations of The First Anniversary, and then powerfully reinforced by the five three-part meditations of The Second Anniversary, have been, by this time, completely frustrated.

A simple example may make this situation clearer. Among other items of cultural baggage, we carry with us, to the theater or to the library, the alphabet. The alphabet comes to us, and with us, prepackaged, an invariable series whether from Alpha to Omega or from A to Z. This fact—that we are prepackaged bundles of habituations—allows the poet to manipulate any number of items that we carry about with us in our cultural rucksacks, everything from feelings about couplets to feelings about coupling. The poet gives us ABC, and our cultural background leads us to expect D; if we get D, we receive the satisfaction that comes from expectation fulfilled, but Donne has—it seems deliberately—in this case crossed our cultural wires.

Apart from the prepackaged truths and beliefs—some more private than public, some more public than private—that we bring to the work of art, there are the meanings that the poet packages for us in the course of writing the poem and that we experience in the course of reading the poem. Donne's couplets belong mainly to the previous category, and his treatment of them is invariable in the sense that our expectation of one couplet followed by another is invariably fulfilled. Donne's structural repetends—his refrains, his colloquies, his morals—belong mainly to the latter category. These repetends, gathering momentum as we read, constitute the main source of the expectations the poet arouses in the course of the work; and they are analogous not to the alphabet but to the *use* the poet makes of cultural habituations like the alphabet. The poet may repeat ABCABCABC until he has established a structure *within the work itself,* until he has constructed a norm out of, say, "shee, shee is dead," against which we may then assess significant variation. Meaning resides in the perception of difference, and while in theory we must concede that the meanings are in an absolute sense endlessly deferred, in practice we extract meanings, and artistic satisfactions, as we proceed. Otherwise, we wouldn't bother; we read for the sake of meaning, and experience. Of course, if we do not see the structural norms that the poet has established through his repetends, we cannot see the variations. Indeterminacy lies in the eye of the beholder.

If we cannot see the variations we must impose meanings from without, reaching into the cultural rucksack in our insatiable search for meanings and extracting, according to the exigencies of the moment, still another "structure" (Jesuit meditation, the Seven Seals of the Apocalypse) and yet another "name" (Logos, Astraea, or the "poet himself") for Elizabeth Drury.

The tricky question will always be to distinguish meanings imposed from meanings discovered, and the distinction between the two can never be absolute because the two activities are inseparable in practice. Yet the distinction itself has absolute importance, for the relative weight that we give to the two activities means the difference between imposing our terms on the other person and allowing the other person a right to her own meanings. Our ancestors and our bedmates differ in all the obvious ways but not, I think, to the extent that the differences diminish their right to be known in their own terms, a piety that always derives its force from the kind of injunction that Ben Jonson delivers "To the Reader":

> Pray thee, take care, that tak'st my booke in hand,
> To reade it well: that is, to vnderstand.

Since the players of Shakespeare's day had to make it their business to remain constantly aware of their audience and the value of the product, it is no accident that John Heminge and Henrie Condell, the editors of the First Folio, address themselves "To the great Variety of Readers"—from "the most able, to him that can but spell"—and then make explicit their answer to the question of literary value: "Reade him, therefore; and againe, and againe: And if then you do not like him, surely you are in some manifest danger, not to vnderstand him." If we do not understand Donne (not in some absolute sense but in the way I am trying to describe), we consign ourselves to the kind of literary repetition compulsion —the unconscious equivalent of literary "deconstruction"—that forces us to provide an endless series of new labels for his "structure" and new names for what Elizabeth Drury supposedly "symbolizes." Indeterminacy is in this respect relative, and lies in the eye of the beholder.

If we were dealing with a poet of the earlier twentieth century, we might be tempted to speculate that Donne's sudden departure from triadic form into formlessness—the amorphous travesty of "structure" in which reason, memory, and will are commingled rather than distinguished and ordered in sequence— imitates the formlessness, the meaningless chaos, of modern life. If with a poet of the later twentieth century we might speculate that she had "deconstructed" her work before a francophiliac critic could have a proper go at it. If we were dealing with a lesser poet, we might speculate that he had simply lost control of complicated, recalcitrant materials.

Yet Donne is, as we know, a major poet, for whom "beauties best" is "proportion," and in consequence his procedures require elucidation rather than speculation. Fortunately, this is easy enough to do if we allow ourselves, for the sake of experience, to think for a moment in the precise terms of Donne's conceptual archetypes. We cannot "lodge an In-mate soule" but must attend to "glassie Essence."

While in the body the soul remains dependent on "sense, and Fantasy"; while in the body the soul must meditate through the exercise of reason, memory, and will. While in the body the soul can only "know *per species,*" as Donne puts it in a sermon that relies on the optical terminology that pervades The Anniversaries. While in the body the soul knows only "by those resultances and species, which rise from the Object, and pass through the Sense to the Understanding." And, adds Donne, "that's a deceiveable way, both by the indisposition of the Organ, sometimes, and sometimes by the depravation of the Judgment" (*Sermons,* IV, 127). In short, we may apprehend the sensible species imperfectly; and even if there is no "indisposition of the Organ" of sense, we may nevertheless fail to comprehend the intelligible species—the "Idea of a Woman" reflected through the agency of the active intellect in "glassie Essence." When out of the body, however, in *extasis,* the soul may aspire to knowledge *per essentiam;* the soul now has the kind of sight that approaches the vision of Sir Thomas Browne's deity, "who lookes not on us through a derived ray, or a trajection of a sensible species, but beholds the substance without the helpe of accidents, and the formes of things, as we their operations." [3]

No longer dependent on the "accidents" and "operations" apprehended by "sense, and Fantasy," the soul need no longer exercise the meditative faculties in order to see and know and will the good. As Bryskett, following Cinthio, puts it: "And right true it is, that whiles she is tied to the bodie, she cannot vnderstand but by the meanes of the senses: but that being free and loosed from the body, she hath not her proper operations, that is most false.

For then hath she no need at all of the senses, when being pure and simple, she may exercise her owne power and vertue proper to her, (which is the contemplation of God Almightie, the highest and onely true good) nor yet of any other instrument but her selfe."[4] It is to this point—"Returne not, my soule, from this extasee"—that Donne has by poetic *fiat* brought the soul in The Second Anniversary.

In his poetic "Progres of the Soule" Donne has worked the soul up to its "first pitch againe," and the soul may now, having gone beyond "discourse" of reason, "intuitively" contemplate the "Idea" behind that "shee" in whom "reson" did not "o'erthrow, but rectifie her will." She had "kept

> Gods Image, in such reparation,
> Within her heart, that what decay was grown,
> Was her first Parents fault, and not her own. . . .
> (Second Anniversary, 456–58)

The locution "Gods Image" refers not to some generalized notion of Calvinist regeneration but specifically, as the lines about "reson" and "will" indicate, to the "trinity from the Trinity"; she keeps the image "in such reparation" (expiatory repair) in her heart and memory that "one might almost say" that "her bodie thought," that in her person it might almost seem that she had closed the great wound that had opened between Sidney's "erected wit" and "infected will"—not by using her "reson" to "o'erthrow, but rectifie her will." To "o'erthrow" the "will" is to repress the passions, the feelings, and to suppress the faculty of choice; it is the way of the anchorite. To rectify the will is to make it "straight" in relation to reason; reason and will become the same, will and reason become one. The relation becomes one of identity. This is her "integrity."

For Donne, in the sermons and in these poems, "Gods Image" refers to that "trinity" of faculties modeled on the Trinity, the three faculties of memory, understanding, and will that ought to function as one but are (as St. Paul lamented) often in conflict because of the Fall. Sir Thomas Browne observes that "it is the corruption I feare within me, not the contagion of commerce without me. 'Tis that unruly regiment within me that will destroy me, 'tis I that doe infect my selfe, the man without a Navell yet lives in me"; and he notes that "there is in our soule a kind of Triumvirate, or Triple government of three competitors." When we, like Elizabeth Drury, manage "to compose those fewds and angry dissentions," the "competitors" may then "bee all Kings, and yet make but one Monarchy."[5]

She may "for life, and death, a patterne bee" (524) because in her innocent *integritas* her faculties and powers are more nearly one, and in this her "trinity from the Trinity" more nearly resembles the Trinity. Elizabeth Drury exemplifies the identity sought, the relation of soul to body that constitutes an almost-ecstatic union. In "A Funerall Elegie," probably the first poem that Donne wrote in praise of Elizabeth, the poet speaks of her, before "she yeelded to too long an Extasie" (83), as

> One, whose cleare body was so pure, and thin,
> Because it neede disguise no thought within.
> 'Twas but a through-light scarfe, her minde t'enroule,
> Or exhalation breath'd out from her soule. (59–62)

In other words, she presents to "sense, and Fantasy" an image of near-ecstatic *integritas*. In The First Anniversary the poet registers the union as a kind of alchemical sublimation:

> She in whom vertue was so much refin'd,
> That for Allay unto so pure a minde
> Shee tooke the weaker Sex, she that could drive
> The poysonous tincture, and the stayne of *Eve,*
> Out of her thoughts, and deeds; and purifie
> All, by a true religious Alchimy. . . .
>
> (177–82)

In The Second Anniversary the elements were so mixed in her that nature might stand up and "almost say" that here is the "Idea of a Woman":

> Shee whose Complexion was so even made,
> That which of her Ingredients should invade
> The other three, no Feare, no Art could guesse:
> So far were all remov'd from more or lesse.
>
> (123–26)

And then the poet returns to his religious alchemy, for he must use the images of "sense, and Fantasy" to figure forth the "Idea," magically producing in this case—out of the implied observation of an innocent blush!—some of the greatest lines of this or any period:

> Shee, of whose soule, if we may say, 'twas Gold,
> Her body was th'Electrum, and did hold
> Many degrees of that; we understood
> Her by her sight, her pure and eloquent blood
> Spoke in her cheekes, and so distinctly wrought,
> That one might almost say, her bodie thought. . . .
>
> (241–46)

Even the commonplace image of the book becomes a metaphysical conceit conveying through "sense, and Fantasy" the almost-ecstatic union of soul and body:

> Shee, who left such a body,'as even shee
> Onely in Heaven could learne, how it can bee
> Made better; for shee rather was two soules,
> Or like to full, on both sides written Rols,
> Where eies might read upon the outward skin,
> As strong Records for God, as mindes within. . . .
>
> (501–06)

Such "pure and eloquent" praises are "so distinctly wrought" that they make unforgettable Donne's assertion in "A Funerall Elegie" that she was "cloath'd in her Virgin white integrity" (75)—not only the "integrity" of the virgin but also, "one might almost say," the "integrity," the oneness with inner and outer nature, that Adam and Eve enjoyed before the Fall. This *integritas,* figured forth by the images of "sense, and Fantasy" that shadow Elizabeth Drury, exemplifies what Donne in the first line of The First Anniversary calls "rich soule," so rich "that one might almost say, her bodie thought." The soul in ecstasy, freed from the corruption of what Sidney in the *Apologie for Poetrie* labels "our infected will," becomes a pure example of what he refers to as "our erected wit."

This is the condition of the man whom Donne the preacher calls "Righteous" because he "dies in Christ": "His understanding and his will is *all one faculty* [my emphasis]." And Donne repeats, to emphasize the identification of faculties: "His understanding and his will is all one faculty," for his "memory and his fore-sight are fixt, and concentred upon one object, upon goodnesse" (*Sermons,* VIII, 190). The "infected will" has been "rectified," aligned or identified with "erected wit." This state of the soul recalls the Edenic, that state of *integritas* in which there is no conflict between reason and will, between knowing virtue and being virtuous. In the *Commedia,* after a long period in which the rational Vergil accustoms Dante the Pilgrim to the *habitus* of virtue, the poet of the earthly empire finally crowns and mitres the Pilgrim lord over himself and tells him that now he may do as he "wills," for at this point in his own "Progres of the Soule" the Pilgrim no longer experiences his earlier conflicts between knowing the good and doing the good.

It is the possibility of this ideal balance of elements and faculties that Macbeth relinquishes when he allows his "fantasy" of future imperium to "shake" his "single state of man" and provoke him to the tragic choice that issues in the murder of the saintly Duncan. But when man retains, or recovers, something of his *integritas* or "single state," reason and desire are more nearly one; to see the good is to know the good is to will the good, and there is no need for "reson" to try to "o'erthrow . . . the will." When "his understanding and his will is all one faculty," there is no longer any need to enter into colloquy with one's soul, no longer any need to exhort one's soul to "looke upward" toward "her," and no longer any need to draw attention through the usual refrain to the apposite moral—and Donne does not.

Where "wit" and "will" are one and the same, the office of memory becomes "concentred" in the act of contemplation, and the soul, now "growne all Ey" (200), leaves behind its three-part meditations and becomes "concentred upon one object, upon [the] goodnesse" of deity. At the point of its "first pitch" the soul, liberated from the constraints of the body in poetic "extasee," shares in the beatific vision where this-worldly distinctions between reason and will no longer obtain, and where there no longer exists a distinction between seeing and knowing—or even between the knower and the known:

> Onely who have enjoyd
> The sight of God, in fulnesse, can thinke it;
> For it is both the object, and the wit.
> This is essentiall joye. . . .   (440–43)

This epigrammatic formulation, enacting in its syntax the statement it makes, provides the ultimate gloss on the rhetoric of
reciprocal identity that echoes and reechoes throughout The Anniversaries.[6] In The First Anniversary "Shee's now a part both of the
Quire, and Song" (10), "shee's now partaker, and a part" (434, the
summary line before the Conclusion), and accordingly the poet
imitates Moses in a "last, and lastingst peece, a song" (461). In
The Second Anniversary she has gone, "As well t'enjoy, as get
perfectione" (318); " 'Tis such a full, and such a filling good" (445)
where "more grace, and more capacitee / At once is given" (466–
67); she, "Long'd for, and longing for't, to heaven is gone, / Where
shee receives, and gives addition" (509–10, the summary lines
before the Conclusion). In this life she is the "object" in memory
of our "wit," the almost-ecstatic union of body and soul that,
before she "yeelded to too long an Extasie," holds the promise of
the time when we too shall be a "part both of the Quire, and
Song." And Donne's rhetoric of reciprocal identification is not a
verbal tic but the necessary expression of the epistemological conceit, the identity of knower and known, that provides the conceptual "hinge" on which The Anniversaries turn.

In the final portions of The Second Anniversary the "trinity" of the soul—reason, memory, and will—becomes "one" or
"Trinitarian," *imitatio dei* in poetry of the God Who is Three
Persons in One. The corresponding powers of the soul—invoked
in The First Anniversary as "see, and Judge, and follow worthinesse"—have merged in ecstatic union, as the previously separated
parts of the tripartite subdivisions merge in the final portions of
The Second Anniversary to provide a poetic imitation of the soul
in "extasee." Structure speaks, "of gladnesse vnspeakable."

In short, Donne uses the three-part divisions of the five
main sections created in The First Anniversary as the basis for the
meaningful variations created in The Second Anniversary. And
then, in a dazzling display of metaphysical wit, the poet leaves
behind this carefully articulated system of comparisons and con-

trasts to simulate the nature of the soul in ecstasy, using structure first to imitate the three-part movement of reason, memory, and will in this-worldly "meditation" and then using the calculated conflation of the elements of that structure to mimic the activity of the soul in other-worldly "extasee." There is no comparable *tour de force* in English poetry until the composition of *Lycidas,* which also enacts, in its own tripartite structure, what it says.[7]

Conclusion

Ben Jonson, and many of his contemporaries, felt that "language most shewes a man." Martin Heidegger, and many of his followers, felt that "language speaks man." Although the reversal of roles, in which language swaps places with the human being, implies a good deal about us and our world, the substitution of "language" for what philosophers used to call "mind" or "consciousness" displaces but does not remove the dichotomy between subject and object that has bedeviled us since the Romantics and before.[1] And since nothing can heal the great wound, we must constantly negotiate and renegotiate the extremes. Newly glamorous word, "language"—old problem.[2] As Dugald Stewart put it toward the beginning of the nineteenth century, "Such is the influence of words upon the most acute understandings, that when the *language* of a sect has once acquired a systematical coherence and consistency, the imposing plausibility of the dress in which their doctrines are exhibited, is . . . likely to draw a veil, impenetrable to most eyes, over many of the inconsistencies of *thought* which they may involve."[3] To draw a veil over the old problem (the mock dichotomy between subject and object) shrouds Donne in particular from our view.

It may help, under these circumstances, to turn our attention from "language" to lingoes. Infantile babble becomes, by kinds of imitation and practice that remain imperfectly understood, progressively more coherent and more public, though happily never quite losing the lilt and loll of early speech or the tonalities acquired in playing pet names and rhyming games; we do not learn a language because we are always learning language, and languages. During our lives we assimilate, less or more consciously, vocabularies that may be described variously as sociological, mechanist, psychoanalytical, materialist, agronomist, organicist, mathematical, or whatever. Some of the words living their half-lives in these diverse lingoes—words like true, tolerant, valid, generous, natural—may come to possess strong meanings for some of us, carrying different charges of feeling at different stages in our lives. Some of the feelings associated with particular words may be relatively private (the word "green" for Andrew Marvell, the word "rigor" for Lionel Trilling); some rather more public, their efficacy shifting with the often-imperceptible movements of the tectonic plates of culture (romance, marriage, mutual relationship, significant other, partner). Which is to say that we not only think about words and use them; we also think and feel—their action in us is diachronic as well as synchronic—in them and through them. So did our ancestors, so do our current friends, enemies, and lovers.

There is no such thing, if we would speak strictly, as a literal statement, though some statements feel less metaphorical than others; no such thing as a dead metaphor, for as metaphors lose glamor and gloss through habitual use they can die only a metaphorical death. Cultural history may be seen in this context as the record of the way metaphors combine, interact, disengage—augment or diminish the degree of their "literal" applicability. In the academic profession change usually occurs through the partial assimilation of an explanatory vocabulary imported from an adjacent discipline. (Only rarely do we feel the force of commanding thinkers like Copernicus, Galileo, Darwin, Marx, or Freud who manage to make their vocabularies seem convincing to many people in one or more cultures, with varying appeal and at various times.) Anthropologists like Clifford Geertz and Victor Turner, to take the example current at the moment, acquired the vocabulary of the literary criticism of the 1950s and transformed it into the "language" of culture, with the result that another society, say that of the Balinese, suddenly becomes "thickly" intelligible as a poetic heterocosm, which is to say that it becomes a culture that exemplifies the principles of the New Criticism; and then this process of cross-fertilization may effect change in reverse as literary theorists suddenly discover "liminality" (or whatever) in the lives and works of poets. In this the academic profession resembles one of the ways that change occurs in cultures at large. To adduce the most spectacular instance: Ernst H. Kantorowicz, *The King's Two Bodies: A Study in Mediaevel Political Theology,* has demonstrated the way in which the early Church acquired the bureaucratic language of the Roman Empire, which in turn became the legal language of monarchy in medieval and early modern Europe—and that survives today in the legal language of corporate America.[4] "Engine Charlie" Wilson, in his presidential voice, used to opine that what was good for General Motors was good for the United States, but then he was not aware that his *corporation sole* derived its legal clout from the *corpus mysticum* of Christ, and so he could hardly be expected to think in some other way than the one he found reasonable because it was habitual; it was his theory. Probably the most efficacious way to "feel" outside the conceptual archetypes of our own culture is through the historical study of literature.

Donne wanted to speak of love, whether it was essential or accidental joy; of knowing ourselves, whether we "lodge an Inmate soule" or possess a "rich soule"; of form and matter, whether they could be so constituted as to make it almost possible to say that "her body thought"; of generation and corruption, whether in motion there might be a "long-short Progress"; of the "Idea of a Woman and not as she was." If we learn the lingo, Donne will speak to us, not without what used to be ambiguity and now is indeterminacy—but well enough to be heard and understood.[5]

Whatever Donne's motivations (surely they were many, shifting, complex?), and however the poet arrived at his materials, the problem of composition remains the same: "Poetry is a counterfait Creation, and makes things that are not, as though they were" (*Sermons,* IV, 87), but it *is* "making," and in devising an instrument of witty praise Donne first of all requires a *radical* or "governing" *conceit*—as distinct from the many local "conceits" in the body of the poem—to bind together his diverse materials and to provide the witty "logic" that will explain and justify his praise.

Much of Donne is deliberately outrageous (think of "The Flea"), and The First Anniversary is no exception. Donne makes extravagant claims, but they are well within the range of hyperbole permitted to the elegists of the time. "A Funerall Elegie" makes equally extravagant claims, and no one objects—because in the "Elegie" Donne does not seek to demonstrate the validity of his hyperboles. Donne's hyperboles do not in themselves excite either belief or disbelief; they are recognized for what they are, hyperbole. The problem with The First Anniversary, as with many of Donne's poems, lies not so much in *what* is said but in *how* the saying is done: the poet not only associates the decay of the whole world with the death of Elizabeth Drury, he affects to *prove* it, to *demonstrate* it.

Unfortunately, if one has an impotent receiver, one cannot see the wit of the "logical" demonstration. Emanuele Tesauro is the only critic of the seventeenth century to offer an adequate account of the technique. In *Il cannochiale aristotelico* (1655) Tesauro takes the commonplace trope of The Book of Nature and transforms it into a volume of metaphysical conceits written by the Divine Wit. The kind of wit Tesauro has in mind involves the use of civilized enthymemes, suppressing one or more premises in order to construct *argomenti urbanamente fallaci* or "urbanely fallacious arguments." It was no great trick for the Petrarchan poet to refer to the *donna* as A Saint, but in "The Canonization" Donne through the exercise of urbanely fallacious logic "proves" that the lady is A Saint. It was no great trick for the Renaissance elegist to weep oceans or to take poetic note of the natural cataclysms that attend the demise of his subject, but in The First Anniversary Donne provides an urbanely fallacious argument that appears to *prove* the validity of his hyperbole. It is this that distresses readers who "lodge an In-mate soule."

Donne in constructing The First Anniversary would of course play upon the relation of microcosm to macrocosm (he always, or nearly always, did), he would draw upon his usual array of cartographic, alchemical, and astronomical conceits, and in this case he would also exploit a series of lesser-used conceits based in musical and geometrical analogies. Nevertheless, he would still need the basic, the radical, conceit on which all the other elements would turn. To do this he relied upon the assumptions about "seeing" and "thinking" that I have sketched in the preceding pages.

When Donne plays with the notion of a "new world" composed of the "matter" of her "virtue" and the "forme" of "our practise" (76–78), when he claims that from Elizabeth's "influence all Impressions came" (415) or that "soules were but Resultances from her" and "did from her into our bodies go" (314–15), the poet reveals his allegiance to the older epistemology that provides him with the terms of his radical conceit. When Donne claims that Elizabeth is "all color, all Diaphanous" (366) or that "now no other way there is" but "goodnes, to see her" (16–17), his terminology is technical, exact: not hyperbole but metaphysical truth. This is *metaphysical* wit, to base the companion poems in the conceit that sight, thought, and virtue are one: this is the view from the "watch-towre," necessarily imperfect in this life but a sure adumbration of the kind of knowing achieved when, according to St. Paul, we shall know as now we are known. Donne describes the perfect, and final, form of this kind of union in The Second Anniversary (440–43):

> Onely who have enjoyd
> The sight of God, in fulnesse, can thinke it;
> For it is both the object, and the wit.

The "sight of God" is what is seen (and thought)—because God's sight, which we share, enables us to see "it" and think "it"; that "it," through grammatical and metaphysical ambiguity, is both— "both the object and the wit." This is the union of the beatific vision, which may be approximated in this world by taking sight from the "watch-towre." Sight is thought, thought sight; and not just in the sense that Plato could speak of the "eye of mind," or that we may use "I see" to mean "I understand." The operation of sight provides the model, from Aristotle to Donne, not only for sensing in general but also for the way the mind, the human intellect, performs its cogitations, acquiring and using its "ideas."

This epistemology encourages certain habits of mind, and may be said to dictate others. In this epistemology the *images* of The Anniversaries correspond to "sense, and Fantasy"; they are "color" or beauty but not "beauties best," which means that the reader must use them not as ends in themselves, as if they were specimen-illustrations of the Imagist Manifesto, but rather as the means by which to ascend into the "watch-towre" of the intellect where the images, stripped of material accidents, reveal their "formes," "ideas," "essences": then they exhibit "proportion" or "beauties best." Beauty is in this sense objective, visible to those of "better eyes" in a world created according to the divine wisdom of number, weight, and measure—and visible as well in a poem that exhibits number, weight, and measure. This is the case, declared Donne, with Psalms, "which is such a form as is both curious, and requires diligence in the making, and then when it is made, can have nothing, no syllable taken from it, nor added to it: Therefore is Gods will delivered to us in *Psalms,* that we might have it the more cheerfully, and that we might have it the more certainly, because where all the words are numbred, and measured, and weighed, the whole work is the less subject to falsification, either by subtraction or addition" (*Sermons,* II, 50). Proportion is "beauties best" in Psalms, or in the "little world[s] made cunningly" of Donne's poems, because it mirrors the divine order of the cosmos. Donne, to make his case, alludes to the apocryphal Liber de Sapientia or Wisdom of Solomon (11.21), which declares that God has created everything according to number, weight, and measure (omnia in mensura et numero et pondere disposuisti). It is this divine principle that allows Jonson to find that because of "weight, measure, number" in "small proportions, we just beauties see" and that affords Marvell the opportunity for his witty defense of *Paradise Lost:*

> Thy verse created like thy *Theme* sublime,
> In Number, Weight, and Measure, needs not *Rhime.*

As Abraham Cowley puts it in his learned annotations to his *Davideis:* "And the *Scripture* witnesses, that the World was made in *Number, Weight,* and *Measure;* which are all qualities of a good *Poem.* This order and proportion of things is the true *Musick* of the world."[6]

When it comes to poetry, it may be that most poets practice medieval realism, pretending to be convinced not only of the "thinginess" of words but also of their "essential" meanings. Think of what has become, along with Pound's "In the Metro" and Carlos Williams' "Red Wheelbarrow," a poem for all seasons—Stevens' "Anecdote of the Jar."

> I placed a jar in Tennessee,
> And round it was, upon a hill.
> It made the slovenly wilderness
> Surround that hill.
>
> The wilderness rose up to it,
> And sprawled around, no longer wild.
> The jar was round upon the ground
> And tall and of a port in air.
>
> It took dominion everywhere.
> The jar was gray and bare.
> It did not give of bird or bush,
> Like nothing else in Tennessee.[7]

Among the "Adagia" of Stevens' *Opus Posthumous* we find that "poetry must resist the intelligence almost successfully" (so also in the poem "Man Carrying Thing") and that a "poem need not have a meaning and like most things in nature often does not have." In my mischievously anecdotal history of poetry, says the poet, you may glimpse Donne's "well wrought urn" and Keats' "Grecian Urn," but you will find that my artifact of "gray and bare" clay is neither a chronicle in verse exemplifing the circle of perfection nor a "sylvan historian" displaying "marble men and maidens over-wrought." No jug but no urn, either.

Perhaps my poem will resist your intelligence unsuccess-fully and you will manage to persuade yourself that I mean to record the victory of poetic imagination over "slovenly" reality, of orderly art over disorderly nature, or even of sterile rationalism over a vital wilderness of truths.[8] And yet, perhaps after you have begun to reconsider the way you have reduced my (perfectly justi-fied) ambivalences to your either-or propositions, I hope that at last and at least you may come to appreciate, first of all, that my poetic anecdote is implicitly a circle, moving from Tennessee to Tennessee in playful mockery of well-wrought literary urns in general and of my rotund subject in particular, and, second, that my round jar "took dominion everywhere" only by means of verbal artifice—the etymological quibbles that iterate the form of the circle. The jar, "round it was," is "round upon the ground" so that the wilderness "sprawled around, no longer wild." The "wilderness rose up to it," and the jar made the "slovenly" wilderness "Surround that hill": the wilderness "surrounds" or encircles the circular jar, but also it becomes, by verbal contagion, sur- or supra-"round," imitating the jar yet again in being "round upon the ground." The "Anecdote," with its irregular rhymes and its "irregular" dimeter and trimeter tucked away unobtrusively among the prevailing tetrameters, implicitly questions in its own formal features the circle of artistic perfection that Donne imitated in "The Canonization," but Stevens in his own well-wrought though not perfectly circular jar (poets, unlike mortgage bankers, do not seek "closure" in this life) works tricks with words that Donne would have admired.

Donne's epistemological principles encourage these tricksy tendencies, perhaps require them. When in The Second Anniversary Donne assures us that the "rich soule" of Elizabeth Drury does "by Death, survive" (379), we are being told not only that her death has brought her eternal life but also that the "idea" of the word "survive" is "live above"—where she now lives, so that etymology becomes essence. In The First Anniversary Donne is working his way toward one of his favorite medical jokes, that every sexual climax takes a day off one's life (that deep pun, on "die"), but pauses en route to exercise his metaphysical wit on the Fall:

> We are borne ruinous: poore mothers crie,
> That children come not right, nor orderly,
> Except they headlong come, and fall upon
> An ominous precipitation.
> How witty's ruine!

Ruin is indeed witty (the word "ruin" is, for Donne, only half way to its modern significance, retaining for him the sense of "fall," as in the "ruined [fallen] woman" of bad nineteenth-century novels). Because of the Fall, children "come not right," which is to say that they do not emerge feetfirst in order to land right-side-up. Instead "they headlong come" in "ominous precipitation," which is to say that it is a bad omen to fall so suddenly out of the womb in such inverted fashion. But also the word "precipitation" reveals in this context "how witty's ruine": *prae-caput* or headfirst is the etymological "essence" of the word.

Such examples may seem trivial rather than witty, though I assume that most of us would agree that it is no trivial pursuit to reanimate the language of the tribe; but in any case I invite you to consider in this connection the extraordinary series of similes that make up the first half (precisely twenty-two of forty-four lines) of the "entrance" to The Second Anniversary. The first six lines establish the witty context:

> Nothing could make mee sooner to confesse
> That this world had an everlastingnesse,
> Then to consider, that a yeare is runne,
> Since both this lower worlds, and the Sunnes Sunne,
> The Lustre, and the vigor of this All,
> Did set; 'twere Blasphemy, to say, did fall.

So far, the familiar Donne, beginning with an ironic glance at Aristotle who supposed the world to be eternal, then effecting the usual reversal of the microcosm-macrocosm relation as in so many of the love poems, and ending with the usual genuflection to what must not be said, or if implied or said, should not have been ("'twere Blasphemy, to say"). (Compare "A nocturnall upon *S. Lucies* day," where Lucy becomes the "Sunne" that eclipses the "lesser," the astronomical, "Sunne," and where, when the poet speaks of her "death," he must add, "which word wrongs her.") Having completed his witty preamble, Donne spins out the most spectacular string of similes written by him, or by any other, metaphysical wit:

> But as a ship which hath strooke saile, doth runne,
> By force of that force which before, it wonne,
> Or as sometimes in a beheaded man,
> Though at those two Red seas, which freely ran,
> One from the Trunke, another from the Head,
> His soule be saild, to her eternall bed,
> His eies will twinckle, and his tongue will roll,

As though he beckned, and cal'd back his Soul,
He graspes his hands, and he puls up his feet,
And seemes to reach, and to step forth to meet
His soule; when all these motions which we saw,
Are but as Ice, which crackles at a thaw:
Or as a Lute, which in moist weather, rings
Her knell alone, by cracking of her strings:
So strugles this dead world, now shee is gone;
For there is motion in corruption.

Although I find that lute endearing, I confess to a particular affection for the beheaded man. He exemplifies what an older generation of scholars sometimes referred to, often citing "a bracelet of bright haire about the bone," as the "metaphysical shudder." The beheaded man shows Donne at his best, master of macabre jocularity; and it is also an extreme example of the "alliance of levity and seriousness (by which the seriousness is intensified)" that Eliot attributed to Andrew Marvell and, by implication, to the other metaphysicals.[9]

The beheaded man appears to be egregiously jolly, his eyes all a-twinkle and his tongue rolling in mimicry of an arpeggiolike trill of seventeenth-century *jouissance*. The eight lines that lead into the enjambed "His soule" begin, innocuously enough, with a regular iambic pentameter, slightly varied by the shadow of a standard cesura after the first two feet and the hint of a trochee in the third foot. The next two lines, however, rapidly gather momentum, as the late cesura (last two feet) of the first line of the two rotates into the early cesura (first two feet) of the second line. This metrical gambol reaches a momentary climax in the next two lines, which are marked by heavy cesuras in the unusual position of the exact middle of each line, splitting the third foot in violation of convention in order to divide the lines into precisely equal numbers of syllables marked by the forward-lunging "ands":

His eies will twinckle, and his tongue will roll,
As though he beckned, and cal'd back his Soul. . . .

This unusual way of achieving metrical parity with syntactical parallelism not only mirrors the spasmodic jocularity of the divided body as it rocks forward from its heels but also sets up a strong contrast with the standard cesuras of the next lines, which lend metrical emphasis to the "ands" that smooth the spastic movements into a salvific series of rolling motions:

> He graspes his hand, and he puls up his feet,
> And seemes to reach, and to step forth to meet
> His soule. . . .

The metrical rollick seems to be the perfect vehicle for the guillotine-humor, but the brilliance of the macabre vignette can only be appreciated in relation to the rest of the similes. Imitated from Lucretius, the image of the beheaded man, considered in itself as a humorously grotesque object of "sense, and Fantasy," can mean no more and no less than it does in *De Rerum Natura* where it functions as an illustration of the *mortality* of the soul.[10] Donne's allusion to the "two Red seas," however, intimates that the head and the trunk of the body will have their own exodus, using division to cross into the Promised Land—and thus to reverse the Lucretian meaning of "division."

I am not at all sure what a "new historicist" or a "cultural materialist" might make of these comparisons. It would not do to propose that the peculiar extravagances of the similes represent a reaction formation induced by the patronage system, and no one (I am trying to imagine) would be likely to "theorize" the gender of this particular beheaded man. It might be possible to have recourse to some kind of "thick description" in the manner of Clifford Geertz, relating this "dismemberment" to the "dismemberment" of the lady in the literary genre of the *blazon*,[11] to the "dismemberment" of the body politic by the pre-revolutionary Parliaments, to the "dismemberment" of the autonomous subject in Jacobean drama, and to Elizabethan practices of drawing-and-quartering, public executions, display of the monarch's power, and so on. It would certainly be possible to bring into play Victor Turner's concept of liminality! I am also quite certain that it would be easy enough to "deconstruct" the tropes and demonstrate how their internal contradictions eventuate in the "aporias" endemic to the logocentric tradition. Nice work and you can get it—but not likely to reveal much about the wit of the poet Thomas Carew proclaimed to be The Monarch Of Wit.

If I were a formalist who had the Imagist Manifesto by heart before I even came to practice the "new criticism" recommended by Cleanth Brooks, I would have an easy time of it. The poem as a whole is heterocosm, a little world made cunningly, and this portion of it, if it is a good poem in this particular universe of discourse, may be expected to display the symbolic system of internal levers and wheels that make it too, though in a lesser register, an artistic unity. The similes must exhibit Kenneth Burke's "qualitative progression," must be expressed in the "language of paradox," and must contain images susceptible of analysis in relation to other images. And indeed the imaginative connections are everywhere in evidence, for we note that the "yeare is runne," the ship "doth runne," and the blood of the beheaded one "freely ran"; that the ship "hath strooke saile," and the beheaded man's "soule be saild"; that the ice "crackles," and the lute is "cracking"; and so on. Most of all I would observe, as Cleanth Brooks and John Edward Hardy did in their close analysis of *Lycidas,* that all these images are really about *water,* for the ship continues to move on water, the beheaded man is explicitly associated with the Red Sea, the ice thaws into water, and the lute rings its own death knell in "moist weather." I do not mean to travesty the endeavor; the verbal associations are remarkable and worth remarking, and they testify to conscious or unconscious processes in the poet that excite, I think we may assume, subliminal satisfactions in many readers. Moreover, this kind of close reading makes it easier to point to aspects of the similes that might otherwise appear to be inaccessible to "sense, and Fantasy"; and yet this method of analysis will not reveal the intelligible species or "Idea" of the similes. It will not show "how witty's ruin."

The similes initially represent "all these motions which we saw" to "sense, and Fantasy," and then the poet himself explains the intelligible "Idea" that informs each item in the series, inviting us to look again, this time from the "watch-towre": "For there is motion in corruption." Milgate cites *Sermons* (VIII, 92): "That *body* which . . . is mouldring, and crumbling into lesse, and lesse dust, and so hath some *motion,* though no *life*"—to which we may add the "motion" observable in a "mouldring" body that is "alive" with worms and maggots. True enough for a string of images but not the sufficient truth about a series of intellectual conceits. True enough for "sense, and Fantasy" but not true enough for the "motions which we saw" from the "watch-towre." Ephraim Chambers, in his *Cyclopaedia* of 1728, points out that the "antient philosophers [mainly though not exclusively the Aristoteleans, in commentaries on *Physica* and *De Generatione et Corruptione*] considered *motion* in a more general and extensive manner. They defined it, a passage out of one state into another: and thus made six kinds of motion, viz. Creation, generation, corruption, augmentation, diminution, and lation, or local motion." Although the "wits" among Donne's readers would know that "motion" also may refer to an inward impulse, proceeding from man's free will or from God's extraordinary grace (Milton's Samson makes his final "choise" prompted by "inward motions"), and also-also to refer to a melodic progression of two parts in relation to each other, these subsidiary meanings complement—they do not constitute—the "Idea" that the similes convey: the poet explicitly explains that "there is motion in corruption," which is to say that the "Idea" of the similes refers, in Chambers' words, to the kind of "corruption" that represents a "passage out of one state into another."

"So also is the resurrection of the dead. It is sown in corruption; it is raised in incorruption" (1 Cor. 15.42). The "Idea" or essence of all these similes is "motion in corruption," reformulating in Aristotelean terms the biblical paradox that we must lose life in order to gain it. The "Idea" is not the common denominator of the similes; it is their real significance, otherwise occluded from view by the "accidents" of material individuality. Not the common denominator but that which makes them what they are. To the eye of "sense, and Fantasy" the beheaded man must appear absurdly grotesque, but from the "watch-towre," exhibited in the *claritas* of that which makes him in essence what he is, his spasmodic gaiety reveals "gladnesse vnspeakable." Donne as usual provides us, some lines later, with his own best gloss on the "division" (like "broken," a musical term) of the beheaded man:

> For such approches doth Heaven make in death.
> Thinke thy selfe laboring now with broken breath,

And thinke those broken and soft Notes to bee
Division, and thy happiest Harmonee.   (89–93)

The literal, the Lucretian, division of head from body betokens the
death of the spirit as well as the body, but the Christian music of
"division" by quibbling *fiat* adumbrates heavenly harmony. The
division of soul from body proves to be the happiest harmony.
And why not? for did not the deity himself create by verbal *fiat*?
and if so, do not poets do well to imitate God's "mysteries" (those
ultimate paradoxes) in their earthly paradoxes? So did Jesus, the
man-God and God-man, in himself a walking and talking paradox
—theological oxymoron or, better yet, Freud's primal word. In
theology as in music the "Idea" of "division" is "happiest Harmonee."

One more (extraordinary) example of Donne's way with
a simile, on one of those rare occasions when we must "up unto
the watch-towre get" without the definition of the "Idea" explicitly provided by the poet with an explanatory line like "For there
is motion in corruption." Donne records—and, really, no one can
do it like this—the imagined "progres" of his "soule" in its "long-
short" journey through the stars to heaven:

But ere shee can consider how shee went,
At once is at, and through the Firmament.
And as these stars were but so many beades
Strunge on one string, speed undistinguish'd leades
Her through those spheares, as through the beades, a string,
Whose quicke succession makes it still one thing:
As doth the Pith, which, least our Bodies slacke,
Strings fast the little bones of necke, and backe;
So by the soule doth death string Heaven and Earth. . . .

To "sense, and Fantasy" the parallel similes—the "string" of
"beades" and the "Pith" of "little bones"—must appear sufficiently apt, ingenious illustrations of the contiguous states of the
soul's instantaneous passage from earth to heaven. Yet when viewed
from the "watch-towre" the similes appear paradoxical rather than
analogical: like the beheaded man they reveal "motion in corruption."

Readers of Homer will be familiar, from its iteration in the *Iliad,* with the earliest formulae for what can happen to the "Pith" that "Strings fast the little bones of necke, and backe." The warrior suffers his mortal cut, his body becomes "unstringed," and he falls, thunderously, and his armor clatters upon him. In other words, death *un*strings the body. In the more highly elaborated physiology of Donne's day the pith or spinal cord (the "sinewie thread" of "The Funeral," more generally the "sinowie strings which doe our bodies tie" of "Progress of the Soul") is the main channel through which the "spirits" issue in effecting communication between the head and the body.[12] Since this vital channel and its medulla "strings fast the little bones of necke, and backe," to divide or to cut the pith is to slit the thin-spun life, which means that the "as . . . as . . . so" of Donne's comparisons turn out to include, when they are comprehended in their "Idea," a Christian paradox that says, in the form of a simile, that we must lose life in order to gain it.[13] Since to *un*string the body is to "*string* Heaven and Earth," Donne's witty combination of similes again asks us to recognize that the essence, the "Idea," of "Division" is "happiest Harmonee." The "image" becomes a "conceit"; the visual form of "sense, and Fantasy" yields its cognitive significance, its essential form.

Viewed from the "watch-towre" the similes reveal their essential meaning, the "rich soule" reveals its true nature, and the reader of The Anniversaries reveals whether or not she "lodge[s] an In-mate soule." Donne is the poet who assumes that subject and object, knower and known, become one and the same in the act of understanding: "For it is both the object and the wit." After all and most of all, as his writings everywhere suggest, Donne wanted to work out ways of knowing and loving, in relation to things both human and divine. He shows himself preoccupied, if not obsessed, with the means by which we know another, whether earthly beloved or heavenly deity. Everywhere and always, even in his most skeptical or cynical moments, he betrays his profound concern—sometimes anxious, sometimes assured or even triumphant—for *identification,* for *union.*[14] In the secular poetry the union sought is with the beloved, and finds its most potent means of expression in religious terms: "Us *Canoniz'd* for Love." In the divine poems the union sought is with God, and finds its most sublime means of expression in sexual terms: "Nor ever chast, except you ravish mee." In both cases union means being one with the other in "a dialogue of one," and Donne's kind of union depends upon virtue as well as knowledge; "see, and Judge, and follow worthinesse" as exhibited in "Idea." Robert Greville, Third Lord Brooke, in *The Nature of Truth* (1640), provides the most succinct formulation available for this older complex of thought and feeling: "what good we know, we are: our act of vnderstanding being an act of *union*." [15]

This union may be, generally speaking, of three kinds. There is the intermediate union, of which I have made so much, that occurs in the watchtower: "our act of vnderstanding being an act of union" between the "form" of the object and the intelligible "idea" in the mind. [16] There is the highest kind of union, of which only an ecstatic moment in the watchtower may afford us a glimpse, that occurs "when our soule enjoyes this her third birth, / (Creation gave her one, a second, grace)," and we "behold with glorified eyes" the beatific vision:

> Onely who have enjoyd
> The sight of God, in fulnesse, can thinke it;
> For it is both the object and the wit.
> This is essentiall joye, where neither hee
> Can suffer Diminution, nor wee;
> 'Tis such a full, and filling good. . . .

The lowest kind of union—even this proves impossible for those who "lodge an In-mate soule" and are capable therefore only of "dull sublunary lovers love"—occurs during sexual intercourse when, as in "The Extasie," "to'our bodies turne wee then" in what is still "a dialogue of one": "Small change, when we'are to bodies gone." One might almost say, to borrow the phrasing of The Second Anniversary, that their bodies thought; and if we cannot at least imagine ourselves capable of this kind of experience I am not sure we should practice literary criticism on Donne.

The Beatific Vision is not, I read, for everyone, but I wonder whether we may not, avoiding the extremes of an excess of cynicism or an access of sentimentality, find the account of this particular kind of bodily union in "The Extasie" psychologically plausible from our own experiences? Even a twentieth-century poet may be allowed to make similar observations, unobjectionably I assume, in composing couplets on "The Marriage,"

> And when I found your flesh did not resist,
> It was the living spirit that I kissed,
> It was the spirit's change in which I lay:
> Thus, mind in mind we waited for the day. . . .

And even if we have no ready psychological analogue for the intermediate experience of the "watch-towre," we know what a wondrous achievement it is for human beings to be able to locate the apt abstraction, the pertinent "uniuersall word"; and from this we may perhaps enter imaginatively, though only for the moment, into the belief that an intermediate kind of union may occur in the "watch-towre," our "act of understanding being an act of union" in which the "wit" becomes the "object." Socrates sought the exaltation of definition in the "uniuersall word," and his followers —from the *verbum mentis* of Augustine to the *verbum mentis* of Aquinas—kept that faith. Robert Fitzgerald, meditating on Aristotle's *De Anima,* compared the "knowing" of the *species intelligibilis* of the tree to plunging his arm into the bole, there to grasp the juices of its essence in the fullness of its clarity; and this kind of union may be thought to bear some analogy to the "personal knowledge" of Michael Polanyi.[17] At any rate, when these lower kinds of union—lower only than beatific vision!—are raised to their highest "pitch," then "one might almost say, her bodie thought."

If we knew all along in reading The Anniversaries that we "represent" a "trinity from the Trinity," then all along we were in the know about the trimerous structure of The Anniversaries and this knowledge served to confirm our sense of ourselves as selves; all along, to phrase it negatively, we knew we did not "lodge an In-mate soule." If we did not, on the other hand, happen to know our trinities, we have nevertheless submitted ourselves to the imaginative pressures of The Anniversaries and may now choose, for the imaginative nonce, to number ourselves among those souls "who know they'have one" because we may "see, and Judge, and follow" the "Idea of a Woman" or "rich soule." We may "see, and Judge, and follow" because we are, when we (imaginatively or truly) know ourselves, an image of the Trinity.

In an age before Descartes this would be our principle of certitude; foundationalism before Kant, it would provide an epistemology of the self. Although the scholars and the canonists tend to focus on *The Confessions* and *The City of God,* the *De Trinitate,* composed over a couple of decades, may one day receive attention as Augustine's greatest work. This extraordinary treatise consists in congeries of subtle introspections that range from the way the "bodily species" of a woman may appear in the phantasy with such distinctness that the "genital organs" are aroused, to the way innumerable "trinities" in the world and in man may be said to mirror in an enigma (through a glass darkly) the Trinity of God.[18] The human mind is "commanded to know itself" so that "it might consider itself and live according to its own nature" (301). Augustine proposes as an article of faith—it was to become a theological commonplace—that when God said, "'Let us make man to our image and likeness,' we believe that man has been made image of the Trinity, because it was not said 'to my' or 'to your' image." The mind in knowing itself knows it "has been made image of the Trinity," which mainly though not exclusively consists in *memoria, intelligentia, and voluntas.* It is this "image which is being renewed day by day in the spirit of the mind and in the knowledge of God, not outwardly but inwardly," and it "will be perfected by the vision [of God] itself which will then be after the judgment face to face, but it is making progress towards it now through a mirror in an obscure manner" (445–47). And "when the mind, therefore, knows itself, it alone is the parent of its own knowledge, for it is itself both the object known and the one that knows" (287); in Donne's words, "it is both the object and the wit."

In *De Veritate* q. 10, *De mente, in qua est imago Trinitatis,* St. Thomas effects the synthesis that later appears in Donne: the *mens* or mind takes its means of abstractive cognition from Aristotle's *De Anima* and its ternate "image" from Augustine's *De Trinitate.* Augustine himself knows that he cannot, entirely, do without those Aristotelean "images of corporeal things," the *species* of "sense, and Fantasy."[19] The "species of the body, which is perceived, produces the species which arises in the sense of the percipient; this latter gives rise to the species in the memory; finally, the species in the memory produces the species which arises in the gaze of thought" (337). But when these sensible images are drawn in "through the bodily sense and . . . flow in some way into the memory," Augustine's Neoplatonic Christianity requires him to believe that we judge them "within ourselves by rules that . . . remain unchangeably above our mind."[20] And here—in this mix of Aristotelean cognition and Christian Neoplatonism—lies the rationale for Donne's praise of Elizabeth Drury.

When for example Augustine hears of someone ardent in "defense of the beauty and the strength of faith," he responds— even if the person is not an acquaintance—with a "chaste and genuine love."[21] If he should then learn that the man is in fact not virtuous, Augustine's "love is withdrawn from that unworthy man, yet it *remains in that form* [my emphasis], according to which I loved him when I believed him to be such. Unless perhaps I now love him for this purpose, that he may be such, when I had ascertained that he was not such."[22] (Donne in his letters justifies his praise of Elizabeth Drury in precisely this way, saying that if the ladies who had objected are virtuous the praise will be theirs.) The human mind in knowing itself finds within itself the unchangeable forms of truth, with the consequence that we know how to praise the virtues of a virtuous human being whom we have never met: "our love for a good man . . . , whose face we have not seen," like Donne's praise of a good woman whose face he had not seen, "is based on our knowledge of his virtues, which we already know in the truth itself" (291).

Before the *cogito ergo sum* of Descartes there was the *si fallor sum* of Augustine. Although this epistemology of the self is elaborated most fully in Augustine's *De Trinitate,* the *locus classicus* for the certitude of Christian selfhood appears in *De Civitate Dei* 11.26. In this chapter Augustine makes his famous reply to the skeptics among the Academics who challenge "these truths" that Augustine takes to be self-evident about the self and who therefore ask, " 'What if you are mistaken?' " To which Augustine responds: "If

I am mistaken, I am. For if one does not exist, he can by no means be mistaken. Therefore, I am, if I am mistaken."

From this pre-Cartesian *ergo sum* Augustine develops his principles of self-knowledge:

> And because, if I could be mistaken, I would have to be the one who is mistaken, therefore, I am certainly not mistaken in knowing that I am. Nor, as a consequence, am I mistaken in knowing that I know. For, just as I know that I am, I also know that I know. And when I love both to be and to know, then I add to the things I know a third and equally important knowledge, the fact that I love.

What has not been fully appreciated about this Christian *nosce teipsum* is that it is developed in triads—for example, being, knowing, and loving—and is derived from Augustine's conviction that his own selfhood may only, and truly, be sought in the individual memory that mirrors in ternate variety the Trinity. The chapter opens with Augustine's declaring that we "ourselves can recognize in ourselves an image of God, in the sense of an image of the Trinity," and then, after the obligatory qualification that it is "merely an image," he adds: "Nevertheless, it is an image which by nature is nearer to God than anything else in all creation, and one that by transforming grace can be perfected into a still closer resemblance." To know oneself, for Augustine and Aquinas and for Dante and Donne, is to know the trinity within, the "trinity from the Trinity" that enables us to "see, and Judge, and follow worthinesse" through the exercise of memory, understanding, and will.[23]

Since this trinity of the soul—memory, understanding, will—corresponds to the triadic structure of the subdivisions, repeated over and over, of The Anniversaries, there exists for the knowing reader an exact equivalence between the structure of his mind and the structure of the poem. And since the same kind of tripartite configuration may be posited of the subject of the poems, we must take considered account of a remarkable set of equivalences; all three are "same as," and this series of correspondences may be lengthened to include the poet. In The First Anniversary the poet "invade[s]" his "great Office" to become the singer who "keepe[s] the song still in [our] memory," and in The Second Anniversary he identifies himself with his own instrument, becoming the "Trumpet, at whose voice the people came." The good poet corresponds to the good poem corresponds to the good subject corresponds to the good reader.

The "first and chiefest office of love," Milton observes in *An Apology,* "begins and ends in the soul, producing those happy twins of her divine generation, knowledge and virtue."[24] The allusion is to the long tradition that stems from the passage in *Phaedo* 69a (cf. *Meno* 87c-d) in which Socrates argues for the inseparability of virtue and knowledge.[25] This tradition—explained and justified by the correspondence theory of truth, the correspondence of "object" to "Idea"—teaches that only the good man can write the good poem, "that he who would not be frustrate of his hope to write well hereafter in laudable things, ought him self to be a true poem, that is, a composition and pattern of the best and honourablest things."[26] Strabo, *Geographica* 1.2.5, observes: "Of course we do not speak of the excellence of a poet in the same sense as we speak of that of a carpenter or a blacksmith; for their excellence depends upon no inherent nobility and dignity, whereas the excellence of a poet is inseparably associated with the excellence of the man himself, and it is impossible for one to become a good poet unless he has previously become a good man." As Milton puts it elsewhere in *An Apology,* "So that how he should be truly eloquent who is not withall a good man, I see not."[27] The poet, himself a "true poem," writes the "truly eloquent" poem for the reader who has the "knowledge and virtue" to grasp the "Idea"— not one who remains "by Receivers impotencies, lame."

How does one "see, and Judge" that The Anniversaries are "truly eloquent," written (necessarily) by one who is himself a poetic "composition and pattern"? Precisely in the way that Aristotle toward the end of the *Nicomachean Ethics* tells us that we may know the good man—only by being one. No "in-Mate soule" need apply. You have to be one to know one, and you have to know one to be one: "what good we know, we are: our act of vnderstanding being an act of *union.*" The knowing union has its grateful vicissitudes, its reciprocal identities, for it is "such a full, and such a filling good." This is to be "part both of the Quire, and

Song," to be "now partaker, and a part" of a "last, and lastingst peece, a song" of anniversaries. This is to complete the poetic circuit, in which poet corresponds to poem corresponds to reader —if all are good, and if the reader knows it. "For it is both the object and the wit." The distinction between subject and object collapses into a series of equivalences—between poem and poet, between poem and subject, between poem and reader. Elevated to their essential status as "Idea" they are one and the same. Poet is poem is subject is reader (when the "receiver" is "potent"), the poem enacting in itself, in its very (triadic) structure, the "trinity from the Trinity" that makes the poem what it is and us what we are. That at least is Donne's Idea of the woman and the poems about her.

 Notes

Introduction

1. Fear of closure, of the determinate, even of meaning itself; ultimately a fear, if we may read between the lines of Paul de Man, of death.

2. I will quote, whenever possible, from *The Epithalamions, Anniversaries and Epicedes,* ed. Wesley Milgate (Oxford: Clarendon Press, 1978), which differs only in accidentals from *John Donne: "The Anniversaries,"* ed. Frank Manley (Baltimore: The Johns Hopkins Press, 1963), which improved upon the text printed by Herbert J. C. Grierson in his monumental edition of 1912. John T. Shawcross judiciously considers editorial and textual problems in "The Making of the Variorum Text of the *Anniversaries,"* *John Donne Journal,* 3 (1984), 63–72, and I quote here, as a means of orienting readers unfamiliar with the territory, most of his opening paragraph.

"John Donne's poems usually labeled the 'Anniversaries' should recall three separate poems: 'The First Anniversary,' subtitled, 'An Anatomy of the World'; 'A Funeral Elegy'; and 'The Second Anniversary,' subtitled, 'Of the Progress of the Soul.' Frequently the 106–line elegy is forgotten. It is generally dated December 1610, the date of Elizabeth Drury's death, although it is printed after 'An Anatomy of the World' in the first edition of 1611. This order is maintained in the second edition of both poems in 1612, which adds 'Of the Progress of the Soul,' thus placing the elegy between the two longer poems. (Only Roger Bennett [*Complete Poems* (Chicago: Packard, 1942)] reverses the order.) The second edition added the title 'The First Anniversary' to the first poem and thus called the new poem 'The Second Anniversary.' 'The First Anniversary' is usually dated in early 1611, some months after Elizabeth's death; 'The Second Anniversary,' usually in December 1611, the first-year anniversary of her death and while Donne was in France with the Drurys. The first edition was published, it would seem, in November 1611, some months after Elizabeth's death; the second, by the beginning of April 1612. There is an errata sheet for the 1612 printing, with errata for both long poems. The three poems were reprinted in 1621 and 1625, and in the collected editions of 1633–69. Marginal notes are omitted in the first edition as well as the collected editions of 1633–69. [The notes are present but incomplete] in 1625 and 1633. That is to say, the marginal notes are complete in the early editions only in 1612 and 1621. A study of the text indicates its deterioration from the 1611 and 1612 editions and makes clear that 1633 [used by Grierson] is based on 1625 alone."

3. Although I have no convenient way of demonstrating the validity of the generalization, I can at least provide an example, from among the many that most of us encounter every day or so, to help clarify the kind of thing I have in mind. Walter Kendrick, "Confessions of a Deconstructor," *Boston Review* (June, 1986), pp. 5–6 and 25–26, touchingly recalls the "intense conversations" about Derrida, Foucault, and Lacan that he had with other graduate students at Yale, when these theorists excited "controversy and stimulation." Kendrick records his subsequent disillusionment when it proved impossible "to preserve that vitality [of the 1960s], to channel it and make it productive," and expresses his final revulsion when "in only a few years the underground [became] business as usual throughout American academe," allowing "the establishment [to] co-opt the ideas we used to find subversive." Since this kind of thing happens generation by generation, we should not make fun of it (the New Critics were regarded as "subversive" by the Historical Scholars in the late '40s and early '50s). Kendrick, with the perspective afforded by the kind of hindsight eventually granted to most of us, can go on to point out that the "trouble with deconstruction (shared with psychoanalysis, Marxism, and Christianity) is that it yields the same answer to every question, simply because the answer is known before the question is asked." Therefore, Kendrick concludes, "Derrida no longer practices deconstruction." But then Kendrick goes on to note the fact that should have been his imperative: "His followers are prisoners."

Having liberated himself (no longer a follower, no longer a prisoner), Kendrick became "free" to turn his attention to . . . pornography! "My familiarity with the critical avant-garde led me to look at that old bugaboo in a new light, to see pornography as 'pornography,' a concept, not an object. I was able to interpret its history in social terms, to see 'pornography' as a strategy by those who hold power (principally educated, well-to-do men) for the control of those who have to be kept from power (women and the poor)." And he adds: "To my knowledge, none of the myriad books on pornography portrays it this way; they're all trapped." All but Kendrick, though by now, presumably, he recognizes that he was free only to do the completely predictable—just another habitual response, dictated by the theoretical vocabulary he had absorbed but definitely could not deploy *sous rasure*. That old bugaboo? new light? concept, not object? power? well-to-do men? to my knowledge? Take the clichés of genteel scholarship ("new light," "to my knowledge," not to mention those quaintly "well-to-do men"), blend with a soupçon of strained bonhomie ("old bugaboo"), mix thoroughly with Derrida and Foucault ("concept, not object"; "power"), add a dash of feminism—and you have the recipe for a man who "count[s himself] on the margins of discourse." Margins of discourse? This recipe, just like the last one that Kendrick followed gram-by-gram and pinch-by-pinch at Yale, invariably "yields the same answer to every question, simply because the answer is known before the question is asked," and this case-history of an intelligent, well-meaning scholar would be merely laughable or sadly pathetic if it were not symptomatic of the general malaise. (I have learned recently that Kendrick followed through and published *The Secret Museum: Pornography in Modern Culture* [New York: Viking, 1987].)

4. *Summa Contra Gentiles* III, xlvii, in *The Basic Writings of Saint Thomas Aquinas,* ed. Anton C. Pegis (2 vols.; New York: Random House, 1945), II, 83–84. Thomas argues that while we cannot know God's essence in this life, it is nevertheless possible for us to approach the truth: "that which is known by the soul is true so far as it contains a likeness to that divine truth which God knows. Therefore a *Gloss* on *Ps.*xi.2, *Truths are decayed from among the children of men,* says that *as from one man's face many likenesses are reflected in a mirror, so many truths are reflected from the one divine truth.*" This gloss, based in the commanding trope of the mirror, echoes throughout the centuries from Augustine to Thomas to Dante to Donne. The "human mind" is a "mirror," and the "human mind" sees God, according to the enigmatic glass of 1 Cor. 13.12, "only as in a mirror."

5. R. C. Bald, *Donne & the Drurys* (Cambridge: Cambridge Univ. Press, 1959), first presented the evidence for Anne's having known the Drurys at Hawstead. See also *John Donne: A Life* (Oxford: Oxford Univ. Press, 1970), completed with scrupulous care after Bald's death by W. Milgate. I have gnarled the facts in these sources to offer my worst-case account of the genesis of The Anniversaries.

6. See Victor Harris, *All Coherence Gone* (Chicago: Univ. of Chicago Press, 1949), for a reliable survey with special attention to Donne.

7. Arthur F. Marotti, "John Donne and Rewards of Patronage," *Patronage in the Renaissance,* ed. Guy Fitch Lytle and Stephen Orgel (Princeton, N.J.: Princeton Univ. Press, 1981), pp. 207–34, chronicles Donne's painful, ambivalent scramble for patronage in a system that had places for approximately half of the talented and impecunious aspirants. In *John Donne, Coterie Poet* (Madison: Univ. of Wisconsin Press, 1986), pp. 232–45, Marotti suggests that Donne's retort to Jonson "does less to explain the poems than to call attention to the motives behind the extreme acts of idealization," namely, Donne's "responding strongly to narcissistic injury." So much, then, for this kind of "patronage verse," which "resulted from Donne's feeling that he had been rejected *by* the world"; the explanation, even if true, cannot explain the wit of the poems, and they are, after all, very witty poems. In a wonderfully acerbic essay, "What Was Donne Doing?" *South Central Review,* 4 (1987), 2–15, William Kerrigan points out that we are "not, by and large, getting anywhere with Donne" because we want to talk aobut power—not about wit or love.

8. For a survey of manuscripts of the poems and of the manuscript miscellanies, see Alan MacColl, "The Circulation of Donne's Poems in Manuscript," *John Donne: Essays in Celebration,* ed. A. J. Smith (London: Methuen, 1972), pp. 28–46. Donne allowed himself to publish a commendatory poem printed in *Coryats Crudities* (1611) and an elegy on Prince Henry in the third edition of Joshua Sylvester's *Lachrymae lachrymarum* (1613); so far a gentleman might go.

9. *Literary Criticism of Seventeenth-Century England,* ed. Edward W. Tayler (New York: Knopf, 1967), pp. 215–16 (cf. Drummond's *Works* [Edinburgh, 1711], p. 143). Drummond claimed (here, most probably in the late 1620s) that "*Poesy* is not a Thing that is yet in the finding and search, or which may be otherwise found out, being already condescended upon by all Nations, and as it were established *jure Gentium,* amongst *Greeks, Romans, Italians, French, Spaniards*"; but Drummond, with that strange mixture of uneasiness and fascination that marks the reception of Donne even today, did not scruple to borrow heavily from The Anniversaries in writing his *Cypress Grove.*

10. Grierson, *The Poems of John Donne* (2 vols.; Oxford: Clarendon Press, 1912), I, xx, pointed out long ago that "scholastic theology is made the instrument of courtly compliment and pious flirtation." And it may be made the instrument of elegiac praise as well.

11. "Certain Informations and Maners of Ben Johnsons to W. Drumond," *Literary Criticism,* ed. Tayler, p. 84.

12. *Some Versions of Pastoral* (London: Chatto & Windus, 1935), published in U.S.A. as *English Pastoral Poetry* (New York: Norton, 1938),

p. 84: "Only Christ would be enough; only his removal from the world would explain the destruction."

13. *John Donne and the New Philosophy* (New York: Columbia Univ. Press, 1937), pp. 276–77.

14. "John Donne in Meditation: *The Anniversaries*," *ELH*, 14 (1947), 247–73; rpt. in *The Poetry of Meditation* (New Haven: Yale Univ. Press, 1954), pp. 211–48. Martz had maintained, quite sensibly, that those who thought Elizabeth was Christ or Astraea were just taking Donne's metaphors rather too literally.

15. Marjorie Hope Nicolson, *The Breaking of the Circle* (Evanston, Ill.: Northwestern Univ. Press, 1950). Chapter 3, pp. 65–104, contains the analysis of The Anniversaries and the spectacularly unsound theory of the "double shee," which seems to owe more to Miss Nicolson's fondness for crossword puzzles than to anything in the poems (she was in any case using Grierson's text, which turns the theory into typographical nonsense). For Nicolson, "she" is usually Elizabeth Drury, though "she" may also be the Virgin Mary considered purely as a woman; "shee," on the other hand, may be Astraea, the divine Virgin Mary, or Queen Elizabeth. Miss Nicolson confesses, p. 88, n. 10, that "While I am persuaded that the three chief women in 'Shee' are the Virgin Mary, Astraea, and particularly Elizabeth, I suspect there is at least one other 'She' and 'Shee' I cannot yet identify."

16. Harding, "Coherence of Theme in Donne's Poetry," *Kenyon Review*, 13 (1951), 427–44; and Bewley, "Religious Cynicism in Donne's Poetry," *Kenyon Review*, 14 (1952), 619–46. "Elizabeth Drury alive . . . symbolizes the Catholic Church; but she is dead," and in her walking ghost we have the "image of Anglicanism" (626–27); she is, rather unhappily, a "girl-symbol."

17. *John Donne: "The Anniversaries"* (Baltimore: The Johns Hopkins Press, 1963).

18. "The Woman in Donne's *Anniversaries*," *ELH*, 34 (1967), 307–26; rpt. as Chapter IV of *The Progress of the Soul: The Interior Career of John Donne* (New York: Morrow, 1968).

19. Mahony, "The *Anniversaries*: John Donne's Rhetorical Approach to Evil," *JEGP*, 68 (1969), 407–13, and see also his excellent critique of Nicolson in "'She' and 'Shee' in Donne's *Anniversaries*," *American Notes and Queries*, 9 (1971), 118–19; Stanwood, "'Essentiall Joye' in Donne's *Anniversaries*," *Texas Studies in Literature and Language*, 13 (1971), 227–38; and Lewalski, *Donne's "Anniversaries" and the Poetry of Praise: The Creation of a Symbolic Mode* (Princeton, N.J.: Princeton Univ. Press, 1973), who argues that in his occasional poetry but preeminently in his Anniver-

saries Donne created a "symbolic mode." The Anniversaries draw on traditions of funeral elegy, anatomy, funeral sermon, the hymn, poetry of praise, and Protestant meditation—and then become "symbolic."

20. Fox, "Donne's *Anniversaries* and the Art of Living," *ELH*, 38 (1971), 528–41; and Bellette, "Art and Imitation in Donne's *Anniversaries*," *SEL, 1500–1900*, 15 (1975), 83–96. This "epistemic" tendency, to find that the subject of The Anniversaries is not Elizabeth Drury but John Donne, seems to have been anticipated—but by what kind of cultural osmosis?—by Toshihiko Kusunose in *Ronko* (Kanseigakuin Daigaku), 19 (1969), 101–14. See also A. Voss, "Structure of Donne's *Anniversaries*," *ESA*, 12 (1969), 1–30, who takes the poems themselves as unified by a "strong element of poetic self-consciousness" and "the 'I' figure of the poem as Donne the poet explicitly." Paul A. Parrish, "Poet, Audience, and the Word," *New Essays on Donne*, ed. Gary A. Stringer (Salzburg: Universtität Salzburg, 1977), pp. 110–39, sought to approach these matters through the sermons and by making use of more traditional views of rhetoric. Definitely influenced by Arthur Barker's "An Apology for the Study of Renaissance Poetry," *Literary Views*, ed. Carroll Camden (Chicago: Univ. of Chicago Press, 1964), and perhaps influenced by Stanley Fish's "affective stylistics," Jeanne Shami, "Anatomy and Progress: The Drama of Conversion," *UTQ*, 53 (1984), 221–35, finds the true subject of the poems in a "pattern of developing and slowly corrected response within the speaker"; and Kathleen Kelly, focusing on the "relation between speaker and reader," brings these developments to a predictable conclusion in "Conversion of the Reader in Donne's 'Anatomy of the World'," *The Eagle and the Dove: Reassessing John Donne* (Columbia: Univ. of Missouri Press, 1986), pp. 147–56. I may mention here a promising but all-too-brief essay by Lindsay A. Mann, "The Typology of Woman in Donne's *Anniversaries*," *Renaissance and Reformation*, 11 (1987), 337–50; also influenced by Barker but moving in an entirely different direction from Shami, as well as from Lewalski and the rest, Mann sees "Elizabeth Drury [as] a complex yet consistent symbolic figure whose deepest symbolic significance is biblical" (in the sense of figuralism or biblical typology).

21. *John Donne, Undone* (London and New York: Methuen, 1986), pp. 1, 227, 130, and 229 (which "makes an angel of Donne as well").

22. *The Metaphysical Mode from Donne to Cowley* (Princeton, N.J.: Princeton Univ. Press, 1969), pp. 59–75.

23. As quoted in Lewalski, p. 114, citing Martz, *Poetry of Meditation*, pp. 238–48; the quotation actually appears on p. 239.

24. Martz, in a letter dated 17 February 1990, reminds me that when Lewalski says "Protestant" she generally means "Calvinist," and he

goes on to point out, rightly, that "to fasten upon the *Anniversaries*" a view of "the 'elect' soul, the regenerate soul according to Calvinist standards, . . . contradicts the very reason for the *Anniversaries*, as spiritual exercises contributing in some measure to salvation." Martz documents this position, mainly though not exclusively with respect to George Herbert, in "The Generous Ambiguity of Herbert's Temple," *A Fine Tuning: Studies of the Religious Poetry of Herbert and Milton,* ed. Mary A. Maleski (Binghamton, N.Y.: Medieval and Renaissance Texts, 1989), pp. 31–56; it is a judicious essay, taking account of the book on which Lewalski herself relies, *The Protestant Mind of the English Reformation, 1570–1640* (Princeton, N.J.: Princeton Univ. Press, 1961) by Charles H. and Katherine George, and making explicit reference to Donne's anti-Calvinist stand on predestination. (I should mention that in March of 1990 I sent Professor Lewalski a copy of my criticisms of her interpretations, asking her whether she thought I had been accurate and fair in my assessment of her position and whether there were other parts of the book that I should have brought into the account. As of the date of this copy-editing, January of 1991, I have not been favored with the courtesy of a reply.) The itch to affiliate Donne, who thought variously and on his own, is not of course confined to Lewalski; see, for example, Stanley Stewart's masterly review, *John Donne Journal,* 7 (1988), 273–86, of Paul Sellin's attempts to fabricate a "Dutch Reformed" Donne.

25. "As a result of this focus [on "symbolic meaning and method"] the pyrotechnics of wit and language-play in these brilliant works may receive somewhat short shrift" (7).

O N E: The Idea of a Woman

1. "Certain Informations and Maners of Ben Johnsons to W. Drumond," *Literary Criticism of Seventeenth-Century England,* ed. Edward W. Tayler (New York: Knopf, 1967), p. 84.

2. Marjorie Hope Nicolson was, I believe, the first to argue that the two poems ought, like "L'Allegro" and "Il Penseroso," to be read as companion poems. O. B. Hardison, Jr. and Helen Gardner, among others, have denied the fact, on the grounds that Donne's express intention to write an "anniversary" each year precludes the possibility that the first two of many might be companionate; but Patrick Mahony, "The Structure of Donne's *Anniversaries* as Companion Poems," *Genre,* 5 (1972), 235–56, disposes of their arguments and presents overwhelming evidence of conscious parallelism: "correspondences between the introductions and conclusions" and "correspondences" between the "five meditations" of each poem allow Mahony to conclude that the poems "form a unit" not

"merely complementary but inter-dependent." Since Mahony works with what he calls "theses," which refer to a "group of lines in which a main topic is treated," his argument proceeds in a direction different from my own, which focuses on less debatable and, I would urge, more meaningful matters like the repetends and other formal features.

In an amiable article, "Reading Paired Poems Nowadays," *LIT: Literature Interpretation Theory,* 1 (1990), 275–90, Mary A. Radzinowicz points to the pertinent changes in critical fashion: "The present critical climate is more interested in unresolved than resolved tensions, asymmetries than symmetries, gaps than unity, the social force of poetry than the unique voice, irrationality than transcendence, and complex than simple models of explanation. . . . Equally, the current climate eschews such class or gender-linked evaluations as privilege high culture or a 'masculine line.' . . . Assertions of either scholarly or critical unity [seem] nowadays inapposite." The elegiac tone of these observations may indicate that Radzinowicz knows that she has lined up a series of dummy dichotomies, but in any case—good citizen that she is—she dutifully sets out in this "present critical climate" to accomplish her self-assigned task of tracking "asymmetries" in a number of companion poems, concluding that "as the seventeenth century began, the taste for paired, answer and dialogue poems was great; as it ended, both the taste and the genres satisfying it had changed. At its height, the two pairs were usually related by hierarchy or contrast—soul above body, heaven above earth, or storm against calm, action against contemplation. During the century, the relationship loosened into the historical, social or psychological." Donne's companion poems, which Radzinowicz does not consider, appear to qualify for all categories.

3. See *Greek Philosophy: A Collection of Texts,* ed. C. J. De Vogel (2d ed.; 3 vols.; Leiden: Brill, 1957–60), I, 166; cf. *Simplicii in Aristotelis Categorias Commentarium,* ed. Carolus Kalbfleisch (Berolini, 1907) as the seventh volume of "Commentaria in Aristotelem Graeca." In *Simplicius: Commentaire sur les Catégories D'Aristote* (page numbers keyed to Kalbfleisch), tr. William of Moerbeke, ed. A. Pattin (2 vols.; Louvain, 1971), I, 286, Antisthenes "<<cui Plato, dixit, equum quidem video equinitatem autem non video>>; et ille dixit: <<quia habens quidem quo equus videatur scilicet oculum, quo autem equinitas consideretur, nondum creatum est>>. Et alii autem aliqui fuerunt huius opinionis." Cf. Diogenes Laertius 6.53 (Loeb): "As Plato was conversing about Ideas and using the nouns 'tablehood' and 'cuphood', he [Diogenes the Cynic] said, 'Table and cup I see; but your tablehood and cuphood, Plato, I can nowise see.' 'That's readily accounted for,' said Plato, 'for you have the eyes to see the visible table

and cup; but not the understanding by which ideal tablehood and cuphood are discerned."

4. "Corporeal Ideas in Seventeenth-Century Psychology," *JHI*, 50 (1989), 31–48. The Michaels set it up (31–32) clearly and succinctly, and I hope that the reader will give this medium-sized list the kind of attention that such quotations seldom deserve—keeping in mind the fact that no respectable philosopher is likely to agree with another about Descartes:

"In place of the standard account [as in Kenny and, I would add, the critics of The Anniversaries] of the first modern use of 'idea', . . . we suggest the following: (1) 'Idea' was used by Descartes in his earliest writings to refer to brain impressions and, in the context of his mind-body dualism, to designate the sense experience correlative with a brain event. In the *Discourse* Descartes used the term 'idea' to refer to a purely intellectual notion, i.e., God. By the time of the *Meditations,* he systematically used 'idea' as a technical term to characterize all conceptions of the intellect or mind, those of pure understanding, sensing, imagining, and remembering, but not the corporeal impressions of the brain.

"(2) 'Idea' was used in ordinary language in a broad sense to denote images, plans, or general notions in a human mind, where the term 'mind' is used without clear ontological commitment to a theory of whether the mind is independent of or includes the brain, and without any explicit distinction between corporeal ideas and cognition that is purely intellectual. The term 'idea' is found in some philosophical writings in this ordinary-language sense.

"(3) 'Idea' was used in *philosophical works* as a technical term that was commonly understood to be equivalent to 'image,' 'phantasm,' 'species,' 'sensibilia,' 'simulacra,' which, it was generally believed, are *experienced* not by the understanding or intellect but rather by the brain. For the most part, intellectual cognition was viewed as the activity of an incorporeal and immortal substance distinct from the body, and it was sharply distinguished from the corporeal sensuous cognition referred to by the term 'idea'; this intellectual cognition was described by such terms as 'universal,' 'notion,' and 'conception.' "

5. As quoted p. 31, the view "commonly accepted," from "Descartes on Ideas," *Descartes,* ed. Willis Doney (Garden City, N. Y.: Anchor Books, 1967), p. 227; also Gilson's commentary on *Discours de la Méthode* (Paris: J. Vrin, 1964), p. 319. In this connection, the Michaels might also have cited (they are of course aware of it), *The Works of Sir Thomas Reid,* ed. Sir William Hamilton (6th ed.; 2 vols.; Edinburgh, 1863), one of the strangest and most interesting documents in nineteenth-century intellec-

tual history. Reid died, Hamilton carried on and died, "H.L.M." carried on—to produce in the Supplementary Dissertations (pp. 742–990) pioneering histories of "idea," "species," "consciousness," and the like. Since Hamilton is working from Reid's commonplace books, it is not always easy to determine authority for the various pronouncements, but it seems clear that there might be traced a line from Reid-Hamilton to twentieth-century misunderstandings: the "fortune of the word [idea] is curious. Employed by Plato to express the real forms of the intelligible world, in lofty contrast to the unreal images of the sensible, it was lowered by Descartes, who extended it to the objects of our consciousness in general. . . . Like a fallen angel, it was relegated from the sphere of divine intelligence to the atmosphere of human sense." Descartes, I guess, must be answerable for much, but not for this; the word fell long before.

6. Paul Oskar Kristeller, letter dated 8 November 1989, writes that "Cicero's idea as a perfect notion in our thought I believe to be derived from Panaetius who adapted Plato to Stoicism. . . . After Cicero, the ideas appear as ideas of the divine (not only of the human) mind, a concept found in the doxographers (ps.Plutarch), Philo, Seneca and others and in my opinion originated by Antiochus of Ascalon, one of Cicero's teachers in the Platonic Academy." Cf. Kristeller, "Die Ideen als Gedanken der menschlichen und göttlichen Vernunft" (Heidelberg: Carl Winter, 1989). Plotinus located the ideas in the divine mind, which to Augustine meant the mind of the Christian deity. Ficino and other Renaissance thinkers regarded Augustine's interpretation as authoritative with respect to Plato, though Richard Hooker expresses his doubts and George (?) Puttenham dismisses divine ideas in a clause.

7. Aulus Gellius (9.14.25), that indefatigable tracker of words, notes: "But Gaius Caesar, in the second book of his treatise *On Analogy,* thinks that we should use *die* and *specie* as genitive forms."

8. The Renaissance dictionaries, stemming directly or indirectly from Calepine, are conservative, repetitive, on the relation of "idea" to "species"; and they depend heavily on Cicero. Under "idea" Robert Estienne, *Thesaurus Linguae Latinae* (3 vols.; Basileae, 1576–78), first offers the following: "Forma, figura, species rerum prima & inchoata intellige[n]tia," which is to say the "sensible species" that proceed from the object to the organ of sense and constitute the first stage, so far lacking "form," of knowledge; as Francis Holyoke puts it, *Riders Dictionarie* (3d ed.; Oxford, 1612), "Idea [is] a specie [or] the first shape of things, and imperfect [i.e., incomplete] knowledge." Then Estienne cites "Cic. 1 Acad. 45 [in the Loeb Edition 8.30–31] de mente, Quia sola cerneret quid semper esset simplex & uniusmodi, & tale quale esset, hanc illi ideam

appellabant, iam à Platone ita appellatam [Loeb gives *nominatam*]: nos rectè specie[m] possumus dicere [Because it alone discerns that which is always simple and uniform and true to its own quality; this thing they call "idea," the name already given it by Plato, and we can rightly call it "species"]. Vide Cicero. in Orat. 6." Thomas Cooper, *Thesaurus* (1565), has "Forma, figura, species rerum prima & inchoata intelligentia. Cic." but also gives the "platonic" meaning reduced to the confines of the human imagination: "figure conceived in Imagination, as it were a substance perpetuall, beyng as paterne of all other sorte or kinde, as of one seale procedeth many printes so of one *Idea* of man procede many thousandes of men." Thomas Thomas, *Dictionarium* (1578), and John Minsheu, *Guide into Tongues* (1617), simply tend to repeat Cooper; but Francis Gouldman, *A Copious Dictionary* (3d ed.; 1674), who bases his work on Thomas, Rider, and Holyoke, has begun to sort things out. The part in Latin at first glance seems not to differ all that much from Cooper: "Idea . . . specie. Plato ideas vocat ex quibus omnia, quae videntur fiunt, & ad quas cuncta formantur. Hae immortales, immutabiles, inviolabiles sunt. Quid sit idea i. quid Platonis esse videatur, audi: Idea est eorum, quae natura[m] fiunt, exemplar aeternum; Sen. Epist. 58. Aug. 1 83 Quaest. cap. 46. Vide & Tho. Aquin. *The figure conceiving in imagination, as it were, a substance perpetual, being as a pattern of all other sorts or kinds. As of one seal proceed many prints, so of one Idea of man proceed many thousands of men.*" But Gouldman in the English portion knows that "idea" may refer not only to an "inchoate" image in the "imagination" but also to "the form of any thing conceived in the mind"; and he knows that "species" may refer not only to inner and outer "images" but also to sensible and intelligible ideas (imago externa vel interna, sensibilis vel intelligibilis), with the consequence that he can append to his quotation from Cooper "1. essentia," or Donne's meaning for "idea." The meaning of "idea" as *essence* (or *species intelligibilis expressa*) has finally made its way into the dictionaries, not just by implication but by specification. By the time of Dr. Johnson's first edition (1755) these meanings have been lost: "idea" has become "mental imagination," "species" has become "any visible or sensible representation." No longer intelligible essences, ideas and species revert to their sublunary status as images retained in the imagination or memory.

9. Seneca, following Cicero in an epistle important for later thinkers, displays the same tendencies. He begins with the transcendentally "natural": "Heare I pray you what *Idea* is, and what *Plato* thinketh of it. It is a patterne, and eternall moulde [exemplar aeternum] of all things, which are made by nature: yet will I adde an interpretation to this definition, to the end the matter may more plainly appeare vnto thee, I haue a

will to make thy picture." And here again, by analogy, the divine thought becomes the human thought: "Thou art the patterne of my picture, of which my mind gathereth some habit [not the Platonic *anamnesis* but the Aristotelean *habitus*], which he will delineate in his worke. So that face which teacheth me, and instructeth me, and from which I derive my imitation, is *Idea.*" Epistle LVII, *Workes of . . . Seneca,* tr. Thomas Lodge (1614), p. 258.

10. Erwin Panofsky, *Idea: A Concept in Art Theory,* tr. Joseph J. S. Peake (New York: Harper & Row, 1968), first published 1924, emphasizes (pp. 11ff.) the importance of this passage.

11. For Cicero (4.16–18) the orator must have philosophical training because, among other advantages, it allows him to "distinguish the genus and species" (genus et speciem). Then Cicero immediately moves to *species* in its other sense, as the idea of eloquence in the mind (mente species eloquentiae).

12. Plutarch, *Morals,* tr. Philemon Holland (London, 1603), p. 813, tries, not always successfully, to disentangle the various meanings and their philosophic sources: "Idea is a bodilesse substance, which of it selfe hath no substance, but giveth figure and forme unto shapelesse matters, and becommeth the very cause that bringeth them into shew and evidence.

"Socrates and Plato suppose, that these Ideae bee substances separate and distinct from Matter, howbeit, subsisting in the thoughts and imaginations of God—that is to say, of Minde and Understanding.

"Aristotle admitteth verily these formes and Ideae, howbeit, not separate from matter, as being the patterns of all that which God hath made.

"The Stoicks . . . that our thoughts and conceits were the Ideae."

13. Paul Oskar Kristeller, *The Philosophy of Marsilio Ficino,* tr. Virginia Conant (Gloucester, Mass.: Peter Smith, 1964), remains the standard work on the subject, but see also Michael J. B. Allen, *The Platonism of Marsilio Ficino: A Study of the "Phaedrus" Commentary* (Berkeley: Univ. of California Press, 1984). Donne accepts the interpretation of the Neoplatonists, as did most of his contemporaries; but the verdict, in this as in other matters, was by no means unanimous in the Renaissance, especially when we consider the demurrals of such an authoritative figure as Hooker.

14. Simon Goulart, annotating the hugely popular hexameral poem of du Bartas in *A Learned Summary Upon . . . Bartas* (London, 1621), pp. 8–9, runs through the usual commonplaces and cites the usual authorities in relation to "worlds Idea" ("The French," he says, "is *Archetype*"). An abridgment of his redaction of the commentaries on the *Timaeus* and

the *Parmenides* will serve to indicate the range of contemporaneous opinion: "But considering that the knowledge of God embraceth all things as present, they [the philosophers and theologians] haue said, that hee being the efficient cause of all things, and appearing no lesse in the creations of them, we ought to say, that the *Idea,* the forme and patterne of them was in the Science and Intelligence of God; that is to say, in himselfe from all Eternity: As also the Poet [du Bartas] hath said a little before, that God admired his glory, his power, and iustice. If a workeman maketh any thing, he hath already before-hand the *Idea* and forme thereof conceiued in his braine. . . . It is not therefore altogether besides the purpose, that *Plato* hath held that there were certaine *Ideas,* or Intellectuall formes of all things in God, as Saint *Augustine* and others haue expounded it. *Aristotle* in his third Booke *de anima,* praiseth the Philosopher *Anaxagoras,* for that he taught that we ought to confesse, that there is an Intellect, not intermixed with things created, which vnderstandeth and knoweth all things. But to shorten this discourse, read that which the scholastique Doctors haue written vpon this common place, *of the science and knowledge of God:* amongst others, *Thomas* of *Aquin,* in his Somme of Theology, the I. part, *quest* 4.*art.*9. and question 14.*art.*6. In the first part of his Somme against the Gentiles, *chap.*65 and 66.*ilirus,* in his disputed questions, in the Chapter, *De Ideis:* See also M. *Antony Natta,* in his worke of God, the 7. Booke: where hee . . . expoundeth very amply, and cleerly, that which is aboue said, hauing followed that which *Plato* said, especially in two Dialogues: that is, in his *Timee,* and in his *Parmenides.* . . . He that desireth more, let him reade the Annotation of *Iohn de Serres,* vpon the *Timeo,* and *Parmenides* of *Plato;* for from him it is that I haue drawne that which is aboue written."

15. *The Metalogicon* III, i, tr. Daniel D. McGarry (Berkeley and Los Angeles: Univ. of California Press, 1962), p. 147.

16. F. Edward Cranz, whose important work I cite and discuss at greater length in Chapter 3, offers in his "Renaissance Reading of the *De anima*" a number of interesting examples of the way new and older vocabularies interact and, in effect, struggle for precedence. Johannes Argyropylus produced an "early humanist" translation of Aristotle's *De Anima,* somewhere between the Ciceronian circumlocutions of some later translations and the earlier *verbum e verbo* translation of William of Moerbeke. Argyropylus retains many of William's technical words, e.g., *intellectus, sensitivum, intelligibile, phantasma,* but uses *imaginatio* rather than *phantasia* and consistently translates *eidos* not with William's *species* but with *forma.* When Johannes Eck comes to publish a commentary on this, the first widely read "modern" translation, he discusses *phantasia* where

Argyropylus writes *imaginatio* and comments on the doctrine of *species* where Argyropylus translates *forma*. In rare instances such as these we are allowed a glimpse of the way a new language of thought at first coexists with the more conservative vocabulary of the commentaries and then begins the process of historical evolution that after centuries of interaction eventuates in, say, Coleridge's famous distinction between Fancy and Imagination or Darwin's "origin of species."

17. Pierre Michaud-Quantin, with the assistance of Michel Lemoine, *Études sur le vocabulaire philosophique du Moyen Age* (Rome: Edizioni dell'Ateneo, 1971), pp. 113–50.

18. This tradition, pretty much ignored by historians of philosophy, is based in ocular and optical models of mind, and I shall have occasion to refer to it again. David Lindberg, the scholar who has done most to explore the area, aptly calls the tradition "perspectivist" (i.e., "optical" in the broadest sense, including even what we would think of as epistemological) and has demonstrated its power and continuity over the centuries, not only in libraries but in the statutory curricula of the universities, and has shown how it culminates in Kepler; see *Catalogue of Medieval and Renaissance Optical Manuscripts, Subsidia Mediaevalia* 4 (Toronto: Pontifical Institute, 1975) and *Theories of Vision from Al-Kindi to Kepler* (Chicago and London: Univ. of Chicago Press, 1976). Lindberg, *Theories*, p. 114, observes that Roger Bacon in his effort to synthesize his disparate authorities is prepared to assert that all the "various expressions used to denote the effect of an agent—*lumen, idolum, phantasma, simulacrum, forma, intentio, similitudo, umbra, virtus, impressio, and passio*—are merely synonyms of the word 'species' employed in particular contexts." Although I do not think that Lindberg himself would make the claim, he has in effect rewritten the history of philosophy from the thirteenth to the early seventeenth century. See particularly his "Alhazen's Theory of Vision and Its Reception in the West," *Isis,* 58 (1967), 321–41, and *Theories of Vision,* which show that the influential theories of Bacon, Pecham, and Witelo represent a "perspectivist" tradition that derives much of its intellectual force from Alhazen (ca. 965–1039). See also *Roger Bacon's Philosophy of Nature,* critical edition (Oxford: Clarendon Press, 1983); *John Pecham and the Science of Optics,* critical edition (Madison and London: Univ. of Wisconsin Press, 1970); and Witelo, *Perspectiva, Opticae thesaurus Alhazeni Arabis libri septem,* ed. Friedrich Risner (Basel, 1572), rept. with introd. David C. Lindberg (New York, 1972).

See also Gerard Simon, "A propos de la théorie de la perception visuelle chez Kepler et Descartes: Réflexions sur le rôle du mécanisme dans la naissance de la science classique," *Actes du XIIIe Congrès international* *d'histoire de sciences, Moscou, 18–24 aôut 1971* (Moscow, 1974), pp. 237–45; A. C. Crombie, "Early Concepts of the Senses and the Mind," *Scientific American* (1964), and Harry A. Wolfson's pioneering "The Internal Senses in Latin, Arabic, and Hebrew Texts," *Harvard Theological Review*, 28 (1935), 69–133. No one should, I think, leave this subject without having consulted William M. Ivins, Jr., *On the Rationalization of Sight: With an Examination of Three Renaissance Texts on Perspective* (New York: DaCapo Press, 1983), and the even more brilliantly idiosyncratic study of Cartesian vision and Renaissance perspective by John Hyman, *The Imitation of Nature* (Oxford: Blackwell, 1989).

19. The basic linguistic possibilities, including Sidney's "idea, or foreconceit," already appear in the verbal distinctions of the Scholastics, waiting to be explored, modified, elaborated. Aquinas, *Truth* (tr. from Leonine Text by Robert W. Mulligan, S.J., I [Chicago: Regnery, 1952]), Q.3, art. 1, begins by quoting Augustine (*Octog. trium. quaest.* XLVI) to the effect that we may translate the Greek "ideas" as "*species* or *forms.*" Thomas then attempts to distinguish the proper meanings of these words. "First, it [form] can mean that *from which* a thing gets its form, as when we say that the informing of an effect proceeds from the form of the agent. [But since the effects often fall short of the formal agency] the form *from which* something gets its form is *not* [my emphasis] said to be its idea or form. Second, the form of a thing can mean that *by which* a thing is informed, as when we say [following Aristotle] that the soul is the form of man. . . . [But] we do not usually call it its idea, because it seems that the word *idea* signifies a form *separate from* [my emphasis] that whose form it is [*quia videtur hoc nomen 'idea' significare formam separatam ab eo cujus est forma*]. Third, the form of a thing can mean that *according to which* a thing is informed. This is the exemplary form in imitation of which a thing is made. It is in this meaning that *idea* is ordinarily used [*in hac significatione consuetum est nomen ideae accipi, ut idem sit idea quod forma quam aliquid imitatur,* and this *idea* cannot be realized by chance but must reflect the intention of an agent]. This, therefore, seems to constitute the character of an idea: It must be a form which something imitates because of the intention of an agent [Thomas had earlier drawn on the analogy of the "artist" and the "artistic product"] who antecedently determines the end himself [*Haec ergo videtur esse ratio ideae, quod sit forma quam aliquid imitatur ex intentione agentis, qui determinat sibi finem*]." This is Sidney's meaning, no more exclusively "neoplatonic" than Thomism; cf. Harington, notes to Book XXXIII of *Orlando* (1591), who praises Leonardo, "so excellent in the Idea, or the conceived forme of his worke, that though he could finish but few workes, yet those he did, had great admiration." In Q.3,

art. 3, Thomas again relies on Augustine, this time making the crucial distinction with almost epigrammatic brevity: "As Augustine says, if we consider the proper meaning of the word, an idea is *a form;* but if we consider what the thing itself is, then an idea is *an intelligible character* or likeness of a thing [*idea est ratio rei, vel similitudo*]." This matrix of linguistic possibilities provides the Renaissance writers with their basic lexicon— and their basic analogy: "note that the divine knowledge which God has of things can be compared to the knowledge of an artist, since He is the cause of all things as art is the cause of all works of art. Now an artist knows a product of his art by means of the form [or "idea"] which he has in himself and upon which he models his product. [But] divine art produces not only the form but also the matter, [and] God knows . . . not only universals but also singulars" (Q.2, art. 5).

    20. *de Incantationibus* (Basel, 1567), p. 36.

    21. See his succinct article under "Idea" in Vol. VII of Hasting's *Encyclopedia of Religion and Ethics.* Webb takes most of his primary references from the "dissertations" of Sir William Hamilton, whose sometimes fragmentary notes on passages culled from miscellaneous works and manuscripts by Reid were further annotated by "H.L.M" and which occupy pp. 742–990 of *The Works of Sir Thomas Reid,* ed. Hamilton (6th ed.; 2 vols.; Edinburgh, 1863); see esp. the notes on "idea" (references listed from Reid's Commonplace Book). Although it is sometimes difficult to determine who is responsible for what in this learned edition, the references are invaluable and together constitute—along with Panofsky's *Idea,* cited above—the closest thing we have to a history of "idea."

    22. "Erot. Dial.," *Corpus Reformatorum,* ed. K. G. Bretschneider and H. E. Bindseil (Halle, 1834–60), XIII, 520.

    23. P. 187; cf. *Liber De Anima* (Lipsiae, 1561), R3^r: *nec aliud sunt imagines ille seu ideae, nisi actus intelligendi.* See also *Initia Doctrinae Physicae* (Witerbergae, 1553); in this volume the *De Anima,* dated 1554, has separate title page and pagination: *nec aliud sunt imagines illa seu ideae, nisi actus intelligendi* (136^r). See also *Liber de Anima* (Lipsiae, 1561), R3^r, and *Commentarius De Anima* (Viterbergae, 1542), p. 130: *Deinde ex singularibus eruit uniuersalia, quae Plato vocabat Ideas.* . . .

    24. The section (vi.4), titled "*De Ideis,*" proceeds in terms of substance and accident, which by definition or mode of argument means to Scaliger that Melanchthon has reduced *ideas* to *illustres notiones,* to accidents, whereas Scaliger knows them to be substances (substantia est, neque accidens). *Exotericarum Exercitationem Lib.XV. De Subtilitate, ad Hieronymvm Cardanvm* (Francofurti, 1576), p. 30.

25. *Opera Omnia* (Venetiis, 1574), *De Intellectione,* fol. 130ʳ et passim for the pairing of *ideae & vniuersalia.*

26. *Arte of Logicke* (London, 1619), I, iv; p. 7.

27. There is a problem here—and it remains a problem for those who, for one reason or another, want to be thought of as "individuals." Since the "substantial form" of each member of a class (people, deer, rocks) is the "same as" every other member of the class, differences between Socrates and Plato cannot be ascribed, for a thinker like St. Thomas, to form *qua* form. Although each universal or general idea may be diffentiated from all others, there is no way, in this vocabulary of cognition, that the general idea, as a general idea or abstraction, may become an individual example of itself. When Aristotle considers nature in terms of form and matter, it is the form as final cause that individuates the matter, differentiating this matter, here and now, from the general laws of physics that govern, say, the four elements. The case of human beings, man as the rational animal, is special but subject to the same difficulties: Socrates, Plato, Speusippus, and other important thinkers are recognizable as men in general and as individuals in particular, but since the soul is the form of the (material) body, the pertinent principle of individuation (rational animal) is likewise the principle of speciation—the defining mark of the species. The question then becomes, if one elects to press the question (as Aristotle did not), What differentiates one *psyche* (Plato's) from another (Speusippus')? and here there can be no ready answer in the Aristotelean or even the Thomist universe of discourse. The essence of soul is to be form, the final cause or *entelechia* of body; but in the *Metaphysics* and elsewhere only form or idea may be defined, which means that individuals cannot, by definition as it were, be defined. That leaves, in this conceptual economy, matter—matter as the principle of individuation by which one member of a class may be distinguished from other members of the class. Aristotle did not fuss over the problem (it was not, after all, his problem but ours); but Aquinas boldly, or recklessly, in *De Ente et Essentia* and in the two summas regards *materia signata* (conceived as matter positioned in space) as the principle of individuation, differentiated with respect to its position here or there, or wherever. Human beings—Pelagius, Augustine—are different, and free to choose differently, and partly in consequence Thomas knows that he cannot hope to account fully for individual differences on the basis of matter alone (whether designated *signata* or not). In commenting on *Metaphysics* 1018b33 in relation to Aristotle's *De Anima,* where he hoped he could exploit the distinction between universal abstractions, which in the order of logic are

to be considered prior to definition, and the individuals themselves, which are to be thought of as prior in perception, Aquinas apparently came to believe that he could differentiate Pelagius from Augustine in the order of perception, though he also had to recognize that the *psyche* or soul of these two very individual persons, presumably differentiated by God, cannot be perceived and therefore, in the order of logic, cannot be named and defined as *different* in Pelagius and Augustine. (We are, then, dancing nowadays to an old tune when we essay to speak of "centered" and "decentered" selves, of "subjects" and "subject-positions"—but we've lost the beat.) In the Aristotelean or Thomist universe of discourse, the "individual" cannot be "defined," though one may thumb one's nose at him. The "individual" is a logical surd. If we assume that class-names are "natural," then we may also assume the possibility of defining what Locke called "real essences"; and we might then go on to construct a correspondence theory of truth, but this ontological security would still not give us the means to talk coherently about that cultural precipitate (Morse Peckham's fine phrase) known as The Individual. Aquinas' position is imaginative as well as logical, and The Angelic Doctor boldly accepted the implications of a problem that Aristotle, unknowingly, had bequeathed him; but the possible inferences were unacceptable to thinkers who believed that these inferences detracted from the dignity of the soul. Thomas, however, can even cite (*S. T.*, Ia, 85, 7) Aristotle's *De Anima* to the effect that those with soft flesh have better minds; since there are no innate ideas, since the mind is first a *tabula rasa*, and since all knowledge derives from the senses, a finer, more original mind ultimately depends upon a more refined body (*S. T.*, Ia, 76, 5). The form is what is understood, matter is what individuates; form provides intelligibility, matter the individuality. Thus for Aquinas each (immaterial) angel is the sole member of its species, and soft flesh the sign of a hard mind.

28. *Religio Medici and Other Works*, ed. L. C. Martin (Oxford: Clarendon Press, 1964), pp. 60 and 47.

29. Barbara L. DeStefano, "Evolution of Extravagant Praise in Donne's Verse Epistles," *SP*, 81 (1984), 75–93, seeks to describe a Christian "dialectic" in Donne, which means to DeStefano that the "extravagant praise" of noble ladies should be taken as "literal, not symbolic, that extravagance is the only appropriate means to praise Christian virtue, that virtue is physically incarnate in contemporary Christians, that they are exemplars, and that the poet is the *vates*." This conclusion seems to me to be more or less instinctively right, though I am not always sure what DeStefano means by "dialectic"; nor can I see how this notion of "dialectic" might be used to counter adverse criticisms from Jonson to the

present. My own position, finally, is closer to that of Peter Rudnytsky, "'The Sight of God': Donne's Poetics of Transcendence," *Texas Studies in Language and Literature*, 24 (1982), 185–207.

T W O: The Watch-Towre (1)

1. Donne maintains that if people will pardon his having descended to publication, "I doubt not but they will soon give over that other part of that indictment, which is that I have said so much; for no body can imagine, that I who never saw her, could have any other purpose in that, then that I had received so very good testimony of her worthinesse, . . . it became me to say, . . . the best that I could conceive; for that had been a new weaknesse in me, to have praised any body in printed verses, that had not been capable of the best praise that I could give." *Letters to Severall Persons of Honour,* ed. Charles E. Merrill, Jr. (New York: Sturgis & Walton, 1910), pp. 64–65 and 206. Sir Edmund Gosse prints, *Life and Letters* (2 vols.; London, 1899), I, 302–6, three letters in which Donne defends himself, all from April of 1612. The first two, to George Gerrard, appear to be versions of the same letter; the third, to G. F., reiterates the same line of defense, which impresses modern readers as embarrassed waffling but which would make perfect sense to Augustine, as I will suggest in my Conclusion. See also R. C. Bald, *Donne & the Drurys* (Cambridge: Cambridge Univ. Press, 1959), pp. 92–98.

2. Quotations from The Anniversaries *(An Anatomy of the World* and *Of the Progres of the Soule)* will be cited by line number in accord with *The Epithalamions, Anniversaries and Epicedes,* ed. with introduction and commentary by Wesley Milgate (Oxford: Clarendon Press, 1978). With respect to The Anniversaries, Milgate rightly follows Frank Manley's pioneering edition (Baltimore: The Johns Hopkins Press, 1963), differing textually from it only in accidentals but, I believe, improving on Manley's fine introduction and commentary. (In a rare lapse Grierson used the edition of 1633 for The Anniversaries; Manley's improvements depend upon the use of the editions of 1611–12 as copytexts.)

3. "Valediction: forbidding mourning," ll. 13–14, *The Poems of John Donne,* ed. H. J. C. Grierson (2 vols.; Oxford: Clarendon Press, 1912), I, 50. All quotations of the poetry, except those from The Anniversaries, and unless otherwise indicated, are taken from this edition, referred to as Grierson, *Poems.*

4. Cited below, and quoted at greater length. The literature on the Trinity is extensive, though what is really needed here is a study of the "trinity" as the image of God within man. But see Jaroslav Pelikan,

The Christian Tradition (Chicago: Univ. of Chicago Press, 1971), I, 172–225); and A. M. Ritter, "Dogma und Lehre in der alten Kirche," *Handbuch der Dogmen- und Theologiegeschichte,* ed. Carl Andresen (Göttingen, 1980–83), I, 99–221.

5. *The Divine Comedy of Dante Alighieri: III Paradiso,* Italian text with translation and commentary by John D. Sinclair (New York: Oxford Univ. Press, 1961), pp. 350–53 and 484–85. At least as early as Clement the "image" was conceived to be spiritual or intellectual, though anthropomorphic writers appear in all ages, and painters were often pleased to represent a handsome Christ, acting on the behalf of His Father, creating a lookalike Adam. In relation to Augustine, however, Gerhart B. Ladner, *Ad Imaginem Dei* (Latrobe, Pa.: Archabbey Press, 1965), p. 20, points to "papal portrait iconography of the sixth to the ninth century where, in images of Pelagius II (fig. 16), Gregory the Great (fig. 17), John VII (fig. 18), and Paschal I (fig. 19), increasing triangularity [i.e., "trinitarian"] of the faces can be clearly perceived."

6. 2.2.140–46, *"Measure for Measure"*: *An Old-Spelling and Old-Meaning Edition,* ed. Ernst Leisi (New York: Hafner, 1964).

7. As quoted in J. V. Cunningham, "Idea as Structure: *The Phoenix and the Turtle," Collected Essays* (Chicago: Swallow Press, 1976), p. 197, citing William Oldys and Thomas Birch, eds., *The Works of Sir Walter Ralegh* (Oxford, 1829), II, xlvi. Cunningham's brilliant explication of "glassie Essence" and related matters first appeared in *ELH,* 19 (1952), see esp. p. 266, but has been ignored by those whom Robert Burton would call the philosophunculists of the academy as well as by most students of Shakespeare.

8. *Essays in Divinity,* ed. Evelyn M. Simpson (Oxford: Clarendon Press, 1952), p. 20.

9. *Sermons of John Donne,* ed. George R. Potter and Evelyn M. Simpson (10 vols.; Berkeley: Univ. of California Press, 1953–62), III, 144–45. Cf. V, 149: "God created one *Trinity* in us; (the observation, and the enumeration is Saint *Bernards*) which are those *three faculties* of our soule, the *reason,* the *memory,* the *will.*"

10. This "trinitarian" conception stands at the center of the Jesuit tradition of "meditation," codified in the numerous devotional manuals available to Donne; see Louis L. Martz, *The Poetry of Meditation* (New Haven: Yale Univ. Press, 1954). The reprint of 1962 allowed Martz to draw attention to the importance of Augustine's *De Trinitate* in this tradition.

11. Melanchthon's *Liber de Anima* (1561) is Protestant-Aristotle: *Augustinus, ut monstret imaginem Dei in Anima, tres uires nominat, Memoriam,*

Intellectum, & Voluntatem. For the latest exposition of the Catholic view and a scholarly account of the theory of processions, see D. Juvenal Merriell, *To the Image of the Trinity* (Toronto: Pontifical Institute, 1990).

12. Sir Thomas Elyot, *The Book named The Governor*, ed. S. E. Lehmberg (Everyman's Library; London: J. M. Dent, 1906; 1966), p. 165.

13. *Sermons*, II, 72–73; hereafter cited as *Sermons* in parentheses in text. Manley was, I believe, the first to make this important connection.

14. See David Lindberg, *Theories of Vision from Al-Kindi to Kepler* (Chicago and London: Univ. of Chicago Press, 1976) and also his *Roger Bacon's Philosophy of Nature: A Critical Edition, Introduction, and Notes, of De multiplicatione specierum and De speculis comburentibus* (Oxford: Clarendon Press, 1983).

15. The optical summa of Witelo, despite or perhaps because of its tendency to ignore the subtleties and idiosyncrasies of his predecessors, particularly Alhazen and Bacon, enjoyed great popularity; and the *Perspectivae Libri Decem*, in Friedrich Risner's *Opticae Thesaurus Alhazeni Arabis Libri Septem* (Basel, 1572), was distributed widely and was widely influential. Charles Monroe Coffin, *John Donne and the New Philosophy* (New York: Columbia Univ. Press, 1937), observes that, at Oxford, "To the works of Aristotle were added the writings of Pliny and Plato. Strabo as well as Ptolemy was counted among the authorities on mathematics. The only change effected in this direction by the Nova Statua of Elizabeth was to allow certain alternatives: *Arithmeticam vel Boetii vel Tunstalli vel Gemmephrisii.* 'Vitellio's Perspective may be allowed in Place of Euclid' " (p. 30). And in 1604, when Kepler wrote his great *Ad Vitellionem Paralipomena, quibus astronomiae pars optica traditur,* his title indicates that he saw his work as subsuming and continuing the thirteenth-century Witelo.

16. "17. Meditation," *Devotions upon Emergent Occasions,* ed. John Sparrow (Cambridge: Cambridge Univ. Press, 1923). When Ernest Hemingway quotes part of this meditation on the "idea" or *corpus mysticum* of "*Mankinde*" as the epigraph of *For Whom the Bell Tolls,* he may be thought to have meant pretty much the opposite of what Donne intended.

17. J. H. Randall's *Aristotle* (New York: Columbia Univ. Press, 1960) remains the best introduction to these matters because the author knows the writers of the Middle Ages and the Renaissance, and because he makes tyros like myself aware of the tone and nuance of the Greek texts. Here as elsewhere it is possible to exaggerate Aristotle's departures from his teacher; Aristotle was, after all, one of the first "Neoplatonists" among the Academics, and Philip Merlan, *From Platonism to Neoplatonism* (The Hague: M. Nijhoff, 1953; 3d ed. rev., 1968), is right, I believe, to devote a chapter "to establish the notion of an *Aristoteles Neoplatonicus.*"

18. *Centuries, Poems and Thanksgivings,* ed. H. M. Margoliouth (Oxford: Clarendon Press, 1958), I, 207 and 95.

19. In what follows I rely upon *Aristotle's De Anima: Books II, III,* clearly translated with good introduction and notes by D. W. Hamlyn (Oxford: Clarendon Press, 1968).

T H R E E: The Watch-Towre (2)

1. My account of the reception of the *De Anima* in the West relies primarily on the invaluable researches of Ferdinand Edward Cranz, who has produced various checklists as well as *A Bibliography of Aristotle Editions, 1501–1600* (Baden-Baden: V. Koerner, 1984); see also *Catalogus translationum et commentariorum* (Washington: Catholic University Press, 1960–), and "The Publishing History of the Aristotle Commentaries of Thomas Aquinas," *Traditio,* 34 (1978), 157–91. In "The Renaissance Reading of the *De Anima,*" *Platon et Aristote à la Renaissance,* "XVIᵉ Colloque International de Tours" (Paris: J. Vrin, 1976), pp. 359–76, Cranz offers a masterly survey under two main rubrics: the history of *De Anima* as a book (publications, translations, commentaries), and the history of the way medieval and Renaissance thinkers sought to assimilate and use *De Anima,* mainly though not exclusively in the translation of William of Moerbeke. As I have observed in Chapter 1, Aristotle and his Greek commentators use *eidos* for the "form" of the human being and for the "forms" of sensibles and intelligibles, and Cranz draws attention (370–73) to the notable fact that translations differ in the Arabic and Western traditions (see also Michaud-Quantin, cited in Chapter 1, n. 17). In medieval Latin translations from the Greek, *eidos* usually becomes *species,* whereas in the translations from the Arabic *eidos* becomes *forma,* allowing two separate or at least separable concepts to develop from the one Greek word: form as essence, species as "intentionality." (See also *Avicenna Latinus: Liber de Anima,* a critical edition of the medieval Latin translation of Aristotle, ed. S. Van Riet and with introd. by G. Verbeke [2 vols.; Leiden: Brill, 1968, 1972].) According to Cranz, the old and new terms were "redefined . . . in such a way that they now applied to the dichotomy between what is in the soul as against what is outside the soul," a dichotomy foreign to Aristotle but apparently congenial to (Christian) thinkers who needed to preserve the "duality" of soul and body, mind and external world. The problem for medieval and Renaissance thinkers "was to develop a new universe of discourse which could contain both the contemporary experience of the ineluctable duality of minds and things and also the Aristotelian propositions on the unity of sense and sensible,

of intellect and intelligible." I think that Cranz has here, as well as elsewhere, focused precisely on the problem and has, as usual, clarified its nature; but Cranz also implies that toward the end of the Renaissance, somewhere perhaps between the time of Zabarella and Suarez, the Aristotelean "axiom of unity" that united the mind with the world (Donne's "both the object and the wit") had somehow been weakened, or even abrogated, so that, in Cranz's formulation, "the species, which had served as the main surrogate for the original unity, lost their reason for being." Cranz is probably right in some sense, strictly considered with reference to the history of philosophy; but Hobbes still finds it necessary in the middle of the seventeenth century to inveigh against the institutionalization of the doctrine of intentional species, and this doctrine not only assumes but rationalizes the "axiom of unity." And while it is also true that *species* is not, in Aquinas' terms, "*that which is intellected* but rather *that by which the intellect intellects,*" Cranz does not mention in this context the similar role played by the *phantasm* in Aristotle, which is that by which the intellect intellects, as well as the role of the *species intelligibilis expressa* in Aquinas, which is that which is intellected. Finally, the *perspectivist* tradition clearly shows that the rupture with the past could not have been absolute or even widespread. Certainly the break with the fiction of the "species" was more or less absolute for "intuitionist" and "nominalist" thinkers from Ockham to Hobbes; certainly it was not for thinkers like Donne and Robert Greville.

2. The most important sources, revealing the significant interaction between Moerbeke's Aristotle and the acute analytical intelligence of St. Thomas, may be studied conveniently in *Aristotle's "De Anima": In the Version of William of Moerbeke and the Commentary of St. Thomas Aquinas,* tr. Kenelm Foster and Silvester Humphries (New Haven: Yale Univ. Press, 1954). I owe the reference to Elizabeth Patton.

3. *Religio Medici and Other Works,* ed. L. C. Martin (Oxford: Clarendon Press, 1964), p. 33.

4. A standard summary may be found in Burton's *Anatomy of Melancholy* I.i.2.2.

5. *John Milton: Complete Poems and Major Prose,* ed. Merritt Y. Hughes (Indianapolis, Ind.: Odyssey Press, 1957). Even within the same author terminology may vary—often "intellectual" for "animal," sometimes "animal" for "vital" or "sensitive"—but since the tripartite distinctions seldom or never varied until later eras, the context generally rescues the sense.

6. David Lindberg has published extensively on the "perspectivist" tradition, and I have cited his pioneering work at some length in

Chapters 1 and 2, but I should probably repeat at least one citation here, with the reminder that most of what I have to say about this tradition derives from Lindberg's studies and his editions of the primary texts. See particularly, in the present context, "Alhazen's Theory of Vision and Its Reception in the West," *Isis,* 58 (1967), 321–41, which shows that the theories of Bacon, Pecham, and Witelo represent a kind of medieval synthesis that derives in its more important aspects from Alhazen (ca. 965–1039).

7. *The Epithalamions, Anniversaries and Epicedes,* ed. W. Milgate (Oxford: Clarendon Press, 1978), p. 115; Milgate cites *Marsilio Ficino's Commentary on Plato's Symposium,* ed. and tr. Sears R. Jayne, "Univ. of Missouri Studies," 19 (1944), 222.

8. See the early work by Elsie C. Graham, *Optics and Vision: The Background of the Metaphysics of Berkeley* (publ. Columbia diss., May, 1929). The copy I used, courtesy of my student Sherri Geller, was inscribed to Ernest Nagel and was written under the supervision of F. J. E. Woodbridge! Graham notes (58): "There had been the Epicurean *eidola* and then the Aristotelian *species* [actually the non-Aristotelean "species"], debased by the unsubtle into something almost as crude. How prevalent the conception was in the time of Descartes is evidenced by his warning not to fall into the common error of supposing that 'pour sentir l'âme ait besoin de contempler quelques images qui soient envoyées par les objets jusques au cerveau.' " Vitellio, called "Alhazen's ape" by Porta, illustrates the process of simplification that occurs again and again in the history of thought. Although Vitellio thinks of himself as an Aristotelean, his systematization of Alhazen, with its *petitiones, definitiones, et theoremata,* transforms the rich subtleties of his master into physical explanations of how retinal images are literally refracted by means of the "spirits" along the nerves and into the brain, or how the perception must be a literal likeness of the object. A kind of literal Lucretianism has infiltrated the thinking of Vitellio, and through him, the university curricula. Graham shows herself everywhere sensitive to these developments and to the cognitive implications of Porta's *camera oscura,* Locke's "chamber," and other determining tropes of mind. As she herself observes (7), Berkeley "was the first formidable opponent of the so-called Newtonian cosmology, and . . . he launched his attack upon it by an *Essay towards a New Theory of Vision.* Few . . . have paused to question this coupling." Few but Elsie Graham.

9. William of Ockham, for example, forcibly rejects the doctrine of intentional species in his lectures on Peter Lombard's *Sentences* in 1317–19 at Oxford, but as the researches of David Lindberg suggest, and as Katherine H. Tachau has ably demonstrated, Ockham's "nominalist" attack proved to be a signal failure, and the doctrine survived not only

Donne's stay in Hart Hall but Hobbes' later attack. In Tachau's formulation, fully documented in *Vision and Certitude in the Age of Ockham* (Leiden and New York: Brill, 1988), "Ockham did not establish a school of Ockhamists, and he did not succeed in displacing visible species from accounts of cognition even in the *Sentences* commentaries. On the contrary, most scholars defended such mediators precisely because they thought the perspectivist account of vision, and of the psychological processes originating in vision, more adequately accounted for the observed phenomena than did the alternative that Ockham proposed" (xv).

10. I have discussed *species* at some length in Chapter 1; here it may help if I say something about this technical use of the word "intention," which has very little to do with modern-day squabbles among literary critics and perhaps even less to do with the very different modern-day debates among philosophers. Seneca, *Naturales Quaestiones* (2.4.6), in answer to what sets the mind (*animus*) in motion (*agitur*), responds with the (Stoic) rhetorical question: *Quis est ille motus nisi intentio?* Intention represents a kind of inner striving, an urge that begins in the mind and moves toward the external world, and it seems to be posited out of a feeling that neither the perceiver nor the object suffices in itself or even in relation to its contrapart to explain the act of perception. The "intention" of the mind—in Augustine often it is "attention"—must also be involved in the process of perception; in *De Trinitate* 15.3.5 and elsewhere "intention" can refer to the *acies* (edge, point) of thought where the mind is joined to the object of thought. The doctrine of intentionality appears in the West as early as Avicenna's commentaries on Aristotle's *De Anima,* where it is used to establish a distinction between primary intention (the apprehension of particulars) and secondary intention (the comprehension of universals), becoming in St. Thomas *species intentionales* (sensory representations in the imagination of objects in the external world) and *intentio universalitatis* (the universal concept produced by abstraction). In general, *forma* refers to the "objectivity" of the external object (in Donne the "formes from objects flow"), whereas *species* refers to the corresponding "subjectivity" or "intentional" likeness of the object in the sense organ or in the mind. Cf., from another point of view, Kathy Eden's first-rate *Poetic and Legal Fiction in the Aristotelian Tradition* (Princeton, N.J.: Princeton Univ. Press, 1986); vide Index under "Intention."

11. Pt. I, ch. i. *English Works,* ed. Sir William Molesworth (London, 1839), III, 3. See also Pt. I, ch. 2: "Some say the senses receive the species of things, and deliver them to the common sense; and the common sense delivers them over to the fancy, and the fancy to the memory, and the memory to the judgment, like the handing of things from one to another, with many words making nothing understood" (III, 8).

12. Daniel D. McGarry, the translator (Berkeley and Los Angeles: Univ. of California Press, 1962), p. 229, cites Chalcidius, *Comm. in Tim. Plat.* 231. Although D. C. Allen, *The Harmonious Vision* (Baltimore: The Johns Hopkins Press, 1954), pp. 17–18, does not cite either John or the letter from Ficino, he does allude to *Timaeus* 70a and *Republic* 560b and then (p. 18) provides one of those fascinating intellectual vignettes for which he should be celebrated: "Other Greeks seized on the analogy and by transcription it became the *arx* of the Latins. Pliny uses it so [Hist. Nat. XI.134] and Cicero proclaims the mind mirific tower of the body [De Nat. Deor. II.140]. It is one of those self-propagating images and, collated with Hebraic usages, it penetrated the writings of the Christian Church and found a place in English poetry. Spenser knows this tower and makes it the citadel of Alma's house. Donne urges his readers to ascend to the 'watch-towre.' It congregates with the admonition of Isaiah, '*contemplare in specula*' and with the response: 'My lord, I stand continually upon the watchtower in the daytime, and I am set in my ward whole nights.' The earthly tower is equated with alertness, with continued intellectual and devotional occupation."

13. *The Letters of Marsilio Ficino,* tr. Language Dept. of the School of Economic Science (London: Shepheard-Walwyn, 1975), II, 103, Letter 57 (*Stultia et miseria hominum*). W. W. Kerrigan, always mindful of my intellectual needs, graciously supplied the reference.

14. Drummond of Hawthornden, gentleman poet and gentleman scholar, acquired in 1611 "A Discourse of Civil Lyff, by Cod. [*sic*] Bryskett, out of the Italian of Giraldi"; in 1612 "Phillipes de Mornay de la Verité de la Religion Chrestienne," which had been translated by Sidney and Arthur Golding in 1587 and which dealt with the Trinity and the "trinities" in man; in 1613 "Jhone Done's Lyriques," and "Sr Jhone Dauies' Nosce Te Ipsum," which relies on the tradition of Aristotle's *De Anima*. See Appendix A, "Drummond's Reading, 1606–14," in French Fogle's *A Critical Study of William Drummond of Hawthornden* (New York: King's Crown Press, 1952).

15. *De gli Hecatommithi,* a collection of *novelle* that went through many editions and provided Shakespeare with the plots for *Othello* and *Measure for Measure,* first came out in 1565; its second part was entitled *Tre dialoghi della vita civilè* and shows Giraldi's acquaintance with *De Anima*. Giraldi, having graduated in philosophy and medicine from the University of Ferrara in 1531, was immediately appointed lecturer and in 1534 received the Chair of Philosophy; see P. R. Horne, *The Tragedies of Giambattista Cinthio Giraldi* (Oxford: Oxford Univ. Press, 1962), p. 10. It has not been established when Bryskett did the translation or which of several

editions he actually used. Although I used the copy in the Huntington Library, a photo reprint is available and may be consulted in Bryskett's *Literary Works,* ed. J. H. P. Pafford (Amersham, England: Gregg International, 1972). Quotations from Bryskett on pp. 122ff.

16. Aristotle (and Donne) take a similar approach to the relation between knower and known. Instead of Plato's doctrine of *anamnesis* by which the soul "recollects" as best it can the "ideas" it knew before its descent into the prison-house of the body, Aristotle assumes that the mind is initially *tabula rasa*. The *archai* or *principia* acquired by the mind derive from a series of perceptions that persist in the memory long enough for resemblances to become evident and produce *logos* or meaning. Although the mind perceives the *archê* in the particular, the universal "form" becomes fully intelligible only through the repetition that permits the mind to disregard the "accidental" properties of the object.

17. "Which common sense, is a power or facultie of the sensitiue soule, that distinguisheth betweene those things that the outward senses offer vnto it; and is therefore called common, because it receiueth commonly the formes or images with [sic, read *which*] the exterior senses present vnto it, and hath power to distinguish the one from the other."

18. "But as those senses know not the nature of things; so is the same vnknowne also vnto the common sense, to whom they offer things sensible. Wherefore this common sense being (as we haue said) a facultie of the *sensitiue* soule, offereth them to the facultie *imaginatiue,* which hath the same proportio[n] to the vertue *intellectiue,* as things sensible haue to the sense aforesaid. For it [the common sense] moueth the vnderstanding after it hath receiued the formes or images of things fro[m] the outward senses, & layeth them vp materiall in the memory where they be kept."

19. The two intellects use the "facultie *imaginatiue*" to "bring foorth afterwards the vniuersals" in what Aristotle calls The Place Of Forms. (These technicalities may be studied most conveniently in *Aristotle's De Anima: Books II, III,* edited and translated, with a concise introduction and excellent notes, by D. W. Hamlyn [Oxford: Clarendon Press, 1968], cited already in Chapter 2, n.19.) Here and elsewhere in this chapter I shall be offering additional commentary on the commonplaces retailed by Cinthio-Bryskett. The "place of forms" in the soul is somehow "akin to perceiving" (429a13) but nevertheless remains distinct from body, for with certain modifications Aristotle feels that "those [the Platonists] who say, then, that the soul is a place of forms speak well, except that it is not the whole soul but that which can think, and it is not actually but potentially the forms" (429a18). The power *(dunamis)* that belongs uniquely to the place of forms Aristotle calls *nous pathetikos* (in the Latin commentators

intellectus patiens or *possibilis*). This power, infinitely malleable, could become all things; it was in "potency" to the universe. It could understand all things by becoming one with them, not indeed with things as they are "out there" (the stone that Aristotle sees is not itself in the mind) but as they are "possible" of being known—the "form" of the stone. For Aristotle all these forms or ideas had to come from somewhere in the world of sensible particulars; knowledge derives from sensation, not from innate ideas or Platonic "reminiscence." Nevertheless, as I have noted in the previous chapter, Aristotle seems to have retained something of Plato's dualistic assumptions about the nature of the soul, not only that it is a "place of forms" but also that the thinking soul "should not be mixed with the body" (429a18), that while "sense perception is not independent of the body," nevertheless "the intellect is distinct" (429a29). The intellect, "potentially" all things "without their matter" (429b29), is in its "active" aspect, and "alone" or only as "act," "immortal and eternal" (430a18).

20. The results of physical perception, the sensible forms, may appear as phantasmata in the imagination or be retained in the memory. They are in the "mind" but not as *nous* or mental act; particulars may be sensed, universal forms must be known, and only through the operation of the rational *psyche*. Although Wallace Stevens figured that Adam in Eden "was the father of Descartes," cognition since Descartes has been marked by a sharper separation between knower and known than could be imagined by Aristotle and Donne. When Descartes relegated the objective world to extension, everything else, including sense perception, became part of *pensée* or mind. In Aristotle, however, the plastic *nous* functions not by separating itself from the object but by becoming, on the analogy of sense perception, "like" or "same as" the object. As Donne puts it in The Second Anniversary: "it is both the object and the wit."

21. Mind *(nous)*, possessing the power to become the "same as" the *arché* of the *ousia* apart from its material conditions, functions in ways analogous to the operations of sense (especially sight), just as for Aristotle mathematical curves are analogous to sensed curves (Socrates' snub nose, Helen's upturned throat). Since Aristotle assumes that sight is primary, he models sensing in general on seeing—and knowing on seeing. There is the "diaphanous" or the transparent medium that is light *in potentia* and that becomes light *in actu* when set in motion by a source of light such as the sun; the medium "actualizes" color in the object, which is then perceived by the eye. Motion in the diaphanous permits seeing, which is entirely physical; the power to sense, which is common to animals and produces appetite (desire or aversion), is set in motion by the object so

that the organ becomes "like" the object. When the "potential" warm blush of the peach and the "potential" *dynamis* of sight are "actualized" together, the eye receives the "sensible form" of the peach apart from its matter, as wax receives the form of the signet ring (*De Anima* 423a). In The First Anniversary this kind of vision provides the basis for similes: "As to our eyes, the formes from objects flow."

22. As in Aristotle, so in Aquinas, the intellect is itself divided into two principles, powers, or aspects: the "agent" or "actualizing" intellect, and the "passive" or "potential" intellect. The agent intellect "turns" toward the sensible species in the phantasy *(converti supra phantasmata)* and then "illuminates" a likeness of the phantasm, abstracted from its material and individuating conditions, in the potential intellect as *species intelligibilis impressa,* where cognition reaches completion in the *species intelligibilis expressa.* This expressed intelligible species constitutes the end of intellection. The mind has reached a definition or "universal." (Aquinas may call this *intelligible species,* according to context, *verbum mentis* or *conceptus;* the label is then, as we say and as they meant, definitive.) Only then does the knower become identical with the thing known. Only then is the object "intelligible," only then is it "comprehensible." As Donne says, "incomprehensiblenesse" could not "deterre" him.

23. Pp. 122–26. Bryskett adds: "And this knowledge is not principally in man, but in the soule, wherin it remaineth as the forme therof. This is briefly the summe of the order or maner of knowledge, which those that follow *Aristotle* do set downe: who therefore affirme that his sentence was, that who so would vnderstand any thing, had need of those formes and images which ther senses offer to the fantasie. . . . And right true it is, that whiles she is tied to the bodie, she cannot vnderstand but by the meanes of the senses: but that being free and loosed from the body, she hath not her proper operations, that is most false. For then hath she no need at all of the senses, when being pure and simple, she may exercise her owne power and vertue proper to her, (which is the contemplation of God Almightie, the highest and onely true good) nor yet of any other instrument but her selfe."

24. Donne's words describe the Beatific Vision, of which the view from the "watch-towre" is but a shadowy counterpart; but the principle of identity, which sustains the analogy between the two kinds of vision, remains the same. Cranz, cited above, quotes (373–74n.) the crucial words about the identity of knower and known from William of Moerbeke's translation of *De Anima* 3.8: *quod omnia ea, quae sunt, quodammodo est anima. Aut enim sensibilia quae sunt, aut intelligibilia. Est autem scientia quidem scibilia quodammodo, sensus autem sensibilia. . . . Animae autem*

sensitivum, et quod scire potest, potentia haec sunt: hoc quidem scibile, illud vero sensibile. Necesse est autem ipsa, aut species esse. Ipsa quidem igitur non sunt: non enim lapis in anima est sed species. In D. W. Hamlyn's translation, cited above: "The soul is in a way all existing things; for existing things are either objects of perception or objects of thought, and knowledge is in a way the objects of knowledge and perception. . . . In the soul that which can perceive and that which can know are potentially these things, the one the object of knowledge, the other the object of perception. These must be either the things themselves or their forms. Not the things themselves; for it is not the stone which is in the soul, but its form" (431b20–431b24). In St. Thomas the formulation (tr. Foster, 457, see citation above) is much the same, but where Hamlyn and Foster have "form," Thomas, like Moerbeke, has "species": "for not the stone itself, but its formal likeness exists in the soul. And this enables us to see how intellect in act *is* what it understands; the form [*species*] of the object is the form of the mind in act."

25. In the course of another argument, Raymond A. Anselment, "Ascensio Mendax, Descenso Crudelis: The Image of Babel in the Anniversaries," *ELH*, 38 (1971), 203–4, suggests that D. C. Allen's view of the *topos* of the watchtower may be limited and limiting and mentions associations with hill and tower that range from fortitude to faith. It may be preferable, in line with the arguments advanced throughout this book, to regard the *topos* as one of those mediating terms, as one of those "middle and participating natures," to which the greater poets found themselves consistently drawn; see next note for some of the poetic possibilities in exploiting the ambiguities of the word "watchtower."

26. The Latin for *watchtower, vision, and mirror* allowed for a good deal of serious quibbling. Augustine, for example, "Select Library of the Nicene and Post-Nicene Fathers," gen. ed. Philip Schaff, VIII, *Saint Augustin. Expositions on the Book of Psalms,* tr. A. Clevland Coxe (New York: Christian Literature Co., 1888), 268, first connects Jerusalem with Sion as meaning vision: "Jerusalem is the very same as Sion; and of this name the interpretation ye ought to know. As Jerusalem is interpreted vision of peace, so Sion *Beholding [speculati],* that is, vision and contemplation," then later (500) effects a typological connection between Sion and the watchtower in us that allows us to look toward the New Jerusalem: "For she [the Church] is Sion: not that one spot, at first proud, afterwards taken captive; but the Sion whose shadow was that Sion, which signifieth a watch-tower; because when placed in the flesh, we see into the things before us, extending ourselves not to the present which is now, but to the future. Thus it is a watch-tower: for every watcher gazes far. . . . Sion therefore is a watch-tower, the Church is a watch-tower." Donne's use of

the word "spectacles" in relation to the "watch-towre" shows the poet wittily aware as usual of etymological quibbles. In *De Trinitate* 15.14.8 Augustine translates 1 Cor. 13.12 as "we see now through a mirror, in an enigma; but then face to face," and interprets "enigma" as one of the Greek tropes. Then, after translating 2 Cor. 3.18 as "We with unveiled face beholding in a mirror the glory of the Lord, are transformed from glory unto glory," he observes parenthetically: "(The word *speculantes* means 'seeing in a mirror', not 'observing from a watch-tower': as is clear in the original Greek, in which the *speculum* that reflects an image is described by a quite different-sounding word from the *specula* or height from the top of which we look out at distant objects, and it is plain enough that *speculantes,* in the phrase *gloriam Domini speculantes* is derived from *speculum* and not *specula.*)"; *Later Works,* "Library of Christian Classics," VIII, tr. John Burnaby (London, 1955). Augustine's careful distinctions do not, of course, prevent him from making etymological connections, anymore than Donne's formidable learning prevents him from using the *specula* of the watchtower for intellectual vision here on earth as well as the identity of "the object and the wit" in heaven. Milton draws on the same complex of quibbles when, at the end of *Paradise Lost,* the angelic historian promises Adam a "paradise within thee, happier far" and signifies that it is time for them to "descend now therefore from this top / Of speculation" (12.588–89)—not only from the Mount of Eden but also from "looking" out toward the future and "thinking" about it. Cf. the "specular Mount" of *Paradise Regained* (4.236) from which, as if from a watchtower, Satan, through "strange Parallax or Optic skill / Of vision multiplied through air, or glass / Of Telescope" and "Airy Microscope" (4.40–43 and 57), shows Jesus the Kingdoms of the World.

F O U R: Beauties Best (1)

1. The definition is commonplace; Donne makes it explicit because he plans to organize two main sections of the poem according to the two main catergories of this esthetic. Sam L. Hynes, "A Note on Donne and Aquinas," *MLR,* 48 (1953), 179–81, points the relevance of some of the more important sources.

2. It may be difficult for some to imagine the excitement, and consternation, produced by this book, which had its antecedents in the 1930s and its parallels with what I. A. Richards, and his extemely bright pupil William Empson, were doing in England with "practical criticism" and poetic "ambiguity" in this decade and after—just as it is extremely difficult for us to imagine, say, "Puritanism" in sixteenth-century England

as a radical and joyful movement, liberating to the spirit. *The Well Wrought Urn* had been preceded by a few tendentious articles written by Brooks and a couple of other displaced Southern Agrarians, which initiated the liberating movement that reached its penultimate peak in Brooks' and Warren's *Understanding Poetry: An Anthology for College Students* (New York: Holt, 1938). The effects of the movement were felt so immediately that John Crowe Ransom could write a book about the practitioners of the "new criticism" in 1941. During World War II Brooks published "The Language of Paradox," in *The Language of Poetry,* ed. Allen Tate (Princeton, N.J.: Princeton Univ. Press, 1942), pp. 37–61, which he later incorporated into *The Well Wrought Urn: Studies in the Structure of Poetry* (New York: Reynal & Hitchcock, 1947). Young people embraced these subversive doctrines with the same enthusiasm as the next generation shinnied up to "theory"; and a lot of the older historical scholars decried the New Critics with the same passion as their descendants now denounce structuralism or deconstruction, and for what now sound like pretty much the same reasons. Graduate students huddled over coffee, murmuring their subversive thoughts, and later drank beer, by the pitcher, to the demise of "historical scholarship" and to the triumph of "literary criticism." Even at The Hopkins, noted Arnold Stein in later years while recalling the excitement of those days, *ELH* dared to publish this new stuff! the stuff that actually dealt with The Work Of Art . . . Those were heady days for some, just as these are heady days, with the usual transvaluation of generational pieties, for some.

　　The old New Criticism, reduced in retrospect to a practice called "formalist," is now seen either as a dead end or as an unending end. In one of those disquisitions on "parergonality" and "self-referentiality" aimed at unnamed critics who supposedly believe in "totalization" and "closure," Jonathan Culler, *On Deconstruction: Theory and Criticism after Structuralism* (Ithaca, N.Y.: Cornell Univ. Press, 1982), pp. 202–5, refers to "Brooks's canonical example" ("The Canonization") and intones that it is now "possible to show that poems which the New Critics have analyzed as instances of the doctrine they [the poems] proclaim are in fact more complex and problematic in their self-referentiality" than the previous generation had assumed. "We have, therefore, not so much a self-contained urn as a chain of discourses and representations: the legend describing the lovers, the verse representation of this legend, the celebratory portrayal of the lovers in the response of those who have heard the legend, the request which the lovers are asked to formulate, and the pattern from above that will generate further versions of their love." Culler offers the rhetorical concession that "this may seem a perverse description of what is happening" but then proceeds—what else?—to add Brooks' analysis to the chain of self-referentialities; this final move is not so much "perverse" as predictable, almost comic in its automatism. Although the predictable response is in general required by the theory of deconstruction itself, it comes into play much earlier in particular instances because of the absence of particular pieces of information. In this instance, it is the lack of historical information about the meaning of the word "pattern," which in this poem refers to the paradoxical circle of perfection and *not* to "the union which the creative imagination itself effects." I am not of course attempting to argue that either the poem or the urn is "self-contained," or that the "meanings" of "The Canonization" are not endlessly deferred in Derrida's sense—only that it's possible to find indeterminacy faster, earlier, and easier in the absence of the relevant lexical information. (To be fair to Culler, I should note that he pursues his little exercise in self-referential oneupsmanship with such brisk efficiency that we know he does not really believe in what he's doing.)

3. *The Poems of John Donne,* ed. Herbert J. C. Grierson (2 vols.; Oxford: Clarendon Press, 1912), I, 14–15. Cf. Dame Helen Gardner, ed., *The Elegies and The Songs and Sonnets* (Oxford: Clarendon Press, 1965), pp. 73–75, who differs—sometimes with huff and puff—mainly in minor details, though in one instance, "extract" for "contract" in line forty, she provides a much-needed clarification of the alchemical comparison, one that might have saved Cleanth Brooks the exercise of superfluous ingenuity.

4. Except what might or might not rub off from historical context. Five is the "marriage" number, or the number of the senses—or the number of Donne's "The Primrose"; and nine (three threes) may be anything from Dante's Beatrice to the cosmological spheres. It is true that Renaissance poets from Spenser to Milton play the numbers-racket indefatigably, but numerological symbolism—notoriously abused—does not seem to me to be structurally significant in this case. See, however, A. P. Riemer, "A Pattern for Love—The Structure of Donne's 'The Canonization,' " *SSEng,* 3 (1977), 19–31, who even dares to speculate that the forty-five lines of the poem may allude to St. Valentine's Day (14 February, forty-five days into the year)!

5. John A. Clair, "Donne's 'The Canonization,' " *PMLA,* 80 (1965), 300–302, mounts the argument persuasively.

6. This paradoxical image, or conceit, which figures so prominently in Cusa, Browne, Ficino, and others, has its origin in the second definition of twenty-four in the twelfth-century, pseudo-hermetic *Liber xxiv philosophorum.* See Dietrich Mahnke, *Unendliche Sphaere und Allmittel-*

punct (Halle: M. Niemeyer, 1937), and Frank L. Huntley, *Sir Thomas Browne* (Ann Arbor: Univ. of Michigan Press, 1962), p. 109, and the references to the basic scholarship cited on p. 262. Lesser writers content themselves with the geometrical circle, the image rather than the conceit, as does George(?) Puttenham when he dutifully rehearses the terms of the commonplace in *The Arte of English Poesie* (London, 1589), p. 98: "The most excellent of all the figures geometricall is the round for his many perfections. First because he is even and smooth, without any angle, or interruption, most voluble and apt to turne, and to continue motion, which is the author of life: he conteyneth in him the commodious description of every other figure, and for his ample capacitye doth resemble the world or univers, and for his indefiniteness having no special place of beginning nor end, beareth a similitude to God and eternity." Cf. Albert C. Labriola, in his learned "'The Canonization': Its Theological Context and Its Religious Imagery," *HLQ,* 36 (1973), 327–39, who relates "patterne" to the "trinitarian unity" exemplified by Father, Son, and Holy Ghost; I would not deny the relevance of this kind of unity to the paradoxes of the poem but would demote these associations to secondary status.

　　　7. "Observations on the 22. *Stanza* in the 9th Canto of the 2D. Book of SPENCERS Faery Queene, written by the Request of a Friend," *Literary Criticism of Seventeenth-Century England,* ed. Edward W. Tayler (New York: Knopf, 1967), p. 206.

　　　8. *Religio Medici and Other Works,* ed. L. C. Martin (Oxford: Clarendon Press, 1964), p. 10.

　　　9. On the circle of perfection, see Marjorie Hope Nicolson, *The Breaking of the Circle* (Evanston, Ill.: Northwestern Univ. Press, 1950), esp. Chapter 2 for a readable survey of the commonplace as realized in the poetry of the time; and Georges Poulet, *Metamorphoses of the Circle,* tr. Carley Dawson and Elliott Coleman (Baltimore: The Johns Hopkins Press, 1966 [first publ. 1961]), esp. the Introduction and Chapter I, "The Renaissance."

　　　10. John Carlos Rowe, "Structure," *Critical Terms for Literary Study,* ed. Frank Lentricchia and Thomas McLaughlin (Chicago and London: Univ. of Chicago Press, 1990), pp. 23–38, sandwiched as he is in the theoretical interstices between essays on "Representation" and "Writing," does not descend even to *mention* the kind of structure employed by Donne to lend shape and intelligibility to The Anniversaries. Beginning with what he takes to be the contradictory etymology of the word (he is not quite prepared to call it a "primal word" in Freud's sense), Rowe moves

to the (predictable) notion that to "*structure* elements" means "heaping or piling them together" (structure without structure?), from thence to a survey of modern theorists centered in Saussure; and Rowe finally adopts Roland Barthes' "definition" of structure as a "*simulacrum* of the object, but a directed, *interested* simulacrum." Rowe, conceding that Barthes has been "very metaphysical" but insisting nonetheless that this "formulation of 'structure' virtually condenses all that I have to say about the ideological significance of the modern use of the term 'structure'," tries to make what sense he can of the word, and of Barthes. Rowe, understandably, gets all mixed up, "heaping or piling them together."

11. T. S. Eliot, *Selected Essays: 1917–1932* (New York: Harcourt Brace, 1932), p. 254. Cf. J. V. Cunningham, "Logic and Lyric," *Collected Essays* (Chicago: Swallow Press, 1976), pp. 162–79: "In brief, the general structure of Marvell's poem is syllogistic, and it is located in the renaissance tradition of formal logic and of rhetoric" (171). The label "Conditional or Hypothetical Syllogismes" comes from Pierre du Moulin, *The Elements of Logic*, tr. Henry Hall (Oxford, 1647), pp. 128–29, as quoted in B. J. Sokol, "Logic and Illogic in Marvell's 'To His Coy Mistress', *English Studies*, 71 (1990), 244–52; Sokol's penetrating analysis shows "numerous differences between syllogisms and *reductio* arguments" of the kind employed by Marvell and reveals that du Moulin's label is technically incorrect. Sokol's argument has the effect, for me, of drawing Marvell's "logic" closer to the "urbanely fallacious logic" of Tesauro and Donne, about which I shall have something to say later on.

12. *John Donne: "The Anniversaries,"* ed. Frank Manley (Baltimore: The Johns Hopkins Press, 1963), p. 8.

13. "John Donne in Meditation: *The Anniversaries*," *ELH*, 14 (1947), 247–73; rpt. in *The Poetry of Meditation* (New Haven: Yale Univ. Press, 1954), pp. 211–48. Although Martz later reversed his judgment, he began by accepting the older view ("successful only in brilliant patches") of The First Anniversary "despite [the] careful structure" he had discovered; he even sought to show that The Second Anniversary is "one of the great religious poems of the seventeenth century" partly because it lacked the "careful structure" of The First Anniversary (p. 221). Martz argues that The First Anniversary reveals a "central inconsistency which defeats all Donne's efforts," namely, that "Elizabeth Drury has, basically, nothing to do with the sense of decay in the poem" (p. 229), a line of argument repeated with variations in subsequent criticism; and that Donne's "gradual modification of the strict mold which marked the sections" of the first poem, while writing The Second Anniversary, "suggests a creative free-

dom" from "formal divisions" that constitutes yet another reason for the superiority of the second poem (p. 237), a judgment assumed if not explicitly stated in later criticism.

In "Donne's *Anniversaries* Revisited," *That Subtle Wreath: Lectures Presented at the Quatercentenary of the Birth of John Donne,* ed. Margaret Pepperdene (Atlanta, Ga.: Agnes Scott College, 1973), pp. 29–55, Martz came to the conclusion that, since The First Anniversary was not "meditation" but "satire," it could after all be considered "powerfully successful"—for precisely the reason that it had previously been a failure: "Thus the poem's sharp and precise division into parts, which I once saw as a flaw, now seems quite in accord with the central image of the dissection, the anatomy. In this 'demonstration of parts' the world is appropriately cut up into these clear divisions and subdivisions, in order that we may see clearly the corruption in all those parts" (38). The organization is indeed appropriate to an anatomy, and Martz would also now agree, according to a letter of 17 February 1990, that the "exercise [of] the powers of the soul" (memory, understanding, will) in the three-part meditations remains an important component in our response to the poem, though perhaps he would still hesitate to accept the exact "meditational" significance that I attribute to this kind of "exercise."

14. "Donne's *Anniversaries* and the Tradition of Funereal Elegy," *Journal of English Literary History,* 39 (1972), 545–59.

15. James Andrew Clark, "The Plot of Donne's Anniversaries," *SEL,* 30 (1990), 63–78, for example, wants to oppose what he apparently thinks are the two ways the poems are conventionally construed, and accordingly he proposes that we understand The Anniversaries "neither as typology nor as exhortation but as plot." What is this "plot"? It turns out to be a "teleological reading," uneasily presided over by Walter Benjamin and Peter Brooks' *Reading for the Plot,* that "looks for that narrative wholeness which gives the *Anniversaries* a relation like that between desire and satisfaction." The "story is abstract or allegorical rather than mimetic," and "Donne himself" figures in it as a "narrator and surrogate hero" in the "familiar triangle of the morality plays." This kind of "plot," exhibiting Burke's "qualitative progression" in what Clark calls a "movement through tension to pleasure," requires little if any support from the text of The Anniversaries, and Clark gives it just about that much.

16. "The Argument of Donne's *First Anniversary,*" *Modern Philology,* 64 (1966), 125–31; "*The Anniversaries:* Donne's Rhetorical Approach to Evil," *JEGP,* 68 (1969), 407–13. To make what used to be

called a contribution to knowledge in this mode of critical thinking, it is only necessary to advance yet another category of thought sufficiently broad in application to correspond somehow to the general topics alluded to in Donne's poems. Biblical typology, for example, has been enjoying a minor revival, and Lindsay Mann, "Typology of Woman in Donne's *Anniversaries,*" *Renaissance and Reformation,* N.S., 11 (1987), 337–50, has no trouble in relating The First Anniversary to five pre-patriarchal events in Genesis, and the seven parts of The Second Anniversary to the Book of Revelation! To demonstrate that The Second Anniversary does not in fact have seven sections may be thought to give such writers pause, but scholars of this kind seem to resemble those who ascend the mountain to await the Day of Judgment and descend only to revise the arithmetic of their Doomsday Tables.

17. *Donne's "Anniversaries" and the Poetry of Praise: The Creation of a Symbolic Mode* (Princeton, N.J.: Princeton Univ. Press, 1973). See esp. pp. 225, 228, 248, 284–86. With respect to The First Anniversary Lewalski asserts, as I have noted, that Donne employs a "four-part argument," but since she accepts Martz's contention that "each of the four sections contains three subsections" (p. 228), she is immediately involved in logical (and arithmetical) contradiction: she gets her four sections by combining Donne's parts three and four (both on "beauty") into one long section, which produces a section that has not "three subsections" but *six*—neatly illustrating the confusion between topics and formal features. And thereafter, the disagreements are more important and, I would have to say, more arbitrary. I find Lewalski's account of structures inexplicable. Why ignore the formal features that function as poetic paragraph-markers? Why seek to substitute "four-part" structures for Donne's tripartite or "trinitarian" methods of organization within the sections? How is it possible to say (p. 284) that one is "departing *in some degree* from Professor Martz" (my emphasis) when one has just doubled the size of Donne's introduction and obliterated the tripartite organization of the first main section of the poem? Until I can find more evidence in the book than "in my view" or "I suggest," I must regard Lewalski's departures from the text of the poems as arbitrary and very misleading. It is as if I were to report in a review of her book in a scholarly journal that "in my view" the first section (pp. 11–15) of Professor Lewalski's Part I, Chapter I, "Contemporary Epideictic Poetry," is part of her Introduction (pp. 3–8)—not that it ought to be but that it *is* part of her Introduction.

18. "Donne's *Anniversaries* Revisited," *That Subtile Wreath,* ed. Pepperdene; the outline appears on pp. 42–43.

19. *Poetry of Meditation,* p. 237; Martz, with that flexibility he has always displayed in learning from other scholars, later changed his mind. Cf. Lewalski, p. 228, who tries to defend the first poem on generic grounds—with reference, that is, to its putative source: the "rigid and schematic organization of *The First Anniversarie,* to which Martz objects," may be seen as "wholly appropriate" to the "genre of the anatomy."

20. *The Enduring Monument: A Study of the Idea of Praise in Renaissance Literary Theory and Practice* (Chapel Hill: Univ. of North Carolina Press, 1962), pp. 171–78. Hardison's schematic outline of structure appears on pp. 176–77.

21. The schematic outline of "nine clearly-defined sections," which seem to have been "indicated" for Hardison not by structure per se (or even by Martz's analysis) but by the *topical "marginal notes* [my emphasis] of the first edition," may be found on pp. 180–81. The usual confusion of topical categories with formal features of the text . . .

22. Hardison, pp. 180–85.

23. Hardison, p. 170. The quotations, to which may be added Hardison's tendency simply to equate "Elizabeth's soul (or 'idea')" with Richards' "tenor" and Jonson's criticism, also suggest how closely Hardison's arguments bear on the theses advanced by Lewalski. It may not be immediately apparent why Hardison's sensible warnings about vehicle and tenor, like those of Martz about taking metaphors literally, were not heeded by later critics, but probably the reasons must be sought in current tendencies to make Mistress Elizabeth into A Symbol.

24. *Sermons of John Donne,* ed. George R. Potter and Evelyn M. Simpson (10 vols.; Berkeley: Univ. of California Press, 1953–62), V, 149. See also IX, 83, and III, 145 and 154, for almost identical passages. In commenting on ll. 3–6 of The First Anniversary Frank Manley quotes an even more pertinent version of the commonplace from *Sermons,* II, 72–73, and in his Introduction, pp. 41–42, makes the important point that the tripartite subsections of the main "parts of the poem correspond to the three traditional parts of the rational soul—memory, understanding, and will." The problem lies not with the generality but with what part corresponds to which.

25. See preceding note; and Martz, *Poetry of Meditation,* pp. 25–39, for the sequence prescribed by the Jesuit manuals of devotion: (1) composition of place (memory), (2) analysis (reason or understanding), and (3) colloquy (will). In the epigraph to his first chapter Martz cites Joseph Hall, *The Arte of Devine Meditation* (1606), but without noting that Hall's methods differ markedly from those of the Jesuits. Hall meditates

in Ramist dichotomies, and he begins not with *compositio loci,* not with the use of images drawn from the memory, but with the understanding. "Our Meditation must *proceed* in due order, not troubledly, not preposterously [i.e., not with the last coming first]: It begins in the understanding, endeth in the affection."

26. The method of beginning with "cogitations" and ending with "affections" appears not only in the *Arte* but also in *Meditations and Vowes* (dedicated 4 December to Sir Robert Drury from "your Halsted" but no title-page in the copy I used in the Huntington Library), in *Second Book of Meditations and Vowes* (dedicated to Lady Drury in 1606 from "Halsted"), and *Third Century* (dedicated to Sir Edmund Bacon, Lady Drury's brother, in 1606). Although Hall's commendatory poems prefixed to The Anniversaries show that he understood, and respected, what Donne had attempted, his own methods are more nearly Protestant and Ramist than Donne's, whose methods represent a kind of meditational hybrid and are more nearly his own. Hall also wrote an *Anathomy of Sin, discovering the Whold bodie of Imperfection and pollution* (London, 1603). The *Arte of Divine Meditation* (London, 1607), which appeared after Hall had left the employ of Sir Robert, is dedicated to Sir Richard Lea and seems to anticipate the kind of colloquy Donne used in The Second Anniversary: "What wilt thou *muze* vpon, O my soule? . . . Vp then my soule, and mind those things that are aboue." Although Donne knew Hall's meditations and valued the literary association, he nevertheless relied upon his own versions of the three-part meditation in preference to Hall's two-part exercises.

27. F. L. Huntley, *Bishop Joseph Hall and Protestant Meditation* (Cambridge: D. S. Brewer, 1979), shows that the Protestant "rule" of Hall's meditations utilizes Ramist bifurcations, and he quotes Richard Baxter (p. 54) on how the Jesuits err: "They have thought that Meditation is nothing but the bare thinking on Truths, and the rolling of them in the Understanding and Memory," whereas "I joyn all these together because though in themselves they are distinct things, yet in the practice they all concure to the same action." Huntley also shows (pp. 55–56), citing parallels between Donne's poetry and Hall's prose, that the two "were partners in literary exercise," which makes it even more significant that Donne chose to go his own way in The Anniversaries, preferring his own "trinitarian" patterns, whatever their associations with the Jesuits, to the Protestant methods espoused by Hall.

28. See Robert Bozanich, "Donne and Ecclesiastes," *PMLA,* 90 (1975), 270–76; and his "Solomon's Method" (unpubl. diss., Columbia Univ., 1970).

F I V E: Beauties Best (2)

1. Barbara Lewalski, *Donne's "Anniversaries" and the Poetry of Praise: The Creation of a Symbolic Mode* (Princeton, N.J.: Princeton Univ. Press, 1973), assembles (pp. 277 ff.) a very useful number of references.

2. In a well-argued essay Ralph Maud, "Donne's *First Anniversary*," *Boston University Studies in English*, 2 (1956), 218–25, takes exception to the adverse criticisms leveled by Martz against the "entrie"; and Martz, with his usual honesty and generosity, appears to have been convinced ("Donne's *Anniversaries* Revisited") by Maud's arguments, which do indeed help a great deal in making sense not only of the "entrie into the worke" but of the relation of the "entrie" to the rest of the poem. In the course of his defense Maud divides the introductory section into three main parts, the "world's sickness and death" (1–54), "concerning the anatomy" (55–62), and the "new world" (63–90); yet Maud's divisions are not precisely those of Donne, who here as elsewhere organizes according to *ratio* or "proportion," i.e., the three "proportionable" elements of thirty lines each that I delineate. (In the "entrance" to The Second Anniversary, *ratio* remains the principle of construction, but here the proportion is 1:2 or forty-four lines divided precisely into two halves of twenty-two lines apiece.)

3. *Religio Medici and Other Works*, ed. L. C. Martin (Oxford: Clarendon Press, 1964), p. 61; cf. pp. 47 and 167.

4. *Literary Works*, ed. J. H. P. Pafford (Amersham, England: Gregg International, 1972), pp. 125–26.

5. *Religio Medici*, pp. 69 and 19.

6. Exemplifying the Parmenidean maxim (perhaps Eastern in its origins?) that thought is its own object. It is foolish to try to provide a source for this kind of resonant commonplace, so elegantly rendered as to make mockery of source-hunting; but the quasi-religious *locus classicus,* apart from the formulations of the identity of "the object and the wit" in *De Anima* and their endless refinements among Neoplatonists and the Scholastics, is doubtless *Metaphysics* 1074b–1075a: "It must be of itself that the divine thought thinks . . ., and its thinking is a thinking on thinking. [But it may be objected that] to be an act of thinking and to be an object of thought are not the same thing. We answer that in some cases the knowledge is the object. In the productive sciences it is the substance or essence of the object, matter omitted, and in the theoretical sciences the definition of the act of thinking is the object. Since, then, thought and its object are not different in the case of things that have not matter, the divine thought and its object will be the same, i.e., the thinking will be one with the object of its thought." The identification of the "divine

thought and its object" is simply the grandest version or pattern—"differ-ing but in degree, of kind the same"—of the human identification of knower and known in the watchtower of the mind: when the object, as in the productive sciences, is the "substance or essence of the object, matter omitted," through the interaction of the active and passive intellects, then "the knowledge is the object"—and the "object is the wit."

7. See the chapter *"Lycidas* in Christian Time" in my *Milton's Poetry* (Pittsburgh: Duquesne Univ. Press, 1979).

Conclusion

1. John Ruskin noted, early on, that "German dulness, and En-glish affectation, have of late much multiplied among us the use of two of the most objectionable words that were ever coined by the troublesome-ness of metaphysicians,—namely, 'Objective' and 'Subjective.' No words can be more exquisitely, and in all points, useless." *The Genius of John Ruskin,* ed. John Rosenberg (Boston: Houghton Mifflin, 1963), pp. 61–62. It's a tough life, but as we know and live this life, we know that we have to deal in mock dichotomies (whatever their vintage, whatever their provenance), making shift as best we can to distinguish subjective from objective, inner from outer, concepts from words, foreground from back-ground, map from territory, words from things, meanings made from meanings found, picture from frame, container from thing contained, life from art, or form from content, though as we also know—to instance only the last false dichotomy—so called content can only refer to the general characteristics of so called form, . . . and so on. The theoretical situation remains as described in the nineteenth century by the logician Alexander Bain: "The essential relativity of all knowledge, thought, or consciousness, cannot but show itself in language. If everything that we can know is viewed as a transition from something else [ultimately its opposite, I would guess], every experience must have two sides; and either every name must have a double meaning, or else for every meaning there must be two names." Bad news for some theorists, good news for most poets, especially the poets who, like Donne, do a considerable amount of their thinking in wordplay. See *Logic: Deductive and Inductive* (rev. ed.; New York, 1889), p. 54; and cf. Freud's "The Antithetical Meaning of Primal Words," *Standard Edition,* tr. James Strachey, Anna Freud, Alix Strachey, and Alan Tyson (24 vols.; London, 1953–74), 11 (London, 1957), 155–61.

2. It may seem that I am reversing the priority that I have assumed earlier—that it is the "words" and not the "problem" in thought

that must receive first consideration; but I guess I believe that focusing on the words cannot obviate the fact that hovering over the two alternatives must be accepted as part of the human predicament. The current rage for chiastic formulations (spectacle of power and power of spectacle—that sort of thing) acknowledges the difficulty but cannot provide anything more than what Robert Frost called a "momentary stay against confusion"; and in any case, most of us would prefer to gain our moments of order from a poem rather than from a verbal tic. By the time this book is published novel "discourses" will, doubtless, be "interpellating" human "subjects" in new—I hope not uncomfortable—"subject-positions," in which case these new subjects will simply have to start thinking once again about who and where they are in relation to the ersatz dichotomies mentioned in the previous note; as Vonnegut says, And so it goes.

3. *Philosophical Essays* (2d ed.; Edinburgh, 1816), pp. 573–74.

4. (Princeton, N.J.: Princeton Univ. Press, 1957). Change in the academic profession also occurs, though slowly and often imperceptibly, through the practice of historical scholarship, which may offer plausible descriptions of how our own culture acquired the presuppositions, the conceptual archetypes, that more or less unconsciously dictate our responses to other people and to works of art. This kind of knowledge may lead to conscious choice, if not immediately to change.

5. Although the language of the Schools, on which Donne relied in delineating the mode of "seeing" pertinent to the "Idea," suffered periodic attacks by the Humanists and appeared to receive its deathblow from Hobbes, nevertheless Locke, who could not bring himself to believe in "essences," worried the thought that there must be *something* there to hold all those secondary qualities together . . . Vocabularies die hard, and one that has received its quietus in one area may live a half or even a full life in another. John Wilkins wanted to follow "nature" in the virtuoso manner of the Royal Society, but he also wanted to provide the new age with mnemonic categories that would enable men of science to hook their "notions" to the essences of "things" in his proposed "Real Character and Philosophical Language." He even convinced the experienced naturalist John Ray, who knew better, to distort his natural classification of "herbs" to make them fit Wilkins' "Philosophical Language"; and Hooke actually employed the outmoded categories in arranging the collections in the museum of the Royal Society. It was only in 1700 that the mathematician Thomas Baker remarked the incongruity: "When Bishop Wilkins undertook this design *Substance* and *Accidents* were a receiv'd Division, and accordingly in ranking Things, and reducing them to Heads . . . he proceeds in the Scale of *Praedicaments;* but were he to begin now, and would

suit his Design to the Philosophy in vogue, he must draw a new Scheme." See Benjamin DeMott, "Science versus Mnemonics: Notes on John Ray, and on John Wilkins' *Essay toward a Real Character, and a Philosophical Language,*" *Isis,* 48 (1957), 3–12; quotation on p. 12, n. 25. Similarly, the mode of "seeing" persisted in some quarters well into the eighteenth century, despite the convincing rebuttal of Descartes and the devastating attack by Antoine Arnauld.

6. *Poems,* ed. A. R. Waller (Cambridge: Cambridge Univ. Press, 1905), p. 276.

7. *Collected Poems* (New York: Knopf, 1955), p. 76. Reacting against the "idealism" of his day, Stevens' teacher William James liked to tell his students that "ideals taken by themselves give no reality," no more than Tennessean jar can "give of bird or bush."

8. The poem, like The Anniversaries, functions as a cultural barometer for all seasons. In the most recent of the many interpretations I have encountered, Frank Lentricchia, "In Place of an Afterword—Some one Reading," *Critical Terms for Literary Study,* ed. Frank Lentricchia and Thomas McLaughlin (Chicago and London: Univ. of Chicago Press, 1990), pp. 321–38, attempts to use the poem to illustrate various ways of reading and ends up with a Wallace Stevens who "insists we see [that Jar of "plain old democratic American jars"] as figuring a work of oppression," though one that—fortunately or unfortunately?—"cannot be explained in classic European terms of class relations (in classic Marxist terms)"!

9. "Andrew Marvell," *Selected Essays: 1917–1932* (New York: Harcourt Brace, 1932), pp. 251–63; the sheer outrageousness of this conceit probably offended Eliot at least as much as the "salmon-fishers moist" of *Appleton House* who, "like Antipodes in shoes," have "shod their heads in their canoes." Since it is no longer necessary to protest that Eliot's view of the seventeenth century is unhistorical, or to insist that the attempt to define "wit" in the "elucidation of Imagination given by Coleridge" is a piece of anachronistic impertinence, it may be the proper moment to acknowledge that Eliot writes highly intelligent criticism and that at least one of his graceful generalities about "wit," in addition to that "alliance of levity and seriousness," will prove to be of continuing value: "It involves, probably, a recognition, implicit in the expression of every experience, of other kinds of experience which are possible. . . ."

10. Grierson (II, 273), seconded by Milgate, cites Lucretius (3.624ff.), who proves that the mind is not immortal by showing that if the body is divided (arm, leg, or even the head, *caput adscissum calido viventeque trunco*), though it may retain for a short time the spasmodic

appearance of life and movement, it must inevitably suffer dissolution and then, and at the same time, the spirit too must suffer its final "division"—and what can be divided cannot be immortal. Donne will demonstrate in his beheaded man that "division" means precisely the opposite of what Lucretius thinks it means.

11. I am not being facetious. See the literal-minded analysis of "To His Coy Mistress" in Francis Barker, *The Tremulous Private Body* (New York: Methuen, 1984).

12. Timothy Bright, *Treatise of Melancholy* (1586) picturesquely describes "spirit" as a "true love knot to couple heaven and earth together"; the soul is "not fettered with the bodie, as certaine Philosophers have taken it, but handfasted therewith by the golden claspe of the spirit." All in all, a nicer way to be connected with oneself than Descartes' pineal gland.

13. Christian similes quite generally contain a negative element that moves analogy toward paradox, as in Paul's asseveration that "as by one man's disobedience many were made sinners, so by the obedience of one shall many be made righteous" (Romans 5.19). This means that the better Christian similes may well combine—the result is paradox—the two main ways the medieval and Renaissance writers sought to write the unspeakable: Browne calls them the "negative" (God is not this, God is not that) and "comparative" (God has an "arm," but His extends to infinity) "ways."

14. Cleanth Brooks, *The Well Wrought Urn* (New York: Reynal & Hitchcock, 1947), p. 18, remarked the obsession early on, though he concerned himself mainly with the way his view of poetry as "paradox," based in Coleridge's view of the Imagination, might be contrasted with "science": "For us today, Donne's imagination seems obsessed with the problem of unity; the sense in which the lovers become one—the sense in which the soul is united with God. Frequently, as we have seen, one type of union becomes the metaphor for the other. It may not be too far-fetched to see both as instances of, and metaphors for, the union which the creative imagination itself effects. For that fusion is not logical; it apparently violates science and common sense; it welds together the discordant and contradictory. Coleridge. . . ." Brooks, like most of the New Critics and even scholars like George Williamson, rightly noted the obsession with union but had been misled as to its significance by Eliot's essay on Andrew Marvell, which had referred the elucidation of "metaphysical wit" to Coleridge's distinction between Fancy and Imagination.

15. Subtitled "Its Union and Unity with the Soule." Although Greville thinks of himself as a platonizer and shows his distaste for Scho-

lastic distinctions, his "God is the God of Order, and not of Confusion" (*Discourse Opening the Nature of Episcopacie* [London, 1642], p. 104), and he is as convinced as Aristotle or Aquinas of the primacy of vision and the identity of knower and known. The first chapter of *The Nature of Truth* is entitled "*The Vnderstanding and the Truth-vnderstood, are one*": "*life* is *light*, and *light* is Truth, and Truth is conformity to God; and the vnderstanding . . . is this *light* to the soule, the *Vnderstanding* and Truth can be but one" (4–5), so that "the act of the Soule is but seeing or discerning" (150).

16. It may be worth emphasizing again that this kind of cognitive union is not exclusively Aristotelean or Thomist. Marsilio Ficino slips easily into the usual jargon and the usual analogy of the architect in his *Commentary on Plato's Symposium*, ed. and tr. Sears R. Jayne, "Univ. of Missouri Studies," 19 (1944), 172: "In the beginning, an architect conceives an idea of the building, like an Idea in the soul. Then he builds, as nearly as possible, the kind of house he has thought out. Who will deny that this house is a body, and that it is very much like the incorporeal idea of the builder in likeness to which it was made? Furthermore, it is to be judged like the idea more because of a certain incorporeal plan than because of its matter. Therefore, subtract its matter, if you can. You can indeed subtract it in thought, but leave the plan; nothing material or corporeal will remain to you. On the contrary, these two will be exactly the same internally, both the plan which comes forth from the builder [into the physical house] and the plan which remains [unmaterialized in the mind of] the builder." Then the Idea of house (or poem) "will be exactly the same as" the Idea in the mind of the architect (or poet) after you "subtract its matter"—and "will be exactly the same as" the Idea in your (the reader's) mind. So also with Sidney's "idea, or fore-conceit." The most useful study of the kind of syncretism encountered everywhere in the period—and, not incidentally, the best investigation of the "affinity" between knower and known, subject and object—may be found in Eugene Hill, "Image and Argument in an Elizabethan Syncretist: A Study of Everard Digby's *Theoria Analytica*" (Princeton diss., 1980). The title does not reveal either the depth or the range of Hill's scholarship, which gives us Digby as representative of his age, though as Hill is careful to note an "extreme" representative.

17. See Marjorie Grene, *The Knower and the Known* (Washington, D.C.: Univ. Press of America, 1984), esp. pp. 55–63.

18. *The Trinity*, tr. Stephen McKenna (Washington, D.C.: Catholic Univ. of America Press, 1963), "Fathers of the Church," XLV. The bodily species of the woman may be found in 11.4.7; page references hereafter in parentheses in text. Books IX through XV probably consti-

tuted the center of the argument for Donne, and Book X in particular
elaborates the psychological triad of *memoria, intelligentia,* and *voluntas,*
which Augustine had come to prefer to the earlier triad of *mens, notitia,*
and *amor.* Aquinas meditated these matters from the early *Scriptum super
Sententiis,* through *De Veritate,* to the *Summa Theologiae.* The *De Veritate*
and the *Summa* assimilate Aristotle to Augustine.

The first eight books of *De Trinitate* deal with the Father, the
Son, and the Holy Spirit. In Book IX Augustine turns to the trinity of
man: the mind *(mens),* the knowledge by which the mind perceives itself
(notitia), and the love by which the mind loves itself *(amor).* In Book X
these three become memory *(memoria),* understanding *(intelligentia),* and
will *(voluntas),* but since Augustine knows that thinking unfortunately
involves some reliance on corporeal things, he elects to "put off the
discussion about the Trinity, of which this is the image, in order that a
trinity might also be found in the corporeal things themselves." Accordingly, Augustine turns, in Book XI, to sight, the noblest sense, and uses
it, as had Aristotle, as the model for sensing in general. There is the
corporeal trinity consisting of the "body that is seen," the "form im-
printed in the mind," and the "attention of the will" that "combines" the
first two; and from this trinity may be derived another—the "image of
the body which is in memory, the form thence impressed" by the "gaze
of thought," and the "attention of the will" that joins "both [of these]
together"; but even this last trinity, while more nearly "inner" than the
one from which it stems, inadequately mirrors the Trinity because it
remains tied to corporeal images. And therefore, invoking one of his basic
distinctions, Augustine in Book XII distinguishes between *scientia,* the
knowledge of the things of this world, and *sapientia,* the wisdom that
directs the contemplation of incorruptible essence. In Book XIII he finds
an inferior trinity in *scientia,* which though it pertains to the inner rather
than the outer man is nevertheless not yet the sought-for image of the
Trinity; in Book XIV he considers *sapientia,* which is peculiarly the gift of
a God Who created man in His image for the contemplation of eternal and
unchangeable things; and in Book XV Augustine seeks the Trinity in
"eternal, incorporeal, and unchangeable things themselves."

19. But Augustine insists that cognition does not take place
entirely in the Aristotelean manner: "For it is not by seeing many minds
with our bodily eyes that we gather, by way of analogy, a general or
special knowledge of the human mind; but we contemplate the inviolable
truth, whence we can as perfectly as possible define, not what each man's
mind is, but what it ought to be in the light of the eternal types" (279).

20. P. 279. Augustine's example in this instance runs as follows:

"When I call to mind the walls of Carthage which I have seen, and form an image of those of Alexandria which I have not seen, and prefer some of these imaginary forms to others, I prefer them for a good reason; the judgment of truth from above is strong and clear, and remains steadfast by the most incorruptible rules of its own right; and even if it is concealed by bodily images, as by a kind of cloud, still it is not hidden or confused."

21. Augustine appeals to essence, to "Idea"; and he envisages his response on analogy with what may be called the *corpus mysticum* of scholarship, and in terms that must have seemed congenial to the poet who confessed to "an hydroptique immoderate desire of humane learning." Suppose, for example, that a person hears the word *timetum* and knows it for a "sign" of something. "This word of three syllables is . . . already known, and has impressed its articulated species on his mind through the sense of hearing." In the "light of the truth he realizes how great and good it is to understand and speak all the languages of all the countries. . . . The splendor of such knowledge is already seen in his thoughts." If he then "chances to find out that *timetum* is the old word for 'wine,' he may want to remember it out of respect for the old books; but if he does not think the old books are worth the effort," he will forget the word because "he does not perceive any connection between it and that species of learning which is known to the mind and upon which he gazes and loves." But if he is in love with knowledge, and if he thinks there may be a connection with the grand "species of learning" in his mind, he may ask the meaning of the sign: "it would [then] seem as if he loved something unknown, but in reality it is not so." For "that species touches the mind, which knows and thinks; it reveals the beauty of minds that have been brought together in fellowship by listening to and answering questions through signs that are [already] known. And this species enkindles him with zeal, who is looking indeed for something he does not know, to which the unknown thing belongs" (291–95). Although desperately metaphysical and of a piece with all those other examples of Augustine's struggle to find, uncontaminated by sense impressions, some principle of immutable certitude within the human mind, this meditation on *timetum* is no austere vision of learning.

22. P. 280. Augustine's illustration is again esthetic, architectural: "Something similar takes place when I recall a beautifully and symmetrically intorted arch which I have seen, for example, in Carthage. In this case a certain reality, which was made known to my mind through the eyes and transferred to my memory, produces an imaginary view. But in my mind I behold something else, according to which that work pleases me; whence also I should correct it if it displeased me. Therefore, we pass

judgment upon these particular things according to that form of the eternal truth, and we perceive that form through the eye of the rational mind. . . . For we form images of bodies in our mind or see bodies through the body in one way, but we comprehend in a different way the types and the ineffably beautiful art of such forms, as are above the eye of the mind, by simple intelligence" (281).

23. *The City of God,* abridged from the translation by Gerald G. Walsh, Demetrius B. Zema, Grace Monahan, and Daniel J. Honan, and edited by Vernon J. Bourke (Garden City, N.Y.: Doubleday & Co., 1958), pp. 235–36.

24. *Complete Poems and Major Prose,* ed. Merritt Y. Hughes (Indianapolis, Ind.: Odyssey Press, 1957), p. 694. Cf. *Reason of Church Government,* p. 670.

25. The best study of one aspect of this tradition may be found in Robert Hoopes, *Right Reason in the English Renaissance* (Cambridge, Mass.: Harvard Univ. Press, 1962).

26. *Complete Poems,* p. 694. Ben Jonson, among others, held fast to the same set of convictions; see the preface to *Volpone.* Cf. Cicero, *De Oratore* 2.8.5.348; and *Institutio Oratoria* 3.7.25, where Quintilian notes that "since the boundary between vice and virtue is often ill-defined, it [has seemed to some] desirable to use words that swerve a little from the actual truth, calling a . . . prodigal generous, a mean man thrifty," and so on. "But this the ideal orator, that is to say a good man, will never do." Strabo, *Geographica* 1.2.3 (Loeb, tr. Horace L. Jones), attacks Eratosthenes who maintains that poets aim only to delight when "the ancients assert, on the contrary, that poetry is a kind of elementary philosophy. . . . And our School [Stoic] goes still further and contends that the wise man alone is a poet." Later (1.2.5), Strabo argues that since "rhetoric is . . . wisdom applied to discourse," and "since Odysseus shows himself master of rhetoric, he and his creator must be wise." Roger Bacon liked to talk about the uneducated young man he picked up, as it were, off the streets; the teenager, because he was a good person, learned the mathematical principles of optics and catoptrics with awe-inspiring rapidity. I should probably confess that I am not terribly distressed by this confusion of ethics with esthetics, life with art. To repeat the Marvin-Mudrick dictum: Books aren't life, but then what is?

27. Columbia Edition, *Works,* III, i, 287.

Index